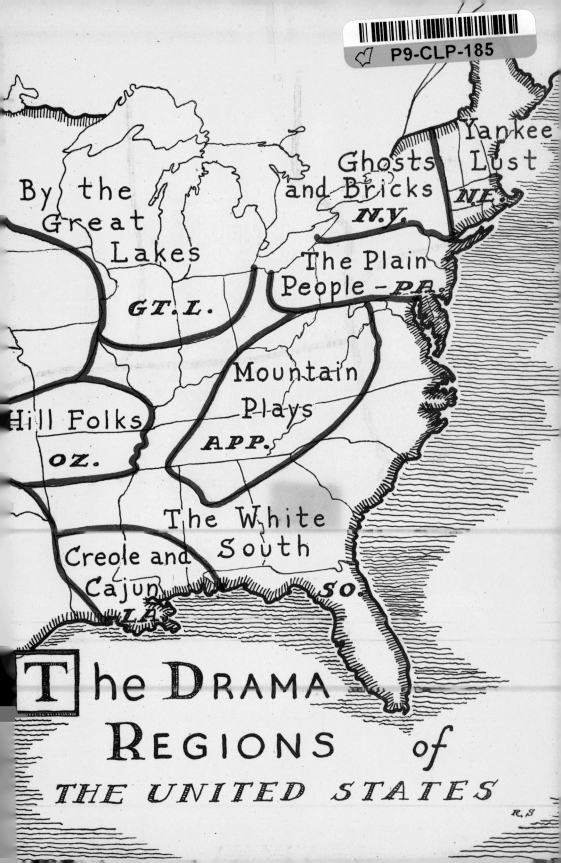

FROM NATIVE ROOTS

The Old Prospector, a wood carving, University of Wisconsin

From Native Roots

A Panorama of Our Regional Drama

by

Felix Sper

ILLUSTRATED

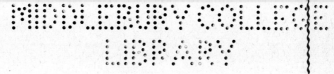

The CAXTON PRINTERS, Ltd.
CALDWELL, IDAHO
1948

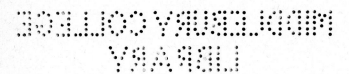
Printed and bound in the United States of America by
The CAXTON PRINTERS, Ltd.
Caldwell, Idaho
61751

ACKNOWLEDGMENTS

To the numerous correspondents who supplied miscellaneous items, to the playwrights who so kindly sent me their scripts, to the directors of the Federal Theatre Project, and to the librarians, without whose assistance this work would have been seriously hampered, the author extends gratitude. Further, to Barrett H. Clark, Professor Arthur Hobson Quinn, the late Frederick H. Koch, E. P. Conkle, Weldon Stone, Benjamin A. Botkin, and Estella T. Weeks, all of whom offered friendly counsel, I express deep, personal thanks.

F. S.

Brooklyn, New York

"We in the United States are amazingly rich in the elements from which to weave a culture. We have the best of man's past on which to draw, brought to us by our native folk and folk from all parts of the world. In binding these elements into a national fabric of beauty and strength, let us keep the original fibers so intact that the fineness of each will show in the completed handiwork."

FRANKLIN D. ROOSEVELT *in a letter to Paul Green, President of the National Folk Festival Association*

Three of these chapters, somewhat condensed, appeared as magazine articles: Chapter II in *Players Magazine,* December 1943, Chapter III in *Players Magazine,* April 1944, and Chapter VII in *Southern Folklore Quarterly,* September 1944.

Contents

Illustrations

NATIVE ROOTS

Our American literature is not a single thing. It is a choral song of many sections.—FREDERICK J .TURNER.

Not one vast, pale figure of America, but several Americas, in many subtle and significant characterizations.—MARY AUSTIN.

All that we did, all that we said or sung
Must come from contact with the soil, from that
Contact everything Antaeus-like grew strong.—WILLIAM BUTLER YEATS.

Locality makes the American drama.—HAMLIN GARLAND.

For all that is creatively significant in national and international life has roots in the local and indigenous.—PERCY MACKAYE.

Dramatize America!—MONTROSE J. MOSES.

All real drama must come from the soil.—FREDERICK H. KOCH.

National in scope and regional in emphasis.—*The ex-American Federal Theatre.*

Native drama is authentic drama.—WHITFORD KANE.

It is only by drawing on the roots of American culture that we shall gather the toughness and courage and self-confidence that will enable us to live through the menacing days that lie ahead.—LEWIS MUMFORD.

The Soil

THE SEEDS of a native or regional drama have been dormant in the American soil for more than a century. While the ground has been arable, few plows passed over it to prepare a crop of plays until this century. At intervals some brave diggers would send their spades into the ground, but they preferred to gaze at far-off horizons. The result was a thin line of scraggly sprouts of uncertain growth.

What prevented the emergence of a native drama at first was the lack of a true sense of place. The region as a fertile unit of background never entered men's minds except in a vague physical sense. The local gods did not whisper to those mortals who expressed themselves in movement and in sound. The dance, the parade, the communal exhibitions were merely those which were ever common to all men. Thus for a long spell local differences or manifestations peculiar to a definite locality did not exhibit themselves in song, pageant, or play.

As bits of lore and legend within a defined area passed from mouth to mouth and later found permanence in the written word, a regional consciousness was born. Native oddities, native manners, native folk-ways became the subject of ballad, of story, and finally of the stage play. By slow degrees the specific American locale began to breed native character types and to appear in celebrations of local events by way of pageantry.

On the formal stage native types of character had

been carved out crudely before the Declaration of Independence, but they sprang from no specific ground. Actually they hung in a vacuum. Gradually, as the republic expanded and the colonists enjoyed the sight of familiar faces on the platform or the stage, a sectional awareness crept into stage performances. To audiences, as well as to scribes, the section meant a group of special qualities associated with a strip of territory north or south of the Mason and Dixon's line. On the stage references to sectionalism appeared as occasional overflow of sectional patriotism. Before and after the Civil War when loyalties and tensions were strained to the utmost, sectional outbursts were not uncommon. For example, in *Neighbor Jackwood* (1857), by J. T. Trowbridge, one character cried out exultantly, "Hurrah for old Vermont and our New England manners and customs . . . our people believe in law and order." But the section as such remained an undifferentiated mass. Not until the time of James A. Herne did the setting of a play mean more than a verbal notation under a title. *Shore Acres* (1892) is definitely planted on Frenchman's Bay near Bar Harbor, Maine. Here the homeowners swear loyalty to their own land and act as if they really lived on the seacoast of Maine. For all that, a genuine consciousness of the region was felt but vaguely.

As the sciences of psychology, folklore, and anthropology contributed their findings to the common pool of knowledge within our century, the playwright began to perceive characteristics that set off a plainsman from a mountaineer; an offspring of the Cavaliers from that of the Puritans; a Spaniard from an *Americano;* a cowboy from a gold prospector. He noted how the human species on his own ground reacts naturally, humanly, and rhythmically. And he became aware of a truth as he examined local variations. *From common physiographic features and common ways of living and thinking is derived the pattern of culture peculiar to a region.*

What is a region? Briefly it is a complex made one by common natural resources and humanized by local beliefs, customs, traditions, myths, and speech in perpetual flux. Even now as the geographic units change, the folk imagination which runs freely in the backwoods never ceases to weave its tissue of superstitions, proverbs, games, jokes, riddles, tales, folk medicine—all compounded from fact and fiction. Today, distributed across the variegated terrain which makes up the United States, there are more than a dozen of these well-defined geographic units which tend to remain relatively stable.

The region as such has erupted an odd assortment of characters as heroes. With each region some folk figure has become identified. In fact, he or she incarnates the dreams and wishes of the common man and transcends the human by performing feats of the impossible. Some of these figures are known only to local residents while others have achieved national reputation. Among such folk heroes may be noted Ocean-born Mary, known in sections of New Hampshire as one who was befriended by a pirate when she was a baby; Old Stormalong of Massachusetts, "the most powerful deep-water sailorman who ever holystoned a deck";[1] Anna Christmas of New Orleans, a powerful giant and tough fighter; Kemp Morgan, boss of the oil drillers of Oklahoma; and two Texas cowpunchers, Pecos Bill and Strap Buckner. Better known to the nation at large is Paul Bunyan, the mighty logger from the North woods "who felled a dozen trees with one blow of his axe,"[2] and who in one afternoon marked off the boundaries of the state of North Dakota. Equally celebrated is his Babe the Blue Ox who had the strength of ninety horses and weighed ten thousand pounds. Famous among the lumberjacks of the imaginary Eel River of West Virginia is a relative of Paul, Tony Beaver. He loved watermelons and grew them as large as trucks. Still another hero who has captured the fancy of the South is John Henry, the "natchal man" and "steel-drivin' giant" who competed with a steam drill in driving spikes into the hard Georgia rocks. As the ballad so mournfully relates, he died "with his hammer in his hand."

Several of these folk heroes, fresh from their native ground, have exhibited their prowess on local stages. Through certain hero plays written in this century they have stormed and bellowed and worked their wonders. Oddly, for reasons of stagecraft, playmakers have had to contract these demigods to human size in order to fit them into the common dramatic molds.

Easier to envisage have been those lesser personalities who, magnified by time and events, fulfilled their earthly destiny. Appearing first in song and ballad, some of these personages in time found their way to the footlights. Once accepted as stage material, their mythical attributes had to be humanized. Among the national heroes to appear in the drama of outlying areas may be named Lincoln, the boy and youth; John Brown, the abolitionist; Daniel Boone, the scout; Davy Crockett, the coonskin Congressman and greatest bear hunter of his day; Johnny Appleseed, who sowed seeds and planted saplings in the wake of pioneers as he traveled down into the wilderness along the Ohio River; Sam Houston, the soldier and statesman from Texas; and a score of others who earned widespread fame in the growing years of our republic.

Finally, the common folk came into literature by

way of fiction assisted by anthropology. In 1880—a
memorable date in American letters—came Uncle
Remus, an aged Negro slave who told traditional fables
of his race in lively, authentic dialect. His creator, Joel
Chandler Harris, inspired other writers from other regions to draw similar characters of the planter, the
cavalier, the mountaineer, backwoodsman, and villager.
It was a brave beginning toward a literature of semi-
realism; an acknowledgment that the men and women
on the soil were as real as colonels and plantation owners. But writers still failed to paint the whole portrait.
Instead, the early local colorists traced shallow, sentimentalized, half-shadowy figures.

Before the stricter demands of regional realism, the
sentimentality of the local-color school faded. The discovery of the folk, their bitter experiences on the farm
and the prairie resulted in the creation of more natural
human types touched with the disillusion of a Hamlin
Garland. But playmakers in the nineties were loath
to fall into the same strain. Only toward the 1920's did
a playwright here and there cautiously prod with a cold
needle the tiller of the soil, move background and
character into some casual relationship, and balance the
outer with the inner. Then came the discovery that the
local oddities of the Kentucky mountaineer or the Oklahoma bandit or the Vermont farm hand were but the
outer dressing of the common man, the universal man.
And regionalism began to burst boundaries.

During the same period began the serious study
of folk culture as applied to the American Indian,
the Negro of the South, and the backwoodsman. It
started with an investigation of the oral ballad and
related folk material found in remote coves and ridges.
Within twenty years a veritable crusade to save from
oblivion the floating, fugitive bits of jests and tales, of

proverbs and songs, was in progress. *The Journal of American Folklore,* founded in the year 1888, became the major repository of source material from all regions of the country. The Missouri Folklore Society was organized in 1906. After December, 1909, under the impetus of Professors John A. Lomax and L. W. Payne, Jr., of the University of Texas, a well-defined regional consciousness was awakened and nurtured. An interest in subjects Texan, as they touched on cowboy lore, and on Indian and Negro folk say in local dialect, set the example for other regions. Inspired by the *Publications* of the Texas Folk-Lore Society, first issued in 1916, many groups undertook to collect ballads, songs, and folk material from specific regions. Soon folklore societies in Tennessee, Pennsylvania, Michigan, and Indiana, not to overlook the American Dialect Society, began to issue bulletins and reports from time to time. Periodicals sprang up to give permanent place to the scholarly findings. Among these may be listed *Nebraska Folklore, Folk-Say, Pennsylvania Folklore Society Publications, California Folklore Quarterly, Tennessee Folklore Society Bulletin, Southern Folklore Quarterly, The Virginia Folklore Society Bulletin,* the *Folklore Foundation Publications* of Vassar College, the *New York Folklore Quarterly,* and the remarkable series of *Folk Studies* undertaken by the United States Works Progress Administration of a few years ago.

Here is God's plenty indeed! In this corpus of folk material, gathered by field specialists, the playwright can find, if he has not already found, scientific confirmation of what experience and contact may have taught him. He may even discover inchoate plots in folk fables. At any rate, here in the records is the raw regionalism he aims to translate into visible, theatrical images.

The value of regionalism was warmly argued in the press during the late thirties. Chief among the exponents and crusaders was the editor of *Folk-Say* (1929), a periodical from Oklahoma which published articles, stories, and poems with a strong Western slant. Benjamin A. Botkin established the claims of the folk and folklore writers. He pleaded ardently for "literary self-determination of regions." The "new regionalism" stressed the marriage of the oral and the written word. Literature, to be revitalized, must dip into the idiom of the folk and emerge as "abundant, resonant, beautiful, laughing, living speech." It was time therefore, he argued, to return to "folk imagination," to "folk idiom," and to "folk metaphor," not narrowly sectional or provincial as in the past, but broadly human and universal.

Oddly, this theory of folk infusion has been voiced throughout history by critics of decadence. With regard to the drama in this country, the bugle notes of Botkin sounded after the event. Regionalism had already been established by dramatists enamored of the folk. Back in 1924, Percy MacKaye had essayed in *This Fine-Pretty World* to revive the idiom of mountain folk. That he merely flaunted verbal tags, instead of carving the texture of speech into sinewy forms as John M. Synge had done before him, is not to discredit the attempt. Other writers throughout the twenties more successfully caught and translated the idiom and acts of the folk into effective stage terms: to name but a few, Eugene O'Neill, Lula Vollmer, Paul Green, DuBose Heyward, E. P. Conkle, and Lynn Riggs.

Sometime before the first World War, three Midwestern college centers had stirred the regional impulse of their surrounding territory. Writers were urged to write about the frontier, the ranch, the prairie, the Indian. Midwesternism became a vital literary doctrine. From Grand Forks, North Dakota, from Fargo, North Dakota, and from Madison, Wisconsin, the call was piped across the prairies. In particular, Frederick H. Koch, Alfred G. Arvold, and Thomas H. Dickinson urged their students and followers to make plays out of native personalities, local legendry, and folk idiom. Ever since, the rural theme, dressed in folk speech, has taken its place in the American drama. The net result thus far has been a library of plays and playlets varying from simple farm problems of medical care, more milk, electrification, soil improvement, recreation, education, and the need to stay on the farm, up to the more complex hungers of frustrated human beings crossed by circumstances, the folly of feuding instead of loving, and the courage to withstand evil forces in nature.

Out of the assembled stage plays which incorporate bits of folklore sometimes shot through with folk fantasy couched in salty folk language, has come a respect for and understanding of the little folks of the soil: the farmer, the backwoodsman, the mountaineer, the lumberjack, the cowpuncher, the riverman, and the prospector, all "rooted in a specific soil" and "controlled by the ways of the outside physical world [rather] than by the ways and institutions of man in a specialized society."[3]

Caught up and placed in his limited natural setting by the practiced hand of the playmaker, the earthbound native with his kin has lived for a moment in a crop of plays whose validity as art and whose value as living documentation must no longer be ignored.

---

1. *The Hurricane's Children*, by Carl Carmer.
2. *The Saginaw Paul Bunyan*, by James Stephens.
3. Paul Green, "Folk Drama," *National Encyclopedia*, XI, 355.

Early Types

IF A SENSE of place was a matter of slow growth, the projection of a genuine native was equally slow. For more than a century the American dramatist tried fumblingly to sketch a credible American. He managed merely to block out a puppet, a caricature, a gawk, a type. Even after Darwin had proclaimed his theory of evolution in 1859, it never occurred to our playwrights to carry over into drama the premise that human animals are conditioned by environment; that nature is to man in the relation of cause to effect. Although Ibsen later showed the world how the locale was tied up with character and personality, our stage practitioners, until the first decade of this century, were loath to learn.

Earliest plantings of indigenous stage types sprouted into the Indian, the Negro, and the Yankee. The three shoots appeared side by side, coming to maturity with almost the same rate of growth. It was natural for pre-Revolutionary playwrights to concentrate their attention upon the Indian as a dramatic protagonist in our history. Despite the fear of massacres, the American craftsman pictured him as the noble savage in a state of nature: innocent, virtuous, and self-sufficient after the doctrine of Rousseau. But the portrait remained not only primitive but static: a figure in a storybook. Side by side with the base British and their snobbish airs, the red man stood out as an exalted chieftain dressed in fine feathers and paint, and poised to swing the dreaded tomahawk.

Our recital begins in the year 1766. The first Indian to appear in an American play was a representation of Ponteach, the Ottawa chief who figured in Pontiac's rebellion. His character is exalted. *Ponteach; or the Savages of America* (1766), by Robert Rogers, established a dramatic pattern. After the republic was organized, the first acted play on Indian life, *The Indian Princess; or, La Belle Sauvage* (1808), by James Nelson Barker, dealt with a set of historic persons taken from annals supposedly apocryphal: Captain John Smith's *Generall Historie of Virginia,* which gave us the Pocahontas story. Loftily the maiden in love with Rolfe spoke in blank verse. The portrait inspired a line of plays which deified the princess. Two decades later, in a play by George Washington Parke Custis, *Pocahontas; or, The Settlers of Virginia* (1830), she was drawn as the Christian who, amid Arcadian woodland scenery, spoke raptly of mercy as an attribute of divinity. She even praised the British as noble creatures in words that reflected the courtly language of current British plays. As a stage type Pocahontas remained for years a doll in a toy shop.[1]

As the nineteenth century advanced, there moved across our stage pale emanations of Indian chiefs, warriors, and maidens, in an aura of romanticism. But in play after play up to 1830 they remain so many puppets in plumes and bangles. In the highly successful *Metamora; or The Last of the Wampanoags* (1829), a tragedy by John Augustus Stone, Indian stolidity and defiance are magnified. In defeat King Philip remained the noble savage in sharp contrast to the unscrupulous British colonists. By 1860, after fifty Indian plays had been staged, the dignified Indian had crystallized.

In those days the playwright knew comparatively

little about the inner life of the Amerindian. No attempt was made to probe his myths and his culture. A remarkable impetus to a deeper interest in the subject was given by the poet Longfellow. *The Song of Hiawatha* (1855), though written in the singsong meter of the Finnish epic, *Kalevala,* stemmed from a strictly native cycle of tales from the Ojibways of the Lake Superior region. The story focused upon a demigod, Manabozho, and confused him with the historic Hiawatha, an Iroquois statesman of the Mohawk tribe. The chief source of this error was the several works of Schoolcraft. Hiawatha, the messenger of the Great Spirit, was sent down in the character of a wise man and prophet, "the personification of strength and wisdom." On the whole, the treatment is more paleface than Indian.[2]

Inspired by the facile, running meter of the poem, numerous adaptations to the stage were attempted by playmongers who chose to turn out stage pieces set to music.[3] For example, one year after the epic appeared, a wag in a few days' time hammered out a musical extravaganza in two acts: *Hiawatha; or Ardent Spirits and Laughing Water* (1856). This "mongrel, doggerel version" by the facile Charles M. Walcot ripples with hilarity and melodies which gently mock the romance, the separation, and reunion of the Indian pair. Character is still negative.

Other variations on the theme borrow a few episodes embroidered with conventional rhetoric. There are the traditional harvest and war dances, solemn councils, and wise addresses by the leader Hiawatha. In one occasional piece Hiawatha receives a message from Manitou the Mighty. As the palefaces have built extensively on the land of the Indians, he must leave for the West. Before going, he urges his chieftains to govern wisely, maintain the peace, live in honor, and keep alive the old traditions.[4]

Minor stage pieces have exploited the properties of lodge, wigwam, canoe, deer, forest. Lyrical lines ape the cadences of the Children's Poet while they act out little scenes against a backdrop of tepee, pueblo, village, and mountain. These dramatized legends remain running lines sprinkled with such show names as Old Chief, White Earth, Young Chief, Medicine Man, and Usama Mondamin. In short, the Indian still fails to come to life.

After the first decade of the 1900's a few playmakers came to view the Indian against his native ground, his folkways, his religion, his consciousness of the unity in all things. It was Mary Austin who opened to white readers the long-closed book of Indian mysteries and gave us our first authentic Indian plays. She noted the religious significance of the dance and divined the basic form consisting of long sequences, dance interludes, and recitatives. In her own plays she tried to mimic the cadences, the speech, and the rhythms which spring from bodily movement. While she understood the Indian, she failed to attain objectivity. As a result, her Indian characters are merely projections of her own rebellious self: mystic symbols who intone a kind of highly stylized, stagey free verse.

Other craftsmen of the theater have approached the Indian theme with the same awe. The poet, William Ellery Leonard, set the Indian amid his tribe within a particular area and a definite time, and also put beautiful words into his mouth. Lynn Riggs angrily re-created the red man's puzzlement in a white man's world and mirrored his secret wish to return to his happy past. The stern indictment implicit in these plots tends to cast shadows over the actors as well as over the scene. Despite the unquestioned skill of these poet-playwrights, the Indian fails to take on fullness or depth.

The play which will picture faithfully and convincingly the heart of the Indian's despair, his true feelings over the invasion of his homeland, his mythology, his religion, expressed in his own way, remains to be written. The plain fact is that the religion which furnishes the clue to Indian character continues to be a sealed abracadabra within a *kiva* on some pueblo.

If the Indian is our first indigenous theme, the Negro is our second. A later comer to these shores, the Negro has played a decisive part in our native economy and culture. Since 1661, when an Act of Council in Virginia made slave traffic a fact, the Negro has been the subject of sentimental study. Not until the period of the Revolution did the drama discover him. In the beginning Negroes like Cudjo,[5] a runaway slave, Sambo[6] (considered the first real American Negro comedy type), and Ralpho[7] sang and danced as they delivered an uncouth, exaggerated speech resembling pidgin English in lines like, "Such a little trick no hurtee me much." Other characters named Cato, Caesar, and Pompey[8] supplied comic relief. More human, though still unreal, mere voices without bodies, were the colored servants like Zeke,[9] who rattled off funny side-remarks, announced guests, and gave vent to such glib observations as "Dem's de defects ob not having a libery education."

Then the buffoon as minstrel mounted the boards. He moved freely in a type of entertainment invented by Thomas D. Rice, a white man, to mimic his black brother. After 1828, black-faced impersonators or burnt-cork artists cut silly capers, farced Negro traits, and mouthed a grotesque dialect. The butt of humor was an aged, decrepit slave, Jim Crow. The interlocutor in the center and the end men, Mr. Tambo and Mr. Bones, all in blackface, carried on a running dialogue, frisked, chuckled, danced, and sang. In 1865 Charles Hicks organized the first all-Negro minstrel show. Despite the comic patter, minstrel sketches like *Old Times Rocks* showed tragic moments on a high level. Black minstrelsy reached its heyday during the nineties with Johnson's *Plantation Georgia Minstrels* and brought into prominence superb comedy teams like Cole and Johnson, Williams and Walker, and others who survived into this century. Today the minstrel tradition lives on in burlesque, in musical comedy revues, in blackface sketches, burnt-cork minstrel shows,[10] the movies, and the night clubs where the onetime interlocutor is now called the master of ceremonies.

As might be expected, the legitimate stage borrowed the singing-and-talking Negro. Stencils like Jim Crow and Zip Coon helped to set a pattern of character. First came the ignorant but faithful Southern mammy, generally called Aunt Chloe. Followed her counterpart, the male slave, "pious, loyal to death . . . sentimental, old or lazy, falling asleep . . . spoiled by indulgence, twisting words for comic effect and believing piously in spooks."[11] This "gemman ob color," loyal to the Southern cause, to his massa and his missey, even went so far as to beg to be allowed to remain with the family without pay after he received his freedom. Along with such stereotypes came the chicken-stealing rascal, the pious deacon exposed as a fraud, the crapshooter and the gin drinker—all of whom have migrated to the movies.

Invested with more human traits sat the martyr in

the shadows, the poor slave of ante bellum plays. His general plight, his foiled attempts to escape, drew sobs and sighs from abolitionist audiences.[12] Of course the most famous slave in our literature is poor Tom from the phenomenal *Uncle Tom's Cabin* (1852) in the dramatic version by George L. Aiken. The pious Negro, conceived in pity and womanly understanding, was more than a stage figure. He became a presence not to be denied; a reality that was inescapable. As he passed from owner to owner until flogged to death by the brutal slave trader, Simon Legree, audiences wept and accepted Tom as real. When in his final agony Tom mumbled, "My body belongs to you, but my soul belongs to God," the pitch of pathos was reached.

By 1909 the stage Negro, whether funny man, mammy, or slave, began to disappear. In his or her place stepped the protagonist struggling against a hostile world to retain personal and racial identity. One outstanding example, *The Nigger,* by Edward Sheldon, developed through poignant situations the theme of mixed marriage, and in the struggle stressed the human side of character. Out of the impact of society upon the ego was born the prototype of the modern Negro. By 1917 the ordinary Negro, in a common setting and talking an everyday language, was no longer a novelty. He was a live resident of a particular section with complex reactions towards his white neighbors and black brothers. Once set on native ground, the Negro spoke and acted plausibly, like any other normal human being. His motives, whether conscious or subconscious, showed the same drive as those of his white associates. While psycho-analysis explored his personal self, the drama, aided by folk study, explored his regional self. Today the

Negro on the stage is neither glorified nor vilified, neither master nor slave, hero nor villain, saint nor sinner. If anything, he is a rebel.

Dig to the roots of our colonial drama and you strike the Yankee: a native folk type destined to rule the American stage for more than a century. It was Jonathan, the blunt, earth-bound New England servant who sang *Yankee Doodle;* Jonathan, the "true-blue Yankee American son of liberty" who summed up the horse sense and shrewdness which the colonists admired and emulated. Begotten by our first dramatist of note, Royall Tyler, this Yankee romped through *The Contrast* (1787),[13] rattling like a magpie and putting to shame the degenerate, city-bred Britons.

Evidently the wag struck a friendly chord in native bosoms. His open ridicule of snobbish stock, his easy, facile humor made him typify the average American's attitude toward European airs and pretentions. Subsequent plays repeated the role under such rustic variants as Nathan Yank, Jonathan Ploughboy, Solomon Swap, Seth Sage, Deuteronomy Dutiful, Jedediah Homebred, Solon Shingle, Horsebean Hemlock, Hiram Dodge, Obediah Whitcher, Gumption Cute, Asa Trenchard, and Lot Sap Sago.[14] The resemblance is unmistakable. Crudely molded is the clay; the label plainly marked; the face whimsically human. From time to time the bumpkin roughly asserted himself, thundered "tarnations," and boasted a Godgiven spirit.

Years later Jonathan, somewhat mellowed and aged, bobbed up in a line of hayseeds from New England. Among these lovable and outspoken uncles to tread the boards, the best-known is Uncle Joshua Whitcomb from New Hampshire. For more than fifty years this hearty clodhopper and apostle of the simple life from

The Old Homestead (1886), written by Denman Thompson and George W. Ryder, touched the hearts of theatergoers. "The very embodiment of honest and rural simplicity" worked hard, slept well, and lived at a time when "money was scarce and luxuries a good sight scarcer." Kin to Joshua is Jed, from Buckport, Maine. *Old Jed Prouty* (1889), by William Gill and Richard Golden, introduced a blunt and kindly keeper of a tavern who lived in a pastoral age. Like his forebears Jed was shown up as the country gawk despised by city swells. But in the end he lived to prove that "honesty snaps fingers at poverty." In the wise and tender Uncle Nat of *Shore Acres* (1892), by James A. Herne, the type comes to flower. Bits of local wisdom and prejudices against "free-thinking ideas" only intensify the frail qualities of this Maine resident. As broad types, these rustics lived on the surface, acted from good motives, and remained elemental as the rocks. Only to a degree were they aware of belonging to a strip of land. Hardly a hint ever comes through that a particular area can influence character.

For a time it seemed as if the Yankee had vanished from the stage. The legitimate theater knew him no more. But stage ghosts depart reluctantly. Of late years he has been resurrected in the shape of the country rube. His major quality is that of rustic shrewdness which operates upon the city slicker and outwits him. Of course he is a shadow of his former self; a pale and spurious emanation to be accepted with good-natured tolerance as a cheap imitation of the true, original Jonathan.

On the Pacific coast about a century ago local, abortive types flashed across the stage. At first it was all fun and mimicry; an open parody of imported and borrowed plots in the desire to break away from theatrical subservience. Influenced by foreign example, plays in California during the 1850's began to catch a glimmer of the common struggles of men and women on their own patch of land. Even when melodrama ruled the boards and the wildest tangle of improbabilities beguiled the rough spectators, the playmaker did carve out an occasional native species with regional traits, mannerisms, and speech. In these tentative beginnings may be found a reaching out toward an independent native drama.

With the changing conception of human nature and of society came a change in the creation of stage types, once only streaked with a few brush strokes and endowed with stage humors. For the American drama the result was the virtual disappearance of the stage Indian, the stage Negro, and the stage Yankee.

---

1. Except in *Pocahontas and the Elders* (1933), by Virgil Geddes.

2. "The Indian Legend of Hiawatha," *Publications of the Modern Language Association*, XXXVII, 128-40.

3. "Mrs. Chapman would appear at Musical Hall (in San Francisco) in readings from *Hiawatha*" writes George R. MacMinn in *The Theater of the Golden Era in California* (Caldwell, Idaho, 1941), p. 149.

4. See "The Passing of Hiawatha" in *Plays of the Pioneers*, by Constance Mackay.

5. *The Fall of British Tyranny* (1776), attributed to John Leacock.

6. *Triumphs of Love* (1795), by John Murdock.

7. *The Candidates* (1798), by Robert Munford.

8. *The Politicians* (1798), by John Murdock.

9. *Fashion; or, Life in New York* (1845), by Anna Mowatt.

10. See scripts issued by Penn Play Company, Philadelphia, Pa.

11. Helen M. Sanwick, "The Development of the Negro Character in American Drama from 1767 to 1934" (Master's thesis, The University of Washington, Seattle, 1934).

12. For example, *The Star of Emancipation*, a collection of poems against slavery which includes "The Fugitives" (1841).

13. First performed in New York on April 16, 1787, and first printed in Philadelphia in 1790.

14. See Montrose J. Moses, *The American Dramatist* (revised edition; Boston, Mass., 1925), pp. 99-102.

Folk Pageant and Play

IT IS NO idle figure of speech to say that whatever touches the earth and sinks roots into it must grow strong. This age-old truism incarnated in the Antaeus myth has been repeated by writers who have given thought to their craft. "It is the soil where all great art is rooted," wrote William Butler Yeats.[1] Similarly Leo Tolstoy and Romain Rolland both testified to the need of drawing "fertility from the folk-soul."[2]

Indeed, the folk instinct for group play, with its outlets in pantomime, dance, song, and speech, merely changes dress from age to age. Long ago the primitive passions had to express themselves in rituals which linked man with the powers above and the demons below the earth. The corn-medicine dances, the vegetation cults, and the thanksgiving prayers for abundance were so many ways of bowing before the unknown; of arousing some response in that inert bosom which nourishes the children of men. Today traces of that primal impulse break through in seasonal celebrations, in flower and fruit festivals, and in harvest pageants throughout our country. Stripped of mumbo jumbo and mystic mumble, the ceremony survives through pageant and parade in scattered areas removed from busy centers.

The less sophisticated a people, the more likely they are to revert to pageantry. Especially strong has been the urge among our foreign-born groups which have not entirely shaken off the influence of their homelands. As a pageant links a people to its past, immigrants willingly have re-enacted Old World customs, dances, and processions in the open. In the Middle and Far West such open-air celebrations have emanated from two motives: a desire to hold fast to that which they have known and loved, and to set forth pictorially their group contributions to the growth of this nation. During and after the first World War, a spirit of self-defense led to a number of exhibitions of folk solidarity.

More articulate than the worship of the seasons is the historic pageant-play which explains as well as pictures a place, be it hamlet, city, or region. As a nation grows and gathers memories of men and events, loyalty to and pride in the land is likely to run to visual representation. The play instinct leads men to reassemble in pageantry past glories symbolized by covered wagons, the march of pioneers, trappers, explorers, miners, and such. If hero there be, he will dominate the action or recital. Theatrical effect will be heightened by eloquence, poetry, costume, and music. The union of these sister arts is essential in the making of the pageant-drama or literary pageant or community masque, as it has been variously called.

It was Percy MacKaye who, inspired by British example, honored the memory of the sculptor, Augustus Saint-Gaudens, in a pageant at Cornish, New Hampshire, in 1905, and thereby set a standard for subsequent civic masques.

Since then, across the length and breadth of this land, innumerable pageants—seasonal, Old World, and regional—have gaily sauntered by. As productions, these examples of a people's art embody the very genius of a locality and enlist the talents and collaboration of writer, scenic designer, player, musician, carpenter, advertiser, and the public.

Themes show infinite variety, while pageant masters
range from the local schoolmaster, who chants the
glories of tobacco raising, to a Paul Green who expends
his gifts upon writing and mounting pieces like *The
Lost Colony* (1937) . Structurally, the finished pageant
has followed the form of prelude, prologue, procession,
an odd number of episodes (in place of acts) , interludes, and epilogue.

If the pageant is stripped of its grandiloquence, the
action isolated and the conflict caged, the core of folk
drama is established. The actor then stands at the
center as protagonist. What he says is more important
than what he does. Carried one step further, the
central character becomes a focus of cross currents
within a region. He may rebel or submit. In the
course of events he will have exposed an inner self
shaped by his own little world. Existence becomes a
tussle between the demands of the ego and the law of
the crowd. The clod may then be identified as the
gaunt and grizzled Ezra or Ethan, the slut Bess, or the
Widow Cagle. Man or woman, each must make decisions as between duty and desire. Once the conflict
is resolved, the curtain falls to a cry of despair, a shout
of denial, or a resolve of fresh hope. Of such are the
varied life figures in the hinterland, the actors in our
living folk drama.

Since 1911 the folk soul in this country has come
under the scrutiny of playmakers. In that year a
visit by a foreign troupe, the Irish Players from the
Abbey Theatre in Dublin, Ireland, caused a dramatic
disturbance. The set of one-act plays on peasant life
they introduced set in motion a current in the theater
which was to culminate in the successful manufacture
of native folk plays. Especially the pieces by John M
Synge suggested to young writers the need of exploit-

ing our own native resources, our folkways, our local history and rural types. Above all, the influence of that great one-act tragedy, *Riders to the Sea,* was felt in a number of plays written soon thereafter, even to the cadence of the lines. It is safe to say that Synge is the godfather of the American folk play.

After this historic visit, the impress on one of our poets was quite discernible. One year later, the impressionable Percy MacKaye essayed to play the role of pioneer on Yankee themes. He preached the need of drawing on known rural types and of portraying them closely. Other playwrights took up the challenge and they have been revealing rural characters of varied shade and hue ever since.

Much has been written and said about the *folk play.* The word has taken on multiple meanings, thanks to our literary historians. Long ago, one form of folk play was the medieval mummer play which dramatized the ballads of Robin Hood, the figures of St. George, the Turkish Knight, the Dragon, the Lord of Misrule, and a host of droll, boisterous types. Such pieces of rhymed rustic foolery, written by unknown scribes, were acted out by companies traveling from barn to barn in the remote hamlets of England and Scotland. In our own time processionals suggestive of such pieces may be witnessed in Philadelphia, in the southern Appalachians, and in New Orleans.

A second variety of folk play is the medieval anonymous *folk pageant* which acted out scenes from the Old and New Testament. Pastoral plays on the birth of Christ and the lives of the saints—called "folk" because they showed the customs and speech of their age—have come down by way of the Spanish invasion of the Southwest. On our own soil such plays are still produced with Old World pomp and solemnity in New Mexico, Colorado, and in some parts of Texas.

A third species—the most recent and more strictly indigenous—depicts life in a definite area and time and within a highly unified pattern of culture. In such plays the folk along the seacoast, in mountain cabins, in lumber camps, on the prairies and on the peaks— these men in overalls and women in calico come to grips with primitive conditions and are driven hard by physical circumstance. Responsible for the naming and writing of this kind of play is the late Professor Frederick H. Koch of Chapel Hill, North Carolina. Rather than use a term like "folk" which suggests so many subdivisions, or accept such used tags as "rustic" or "rural" or "village," this inquiry, in the interest of clarity, hereinafter will use the less controversial term of *regional* play.

At this point a warning must be rung. As in nature poisonous imitations of edible berries spring up in near-by places, so a bastard species of the regional play exists. It is named variously in publishers' catalogues as the "rube" or "hillbilly," "bush" or "R.F.D.," "small-town" or "b'gosh" play. The emphasis is on the boisterous plot or stale jokes, the slapstick, old gags, the lush, exaggerated dialect. High-spirited yokels point laughingly at the poor rustic and his troubles to provide belly laughs for the rural belt. A favorite theme is that of the country boob who outrageously outwits his scheming, slick city cousin. The very titles suggest hilarity: *Dotty and Daffy, Yimmie Yonson's Yob, Howdy Folks, Cheerio, My Deario, Gosh, I Thought I'd Die,* and the rest. Further comment on this false species has been reserved for a later chapter.

What, then, stamps a regional play as authentic? First and foremost, an indicated affinity between man and background. Characters must be rooted and branched like the natural flora of the region. As eelgrass, live oak, sagebrush, mesquite, redwood, and Oregon pine stem from different acres, so the diverse species of homo derive from different geographic strips. Once this correspondence is established, minor considerations of plot and dialogue become less pressing. In brief, the play must be an honest yet dramatic transcript of the folk as they pass their days on native ground.

Some will here interpose an objection that the passions of love, hate, jealousy and such are not bound by time or place. Admittedly, plots and situations resemble one another in fundamental matters and in responses to stimuli. Nonetheless it must be maintained that the *specific* manner of response is determined by the nature of the physical milieu, the regional code, the prevailing mores. In addition, the local idiom not only provides the color and spice but the poetry and the incidental music which render the drama significant as document and sometimes great as literature.

There is no current regional formula or style in drama. Different visions distinguish different craftsmen. One writer sees reality through a camera lens and records conversation on a sound track. Actually, minor playmakers write in this all-too-literal vein. The more reflective observer penetrates the mask of character and probes the quirks and aberrations of temperament in a crumbling world as do E. P. Conkle and Paul Green. Still a third type searches for the symbol behind the fact—the secret behind appearances—and expresses it in folk poetry wrought from the common idiom after the manner of Lula Vollmer and Lynn Riggs. Finally, another brushes character with whimsy and creates an effect not unlike super-realism in painting, in the style of Weldon Stone.

The bulk of plays under review belong to the shorter or one-act form. According to accepted definition, any play taking less than an hour to produce is a one-act play. A lesser number of the examined plays belong to the full-length variety. The dominant mood is that of tragedy. Like nature, the drama frowns more often than she smiles. It is likely, too, that playwrights find it easier to strike the minor chords.

The plays to be discussed in this book were gathered from every available source: pamphlet, periodical, book, and anthology. Sometimes playscripts were read when the writers consented to send them. To separate the regional from the non-regional, the authentic from the spurious, a strict policy of selection, perhaps arbitrarily applied, had to be invoked in the absence of precedent or guide.

To weigh the merits of the homespun products of the backwoods against the polished wares of the Broadway stage would serve no valid purpose. Each has its own place in the drama and need not encroach upon the other. The feud between country and city theater will not be fanned in these pages. Let one image suffice to show the basic difference. The regional drama is a sturdy pine on a bank watered by a running stream; the urban play is a painted screen of flowery design set against a fireplace near an armchair under a ticking clock. Consider *Sun-Up* as against *The Philadelphia Story*.

And now, to a detailed consideration of the plays themselves, region by region.[3]

1. *Early Poems and Stories* (London, 1925) .

2. Romain Rolland, *Le Théâtre du peuple* (Paris, 1903) .

3. See references at end of each chapter for play titles and occasional notations. For a complete listing of regional plays and authors, see Section V of the Bibliography beginning on page 297.

The Regional Drama

I

Yankee Lust

FROM Maine to Connecticut unrolls a line of unsurpassed scenic beauty punctuated by power dams, lumber mills, quarries, sugar maples, tobacco barns, roadside markets, and gift and antique shops. On the land live a medley of nationalities from fifty countries. Although New England once was predominantly of British stock, with an infusion of French-Canadians and later of Irish, the English core had shrunk to about 40 per cent by 1938.

The legendry and balladry remain essentially British, however. From the state of Maine southward into the lower belt a miscellany of song and story and lore has spread to seacoast and farm. Hundreds of ballads starting with the familiar "Come all ye" have been cut and trimmed to acceptable shape by the onetime God-fearing New Englander. Dutifully the descendants have guarded this valuable heritage.

But with new times there have come new manners. The average Yankee may be reticent and practical-minded, but no longer is he ruled by that stern conscience which tradition once affixed to him and which American letters once exalted. His faith in a rigid system of conduct has been shaken by the inroads of science and the traffic in curios, antique furniture, and tourist cabins. Not so long ago, historic-minded brethren nailed up tablets on every ancient tavern, farmhouse, and blacksmith shop with one eye open for the tourist trade.

Ulterior motives aside, the true New Englander

will not and cannot forget the past. Memories still
haunt old waterwheels, old barns, the ancient hills.
Natives filled with ancestral pride miss no opportunity
to celebrate historic events whenever possible through
pageant and play. *The Gloucester Pageant,* written
and directed by the versatile Percy MacKaye, in 1909
initiated a line of spectacles which only two wars have
interrupted. As a matter of fact, about three hundred
such pageants have moved through city streets or been
shown in halls of hamlets and towns. Most impressive
were the numerous celebrations which honored the
tercentenary of the landing of the Pilgrims. Among
these may be named *The Pilgrim Spirit,* a pageant by
George Pierce Baker, and *Merry Mount,* by William
O. Bates, which showed scenes from Boston and Merry
Mount. Such Puritans as John Winthrop, governor of
the colony, members of the Council, Captain Miles
Standish, a planter, a squaw, and a jester throng by.
"These colors on the historical palette" prove less
colorful on the printed page.

While the pageant can give us but the externals of
history, the play must delve into deeper historic layers.
Upon the screen of the past will move somber and sig-
nificent figures. Back in 1824 the witchcraft delusion, a
folk obsession, formed part of the theme of a play. Probably the earliest reference to the "powers of darkness"
occurs in *Superstition,* by James Nelson Barker, a
wild-tangled plot about Puritan persecution, witches,
and Nonconformists. But the witchcraft theme, as
such, does not stand alone; it is buried in a story of
regicides, Indians, and Puritans.

Later in the century an outmoded specimen of
dramatic writing, *Giles Corey, Yeoman* (1893), by
Mary E. Wilkins Freeman, set the action of "this
witchcraft folly" in Salem Village within a framework

of melodrama. The plot moves in a straight line.
After a quiet spinning song and screams over "a witch
in the chimbly," the fear of pursuit by "a beast with
horns and a tail and eyes like balls of fire" bodes ill
for innocent characters. "Afflicted maids" suffer griev-
ous torment from these "powers of darkness." False
accusations against Mother Corey and her daughter
culminate in a trial at the meetinghouse. The rational
plea that "there is no such thing as a witch" is countered
by false charges which spring from jealous and personal
motives. When the mother is jailed, the husband rages
in protest. The horror and pathos of the final moments
are intense. The mother is hanged, the daughter
freed, and Giles Corey pressed to death by weights.
Throughout, the historic background is faithfully
drawn. Dramatically considered, the long passages of
dialogue create a literary rather than a theatrical
effect.

Similar dramatic attempts fail to reach the high
level of attainment in Esther Forbes' *A Mirror for
Witches*. One of these tales has been theatricalized.
The effect is shrill and stark. "The whole country is
stricken with witch-fever," cries one character. A
livid light on the repressed, crazed fanatic who in-
sanely pours out a stream of obscene accusations at her
stepdaughter for playing with her poppet (doll) is
focused on *The Devil's Doll*.[1] Has she not sold herself
to the Devil, the Prince of Lust in the forest! The girl
confesses in a moment of hysteria and expires. In
other playlets characters turn out to be historic puppets
who jabber like Cotton Mather and his kin in strange
Quaker and Puritan lingo.[2] For a moment, too, Judge
Sewall, a rotund figure at sixty-nine, undiscouraged
by rebuff and mixing dowry with romance, stalks
across the scene as he goes a-courting.[3]

These voices from the past seem to emanate from wraiths rather than from bodies despite the touch of earth in the portrait of Judge Sewall. They speak in studied syllables and in formal accents. A freer type was projected in the so-called American folk-plays, *Yankee Fantasies* (1912), by Percy MacKaye. Disdaining the "chill constraint" and "half-outwintered Puritanism" of decadent New England, the poet sought to recreate the free vagabond after the manner of Yeats and Synge. The easygoing, lusty Chuck incarnates pagan virtues as he pipes his pagan melodies along the highways and countryside in defiance of order and restraint. Finally, with fine bravado, the youth carries off his maiden to the White Mountains. Pagan attributes are likewise noted in the unregenerate minister who decides to marry the free Canuck, a wicked, wine-drinking alien. To make matters worse, she offends the scruples of strict churchgoers. Comically drawn is another character, the old paralytic veteran who retells the story of Gettysburg as memorial bugles blow from afar. In his excitement he forgets his palsy and walks off. The poet's indictment of New England righteousness is fully warranted. But his borrowed conception of poetic paganism can hardly sit with ease upon the offspring of Calvinists and such. Daubed as these characters may be with a layer of earth, they remain creatures of fantasy. The unreality is heightened by the fact that they speak a labored and turgid dialogue.

In actuality Yankee fantasy has long been tempered and restrained by the hard sense of the native. Only by pronouncing the supernatural odd and "skeery" and by declaring, "Thur's queer doin's 'round here" does the Yankee accept it. For the drama the result is equivalent to putting a bit in the mouth of Pegasus.

Consider this plot. Out of a well on Connecticut ground rises the ghostly figure of Leather Man, a water sprite, tall, lean, and mysterious. The overworked maiden who chats with him is suspected of "carryin' on's with a ghost." For a moment the play flies along a poetic level, then flops. The mystery is explained. A murderer has long been shielded by his nagging wife. After some signs of awakened conscience and a sermon on the passing of days, the mystery man vanishes. This mélange, known as *Honey Holler,* by Keith MacKaye, hovers like an uneasy phantom between two worlds. The poetry does not soar and the sundry bits of wisdom betray little folk quality.

Even the devil, a favorite folk hero, must be brought down to our human level as a Mr. Scratch. Long has New England wrestled with the flesh and the devil. For generations, from Jonathan Edwards down, questions of guilt and sin, of right and wrong, were clearly demarcated. Desire had to be curbed by duty until new forces released the repressed victims and time softened the iron codes of conduct. Transplant the Faustus legend to New England, re-dress it in homespun, and you get *The Devil and Daniel Webster,* a playlet by the late Stephen Vincent Benét. The scene is Cross Corners in the New Hampshire of 1841. Against a backdrop of square dancing and politics, of drinking and merrymaking at a country wedding, the old struggle between body and soul comes to grips. Mr. Scratch, an intruder, has arrived to claim the groom who, ten years before, had exchanged his soul for worldly goods. Then two wits, the one human, the other diabolical, gird for the combat. As two brands of justice clash, a kind of grim humor breaks through. Fervidly, in semipoetic oratory, the great Daniel Webster pleads the case of his client before a

judge and jury summoned by the devil. In the end
Yankee wit wins and the devil leaves, beaten.

In the age-old tussle between the devil and the
flesh many a fine spirit has had to go down. With the
coming of new values, the old values did not surrender
without rending the body they left. Truly, much
agony was suffered by lover and lover, husband and
wife, parents and children. The drama can wish for
nothing better.

Tense yet withal tender are the recordings of such
inner conflicts in the plays of Alice Brown. An unaffected tale of habit and conscience stirred into open
rebellion for a while, but repressed by a sense of guilt,
unfolds with finality in *Children of Earth* (1915).
Within the framework of the old triangle, the right to
love overpowers cupidity. In the company of the
"worthless" man married to an ignorant Portygee,
the woman blossoms. But too soon the shadows of
remorse come between; narrow notions of duty close in
and life relapses into its former drabness. "Not that
way," cries Conscience. Two years before, in *A March
Wind,* the author had presented the case of a woman
past middle age married to a passing stranger with a
child. Spiteful insinuations by a cousin create a tem-
porary domestic rift. But when the husband decides
to leave, the wife joins him. Greater than respectability is devotion. In *The Sugar House* is enacted a
comedy of love and jealousy. In one of the shacks in
a New England wood, used to store sap pans and kettles
for boiling maple syrup, a young woman has decided
to live with the husband of a friend. Soon the two
claimants come face to face; the one anxious to hold
her man, the other insistent on her right to live as she
pleases. When the community learns of this plan, an
aroused vigilance committee makes veiled threats and

quotes from the Bible. The story ends in a show of
remorse by the husband and in victory for the wife.
Though these people make an attempt to follow their
impulses, in the end they too have to yield to conventional morality.

In her quiet, unsensational technique Alice Brown
devised a fit medium for interpreting the folk on the
New England soil. Her sense of the scene coupled
with a warm sympathy for colorless lives made her an
admirable pioneer, a leader of a school of regional
writing. But we missed her cue. The professional
theater gave her little heed and continued to run in
the worn and convenient grooves.

A similar case of the claims of conscience, told by
another scribe, is that of the susceptible lady loved
by one other than her harsh and moody husband.
But duty's chains bind her and she will not consent to
any change in her status.[4]

Indeed, conscience may be an excuse for practicing
cruelty. On the young it is easy for self-righteous
elders to inflict acute suffering by imposing a strict
course of conduct. For example, though circumstances
warrant a divorce, granny insists that "divorce is an
instrument of the Devil."[5] In another instance, a
mother's firmness drives her daughter straight into
what she most dreads. Settled notions of renunciation
and sacrifice pitted against the younger woman's need
to work out her own code join issue. In the course
of the "inquisitorial skirmishing" mother love is ruth-
lessly rent.[6]

Repression breeds the ingrown personality, a regional by-product. Generally the type quotes from
the Bible, suffers delusions, and experiences calm intervals. Sometimes he or she faces crucial moments
when fixed ideas are wrenched apart. In an early play

by the poet, Robert Frost, the habits and ways of a bachelor-recluse are upset. On the plausible pretext of murder in order to escape detection, a criminal's conscience is slowly revealed. At the same time romantic notions about hermits are blasted in *A Way Out*. Though the final movements are blurred, the characters come through as products of the region.

It is not surprising that perverse egos have sprung from the stony ground. The struggle to eke out a living has developed traits of stubbornness and eccentricity. A number of minor plays show up these traits. A heartless husband's refusal to save a dying child, because his luck has never failed him, suffers the agony of seeing his child die.[7] The sick farmer who prefers the mindhealer to a reputable doctor dies after bequeathing the farm to his son, a railroad worker. The son, against his inclination, returns to the farm. Too long he has heard his elders talk about farm duties and farm labor.[8] Far more perverse is the farmer who sees no need of a doctor for his sick son, although he knows enough to hire a veterinarian for his cows. His son, who has been drinking a patent medicine advertised over the radio, continues to drink the stuff and dies as the radio blares on.[9]

The acid personality of the venomous old shrew or gossip from the rural areas has been etched by playwrights old and new. She can work irreparable mischief. There are flashes of satire in the portrait of the crone who convinces her aged neighbors that their runaway son, now returned after thirty years of absence, is only an impostor. As the parents doubt his identity, the prodigal son rushes out.[10] A familiar present-day nuisance is the malicious busybody who lifts the telephone receiver to overhear conversation. She can scare an entire community by spreading false alarms.[11] More tragic is the case of the shy maid who has retired into her shell after caustic tongues cast slurs upon her character. When at long last her man returns from Canada years after his promise to marry, she no longer loves him or wants him.[12]

In the long run, repression can lead to perversity and pride. And pride invites rebuke. To illustrate: a strict church member and her minister combine to ostracize the cynical invalid-husband who jibes at morality. They banish him from the congregation. Before he shoots himself he hurls a blast at respectability.[13] Another proud invalid, when confronted with the necessity of selling the old homestead, is forced to give in.[14] To the same class belong the dignified parents ruffled by news that their son is to marry a Polish maid. They are finally placated by the promise of a dowry.[15]

Extreme pride in turn touches on clannishness. And clannishness is rudely shaken in *Icebound* (1923), by Owen Davis. Proud personalities in the Jordan family resent the fact that the money has been willed to a lowly outsider, a distant relative and domestic. To the surprise of everybody, she hands over the farm and the assets to the black sheep of the family and asks to remain as his wife. This picture of snubbed middle-class folk is drawn in broad, rugged lines.

Conscience, duty, ingrown traits, all projected against a wintry New England landscape, are summed up in *Ethan Frome* (1935), the dramatized version, by Owen and Donald Davis, of Edith Wharton's novelette. The old triangle repeats the theme of frustration among the villagers of Starkfield; in particular the hypochondriac wife, the helpless cousin, and the repressed farmer. Conscience struggles with desire: shall it be wife or cousin? Ethan steals a few hours of innocent pleasure until a fateful decision crumples his hopes. Then the crash of the sled carrying the two into the elm tree settles their fates! Twenty years later, by an ironic twist, the three are still tied together in mutual dependence. In this stage version the stark outlines of the story are accentuated, the scenes tightly compressed, and the passions whipped up. While the pathos is deep, the sense of inevitability is less sustained than in the original novelette.

These assorted hard-bitten New Englanders reach full stature in *Desire Under the Elms* (1924), by Eugene O'Neill. Bleak creatures in a bleak land, they hate and love and stammer out their surging passions in blunt speech. Under the symbolic elms towering over the doomed cottage they carry on the ancient feud between man and nature, and between man and man. Although "we been slaves t' stone walls here," the human will has managed to "make corn sprout o' stones." Once nature has been subdued, the lust for property contends with the lust for the flesh. In pursuing circles move three personalities: a gaunt, hard-working Bible-quoting father of seventy-five; his loutish son, sensual and sentimental; and the newly arrived third wife, primitive and plotting. From the three lines converge hates which finally break. Father knifes son; son knifes father. The last scene is an appendix of horror. After lust has passed into love, raw instinct, to redeem itself, feels forced to commit child-murder. Conceived like a problem in geometry, this three-cornered feud ends in a fatal zero.

When storms of passion abate, man reverts to the simple pursuits of trade and pleasure. The ordinary New Englander has converted his love of old things into cold cash. Certainly the antique furniture racket has obscured traces of the old conscience. Two play-

"Ethan Frome," by Owen and Donald Davis

lets prove the point. Factory-made chairs are sold to gullible city jobbers as antiques. However, when a Paul Revere tankard, the object of search by many buyers, is unwittingly sold to a knowing dealer who sees through the seller's tricks, the cheater is cheated.[16] Equally conscienceless, though justified by sentimental considerations, is the act of the old spruce gum gatherer who sneaks back a valuable pitcher which has been sold to a dealer who would not return it.[17] Such playlets slyly rule out notions of business honor.

One local legend which deals with belief and doubt has found its way to the stage. It is woven into the story of the old man whose granddaughter took sick. Together the two got into a buggy to go to Boston for medical aid. Natives near Boston believe that when such a man calls at any house to ask the fatal question, "Which is the way to Boston?" death will visit that home. The dramatic version involves an aunt and uncle entertaining a nephew and his wife. The younger man accuses the older of being superstitious, of living in the past, and of believing in signs and omens. Meanwhile the aunt is worried over her daughter, now lying in a hospital. A knock! A stranger asks the way to Boston. Yes, it was a man in a buggy and he had a little girl with him. The old folks know exactly what that means. Still, the news that comes by telegram is unexpected. The daughter has recovered, but the shock proves too much for the aunt and she dies. The play of fear and foreboding, the momentary relief over the checker game, the exchange of views are well sustained, though the resolution is artificially consummated.[18]

Along the curving peninsula known as Cape Cod, and in near-by territory, the seafolk present as homo-

geneous a picture as that of any inland or mountain
group. Traditions, customs, beliefs, and tales associated with the sea bind them into one broad identity.
The elemental struggle of the fisherfolk against the
sea goes on grim and fierce as of old. Characters bend
like reeds, sometimes break before the gale. For those
whose kin must part between long voyages, a show of
courage and resignation grows habitual. Whenever
wives must yield up their menfolk, they suffer a crisis.
Those who brood too long go mad. Though these
Cape folk hate the sea, routine or inertia makes them
unwilling to accept change.

Several sea pieces bear out these observations. When
a younger son feels bound to follow the trade of his
elders who lost their lives at sea, nothing will stop him.
In another instance, the son will take the father's place,
and twenty years hence others will watch while *his*
boat comes in.[19] One character observes with the old
sea captain in *Anna Christie* (by Eugene O'Neill),
"It's that old woman sea that takes our men from us."[20]
In the whaling days of Nantucket many a youth must
have pondered the question of landlubber or seafarer.
Should he marry the girl after a delay of seven years,
or put it off again because the sea calls? He decides
to sail.[21]

Brooding too long over lost ones often breeds hallucinations. Grief may cause one to hear the tinkle of bells
and to walk into the sea after a lover who has failed to
arrive with his ship.[22] It may also distract the confined
wife on the Maine coast who dreams of a former
drowned lover and follows his ghost to her death.[23]

The drab life of these seafolk does not rule out
humor inherent in character. Reminiscent of old men
in Irish plays are the two crusty ex-skippers squabbling
to assert their rights to manage a love affair of their

niece. Against a blue sky verbal squalls break out. But the niece has her own plans. She is engaged to a youth unknown to her two uncles. The language of the sea is comically used. "Fog around your jib-boom. . . . Wait! Heave-to! Come up into the wind," and other such phrases are sprinkled through the piece.[24]

Old land portraits of sleepy townsmen who lolled on the steps of the village post office over thirty years ago are revived in *Three Cape Cod Plays,* by Joshua Freeman Crowell. Small-town life before the first World War is gently shown up. The natives crave excitement, manage to get "rousted" from time to time only to relapse into sleep. The rabble-rouser loves to stir up suspicionmongers while the old sea dog takes a fatherly interest in everybody. The village Xerxes, who ties the three plots together, changes his occupation often and believes in the principle of slowness. Finally he wins the girl. The plots may be inconsequential, but the humor is sly and pervasive and the characterization droll.

What distinguishes these sea pieces, influenced, for the most part, by the modern school of Irish dramatists, is the universal outlook, the consequences determined by sea life, and the racy speech uttered by the seafolk along the Cape.

Definitely the drama of New England stems from conditions of living on the rocky, inland soil and along the fishing banks. It aims, within a specific area, to put flesh on human forms marked by regional habits: the baffled, repressed, inbred, perverse, clannish natives. For here characters still cling to stumps like fruity fungus among

These Devil's acres thick with thorns,
with junipers and briars.[25]

The keynote of Yankee drama is sobriety shaken by
cross fire.

---

1. By Mary Margaret Russell.
2. *The Diabolical Circle*, by Beulah Bomstead.
3. *Dowry and Romance*, by Rose C. Meblin.
4. *Maze*, by Arthur Corning White.
5. *Hollyhocks*, by Joseph Philip Fox.
6. *The Conflict*, by Clarice V. McCauley.
7. *Thompson's Luck*, by Harry G. Grover.
8. *A Transfer of Property*, by Mark Reed.
9. *Forever Credulous*, by David O. Woodbury.
10. *Just Neighborly*, by Alexander Dean.
11. *Ring Once for Central*, by Carl Allensworth.
12. *Common Ground*, by Eleanor Whiting.
13. *Blockade*, by Olivia H. Dunbar.
14. *Ancient Heritage*, by Philip Goddard Parker.
15. *Onions*, by Priscilla Ordway.
16. *Grandfather's Chair*, by Walter Prichard Eaton.
17. *Hannah's Pitcher*, by Margaret Miller.
18. *Which Is the Way to Boston?*, by Ronald Lorenzen.
19. *Mis' Mercy*, by Louise W. Bray.
20. *Men Folk*, by Florence Ryerson and Colin Clements.
21. *Greasy Luck*, by Rachel Field.
22. *The Marriage Gown*, by Judith K. Sollenberger.
23. *Rain*, by Dana Burnet.
24. *The Managers*, by Joseph C. Lincoln.
25. From *Ballads of Square-Toed Americans*, by Robert P. Tristram
Coffin (New York, 1933), p. 98.

II

Ghosts and Bricks

FEW AMERICANS ordinarily associate folk say with the state of New York. Yet ghosts, goblins, and witches do flit along the Hudson River and the Mohawk Valley. Thunder Mountain is said to shelter a crew of goblins. Mountain dwarfs, survivors of a Dutch crew, still haunt the shores for treasure, while phantom ships and a phantom oarsman glide along the waters off New Rochelle as well as over those of Long Island Sound.

Legendry is but one manifestation of folklore: the fantasy of the people running free. Over a layer of lore deposited first by the Indian there has been laid a composite heritage brought over by German, Italian, Scottish, Irish, Polish, Dutch, and other nationalities. Ballads which once rang from tanneries, from the shanties of hoopmakers, and from lumber camps still are heard throughout the Catskills. Such old tunes as "Brennan on the Moor," "The Cutting of the Pines," and "The Flat River Raftsman" still float down the years. In addition, a medley of popular beliefs, superstitions, tales which circulate up and down the state among the hill folk in upstate counties and in the folds of the Adirondacks, have not yet been fully recorded.

The regional drama draws its lifeblood from this floating fact and fiction. Tentative playlets based on the life of the Oneida and Seneca Indians appeared in 1900. *Yagowanea,* by Helen P. Kane, a story of vengeance and punishment for violating the laws of

sanctuary, is set against the bluffs above Niagara, with
Lake Erie as the background. *The White Doe of
Oneida* (1907) and *Yot-Che-Ka* (1914), a pageant-
drama laid in the sixteenth century, deal with inter-
tribal relations. Indian songs weave through the plots
and the talk is sprinkled with expletives like *Hi! Ho!
Ohé!*

Three York State folk festivals combine the features
of the harvest festival with those of the song-and-custom
revivals. There is the Polish Onion Festival, held in
Florida, Orange County; the Catskill Folk Festival,
organized as an educational feature by Norman Studer
to pull out of corners the minstrelsy which lingers in
the backwoods of the Catskills; and the spectacular
annual August Indian pageant given, since 1931, at
Ticonderoga under the direction of Tom Cook. It is
intended to preserve Indian lore for the delectation
of the white man. The tenth festival, for example,
was divided into two parts. The first showed Indian
dances, customs, and a thanksgiving ceremony. The
second spectacularly presented the familiar story of
Hiawatha's purpose to end Indian warfare among the
Five Nations by combining the tribes of the Cayugas,
Oneidas, Senecas, Onondagas, and Mohawks into one
common band to "build a long house" that would endure for centuries. The conflict is supplied by the
opposition of the obstinate Atotarho, the warring
chieftain. He is finally won over by a shrewd stroke
when Hiawatha names him as the one best qualified
to act as the head sachem for the league. The following year the festival showed Red Jacket, the famous
Indian orator, in a series of scenes with the customary
Indian accoutrements.

Most widely known of folk characters is Rip Van
Winkle. Though imported from the Harz Mountains

of Germany, the story was mixed with Dutch fragments and squarely set down on the soil of the Catskills
by Washington Irving. The first dramatization in
America was given at Albany in 1828. Later versions
modified the story. At least nineteen dramatic adaptations were made between 1870 and 1916: six serious
plays, five librettos, and eight comedies.[1] The version
which held the stage longest and played throughout
the nation and in the British Isles was *Rip Van Winkle*
(1865), written by Dion Boucicault and altered by the
popular actor, Joseph Jefferson. Rip, a genial and
lovable tippler, speaks a German dialect, quarrels with
his Gretchen, and shrewdly declines to sign the papers
which will turn over the property to the villainous
townsman. Rip's wife thereupon orders him to leave
the house in the midst of a heavy storm. Presently
appears a dwarfish figure clad like a Dutch seaman of
the 1600's in doublet and hose and high-crowned
hat. Henry Hudson and his crew follow. Rip accepts
the drink offered by the dwarfs and falls asleep.
Twenty years later he awakes, trudges to town, is
recognized, and arrives just in time to free and gladden
his wife and daughter. The dramatic version by
James A. Herne stresses the Dutch character of Rip.
Of librettos, the folk opera in three acts (1919) by
Percy MacKaye (with music by Reginald de Koven)
deserves passing mention. In keeping with operatic
license, the poet introduced a touch of the supernatural in the guise of the Magic Flask. He also invented a charming younger sister for Katrina, called
Peterkee. Henry Hudson tells Peterkee how to win
the Magic Flask. Years later, just after his long sleep,
Rip returns on the day his beloved is to marry. Of
course she has remained faithful to his memory. After
a drink from the flask, Rip regains his youth; and the

two are united. In this piece there are no elves, no shrewish outbursts from Katrina, and no poetry to speak of. The action is well wrought, and the entire effect pictorial. Other versions seem to miss fire and fail to stir the will to believe. The elves are no more elves than rocks are ravens.

Among contemporary plays *High Tor* (1937), by Maxwell Anderson, uses the same legendary background. Set on a mountaintop above Haverstraw overlooking the Hudson, a phantom crew of Dutch sailors has been lost for three hundred years. While certain scenes are dreamily folkish, the play as a whole cannot be regarded as truly regional.

From the life of religious sects which retain that single-mindedness making for folk identity have stemmed plays which are definitely regional. One of the earliest sects to take root in eastern soil during the Revolutionary War was that of the Shaking Quakers, or Shakers, founded by Ann Lee. These people, who consecrated themselves and their property to God, led celibate lives, believed in the equality of the sexes, and considered themselves "a body of saints whose mission it was to redeem themselves and others from the sins of worldliness and carnal nature." The first society and fountainhead of Shakerism was organized in 1787 at New Lebanon, New York. Two other settlements, at Watervliet and Groveland, followed. Although the Shakers lived communal lives of purity, austerity did not forbid laughter, the singing of hymns, and religious dances supervised by elders. As for the drama, it is pertinent to note that one prominent elder stoutly denounced the "play." It was therefore left to non-Shakers to stage such plays as might be written. Of three dealing with the society, penned by non-Shakers, two were acted in the East. The settings

are not strictly localized. *The Shaker Lovers* (1849),
written by Samuel D. Johnson, an old melodrama with
a preposterous plot, relates to a period before the
Civil War. Briefly, two Shakers are in love. He pro-
poses a tryst and—what is sternly forbidden—marriage!
He will no longer be "one of the blinded and deluded
people." An elder, the jealous villain, discovers their
plan and exclaims, "She shall be my bride and he, my
victim." After a number of mishaps and foiled attempts
to kill the youth, the lover arrives in time to accuse
the elder and save his ladybird. The author's knowledge of the Shakers is slight and the total effect, regarded in a modern light, maliciously satiric. A more
whimsical playlet in verse, *The Little Shakeresses*
(1923), by Carla F. Rosenthal, presents seven of the
sect and another young man. They are sedately
stirred by the news that the circus is coming to town.
One recalls visiting the circus as a child. When an
agent enters to offer them tickets, what are these good
ladies to do? Give them to the children? Oh, no! But
one by one they agree to go along as guardians.

The change from religious to secular history is like
passing from a quiet church into a busy street. In the
first half of the nineteenth century life to the canallers
on the Erie Canal was, presumably, exciting. Revived
in a play, these boaters—canalboat cook, preacher, bar-
tender, fiddler, and plain person—bustled and quar-
reled and drifted along from Rome to Utica. The plot
of *Low Bridge* (1938), by Frank B. Elser, hinges on a
romance between a ship's cook and a gawk from the
farm. Love wavers until the climactic fight decides
the issue in favor of the rustic suitor. The dialogue
is peppered with references to the rivalry between
canalboat and railroad. A bit of local brag is ad-
missible. "By grab, she's a swarming hive, the Old

Erie Canal is. It's the bowels of the nation. It's the
hull she-bang of life." Drawn in hard, straight lines,
the picture resembles a Currier & Ives' chromo.

The theater of the state owes much to Cornell University. During Farm and Home Week rural dramatic
festivals have been put on in past years. Professors
have stimulated the writing and producing of local
plays. The first batch of nine rural-life plays, written
in 1928, pin down problems in farm economics.
Themes vary. Two deal with disappointed lives, four
with the cruel parent, and three with local matters.
The point is sharply driven, the homely qualities of the
actors plainly outlined, the background roughly
sketched. Definite problems touch upon the son who
has tasted city life and gone to agricultural college;[2]
the county agent who sums up rural wisdom;[3] the
need of organizing farm association bureaus to help
young couples to a fresh start and thus "keep 'em down
on the farm."[4] As plays they use character to demonstrate a thesis, and as such may be dismissed as practical
pamphlet plays.

Other Cornell offerings, presented seven years later,
try to capture a sense of place. Playlets with a dash of
drama deal with matters more personal and local, and
show up rural characters more sharply. There is the
bashful beau who, by the help of a department store
catalogue which advertises dresses and rings, finally
pops the question.[5] The cheese genius, after six
months' effort at making cheese "out o' milk we was
dumpin' during the milk strike," succeeds in winning
the three-hundred-dollar prize.[6] Finally, there is the
aged farm woman who does not follow her intention
to move to a city apartment but stays on the farm to
take care of a neighbor's orphan and her newly arrived
niece.[7]

Since 1919 a New York State Drama Project for the writing and producing of "plays of regional interest" has been conducted by Professor A. M. Drummond of Cornell University. In 1938, the Cornell University Theatre began the project for New York State Plays under the supervision of Robert E. Gard. From legends, ballads, historic items buried in old journals; from countryside tales about witches, giants, Indians, horse thieves and such, competent plays "on the American theme" have been devised.[8] They range in time from 1790 to 1941, and in scene from the manors of the Hudson to the vineyards of Chautauqua County. These chunks of material are frankly theatricalized, with a dash of farce to make them palatable.

The famous Cardiff hoax, perpetuated in 1869, revived a chapter in human folly and credulity and supplied the theme of a long play. In the spring of 1939, *The Cardiff Giant,* written in true circus style by A. M. Drummond and Robert E. Gard, regaled the public at Ithaca. The town of Cardiff lies fifteen miles south of Syracuse in the Onondaga Valley. When the play opens many human types cross the stage: canallers, farmers, rural schoolmasters, Negroes, cracker-box politicians, Civil War veterans, a chief and a squaw, reapers, wives, David Harum, the hoss trader, and Colonel Wood, the preacher. A procession is marching off to see the advertised wonder, a dead giant. People are asking, "How did it get there?" The truth is that this "stunnified fish" had been brought in a box from "Ioway" and buried in a lot. At a well-digging bee, arranged beforehand, the petrified, human giant made of gypsum is unearthed. It weighs one and a half tons and measures twelve feet in length, four feet in width, and twenty-two inches in depth. Amazement! A tent is rigged over the body and the public admitted for a fee. Crowds pour in; poems and testimonials praise this "wonder of the century"; the owners grow rich. P. T. Barnum offers a hundred thousand dollars, but the bid is rejected. Finally the hoax is exposed and the show is over. To judge this processional of stage puppets daubed with primary colors by standards other than the circus would be captious.

An analogous stage piece, based on an upstate legend known in the Finger Lakes country, is *The Lake Guns of Seneca and Cayuga,* by A. M. Drummond, published by the Cornell University Press. "These baffling thunders," these drumming sounds which boom from the lakes, have long mystified residents and strangers. How to explain them is the task of the playmaker. An interlocutor recites the local myths and the geographic wonders of the region. These include the Great Serpent, "Seneca Lake what ain't got no bottom," and the Big Snake that stretched three hundred miles across New York State and flattened down the hills. In the mythical down under, The Man of the Lakes opines that the sounds are made "by ancient stone Indians who wander through the underground and fall off subterranean cliffs." Other hypotheses are offered to a steady beat of minstrel-show hilarity and noisy slapstick. One is tempted to ask why a core of legend must be dressed up with so much hocus-pocus.

Other theater pieces jump from place to place in upper New York State. But the tone is chastened, the craftsmanship competent. Of these dramatized pages from state history, the most notable is *Chenango Crone,*[9] a flash into an odd corner off Cherry Valley Pike near Nine Mile Swamp in the days when organized horse thieves used to terrorize the countryside.

The action is dark and horrendous. Indeed, the story unfolds as story and not as sociology.

Three comedies by Robert E. Gard, done with skill, humor, and dramatic aptitude, return to early state history. Facts dug from musty records flicker into momentary life. The psychology of the frontier maid who reluctantly consents to marry her man only by extending her arm through a hole in a suspended quilt is vivid and plausible.[10] So is the sudden conversion of the unbelieving horse thief by a happy accident which looks to him like a miracle.[11] True to fact is the farcical mixup of rebels and a leader during the antirent strikes in the 1840's.[12] This plain, theatricalized transcript is a workmanlike specimen of historic farce.

Over a period of years, about fifty regional plays have been staged by the Cornell University Theatre. In the main these plays seem cut to set patterns. Characters do not give evidence of being rooted; neither is the region assimilated. A third dimension is lacking. At all costs the actual happenings must be heightened. Therefore, for every ounce of fact there must be a pound of spice. The note of forced heartiness and theatricalism, the nasal twang and the circus stunt, can serve but to perpetuate the popular notion of "rube" comedy. The mere desire to arrest legends and historic episodes in dramatic form, worthy as the wish must be, does not of itself create a valid regional drama or plays of regional interest. There must also be a strong inner urge toward regional expression to guide the pen of the gifted regionalist.

During the summers of 1941 and 1942 a troupe of eight graduates from Vassar College, calling themselves the Valley Vagabonds, toured middle New York State. They offered their original dramatizations of the folklore of the Hudson Valley and presented their plays out of doors. Their playlets belong to ephemera.

Minor one-act plays written by miscellaneous scribes stress character on native ground. In three of these numbers, common misery unites three women. A devoted mother frantically tries to shield her half-witted son against officers of the law and fails.[13] A hard old woman, now blind, bewails her misused past. She finally discovers that "there's loving in the world."[14] A sensitive wife of a boorish husband, a cabbage grower, finds it hard to breathe the air of her native Long Island.[15] Two slighter sketches, cut to the same design, deal with bandits in a storm. In both scenes the intruders are trapped while the storm outside rumbles on.[16]

Among the essays toward a genuine regional drama, one solid achievement of folk portraiture stands out: *Darick Clausen* (1929), by Thomas P. Robinson. Here independent character, bred in the brick kilns of the Catskills and nursed by kindliness, after two centuries at brickmaking turns hard as brick itself. In a fold of the mountains lies Cowenhaven, known for its fine bricks. Baked by simple, genuine folk in old-fashioned kilns, these bricks supposedly retain something of the spirit of their makers. When modernity sweeps in on the skirts of a rich, aggressive newcomer, the townspeople fight all attempts to streamline the brickworks. In fact, one of the foremen will not accept the new machine-made heresy. He clings to his old artistic habits and honesty. Finally comes the test of comparison. The new brick is declared inferior to the old one because it lacks that intangible honesty which once poured naturally into the older mould. Darick feels himself vindicated and bluff integrity wins. At the same time, he and the newcomer are united in wedlock.

What ties these plays together, one-act and full-length, dealing with aborigine, folk figure, history, earth phenomenon, farm, and local record, is the impact of desire and motive against circumstances peculiar to the specific soil of New York State. Shaped by these settings, characters are what they are. Though these plays may lack distinction, the flavor of actuality is unmistakably authentic. Out of such home-grown stuff can eventually come a rich regional drama.

With such articulate promoters of regionalism as Carl Carmer, Harold W. Thompson, A. M. Drummond, and Robert Gard piping the rural horn and luring investigators to tap the rich folk resources stored in libraries and museums upstate,[17] there should be a theatric awakening throughout the state. Thus far the drama of this region has not been orchestrated. Rather it is a playing of separate instruments waiting for the master conductor.

1. According to information obtained from the Office of the Registrar of Copyrights, Washington, D.C.

2. *That Upper Forty*, by Marvin Herrick and Hoyt H. Hudson.

3. *Balanced Diet*, by Elizabeth Lay Green.

4. *The Old Timers' Bureau*, by John H. Munson.

5. *The Catalogue*, by T. M. Morrow.

6. *Cheese It*, by Edna Becker.

7. *A Light on the Crossroads*, by C. E. Van Norman.

8. See *How to Choose a Play and How to Write One (Cornell Extension Bulletin, No. 449)*, published by the New York State College of Agriculture at Cornell University, Ithaca, N.Y., November, 1940.

9. By Edward Kamarck.

10. *Let's Get On with the Marryin'*.

11. *Raisin' the Devil*.

12. *Mixing Up the Rent*.

13. *Joe*, by Jane Dransfield.

14. *Marthe*, by Noel Armstrong.

15. *The Detour*, by Owen Davis.

16. *Spring Storm*, by Frank H. Ordway; *Out of the Night*, by John Smith.

17. Crammed with folklore are the Grosvenor Library in Buffalo, the Buffalo Museum of Science, the library of The State College for Teachers at Albany, the Cornell Library, the Rochester Library, the Syracuse Library, the Vassar College Library, and the numerous museums and county historical society depositories throughout the state, especially that of the New York State Historical Association at Cooperstown and the museum at Ticonderoga.

III

The Plain People

OUT OF THE seed, the fruit; out of the root, the tree. So, too, from the origins of a section, may be fore-shadowed the course of future events. The first settlers of Pennsylvania, that fairest spot among the colonies, brought with them an inbred sturdiness, a friendly spirit toward other men which remained constant. The promise of liberty and equality which William Penn and his one hundred Quakers offered in 1681 attracted other settlers. What the colonists of this model commonwealth would not tolerate was the slightest relaxing of firmness for fear of weakening the established faith. To this end the Quakers, or Society of Friends, whose "faith had been tried in the fires of persecution,"[1] prohibited all "rude or riotous sports" and opposed theatricals on the ground of morality. But with the passing of time, as the human instinct of play asserted its demands, the Quakers came to accept the singing of appropriate airs, then dancing, and, in recent years, even the staging of acceptable plays.[2]

British influence, from colonial days, caused a re-vival of medieval mummery at the beginning of this century. In Philadelphia, an annual street pageant, performed by thousands of masqueraders and dancers in splendid satin marching along under a Lord of Misrule, recalls the old Christmas festivities which long ago amused the British public. The Mummers' Parade on New Year's Day has been an institution which even the war could not suspend.

Returning to historic beginnings, after the British

had settled, other nationalities poured their members into Penn's colony. The Germans, a conglomerate mixture from continental Europe, mainly the Palatinate, flocked there after 1683 and settled in the eastern part of the region. The groups intermarried but held on to the common dialect spoken in the Palatinate and along the upper Rhine. Today their descendants, the thrifty and pragmatic Pennsylvania Germans (wrongly called Dutch) may be recognized by their dress, speech, and doctrine. Men and boys wear broadbrims while women wear bonnets and distinctive apparel of brown, black, or gray. Characteristic is their use of the terminal "ain't" for "Isn't that so?"

They cling rigorously to church dogmas, these devout worshippers. They practice nonresistance, recognize the Bible and personal conscience as their sole guide, but differ on specific points. As a result they belong to a score of denominations: Mennonites, Amish, Dunkards, Moravians or United Brethren, Lutherans, Schwenkfelders, Weinbrennarians, Widerdeifers, Brinsers, and others. Some of these sects agree with the Quakers in forbidding oaths and in refusing to take human life, or to enter the military service. Despite the rigid discipline (as among the Amish) and the ban on theaters, movies, and public entertainments in certain counties, feasting, country-dancing, "singings," and hymn music played on the long zithers are permitted.

Any drama, therefore, which springs from such sources must operate within a framework of religious doctrine and folkways. Native plays are rooted in the faith as well as in the soil. Plays state, if they do not resolve, the conflict bred by divergent viewpoints on church discipline as against worldly desire.

One historic play based on the life of a fanatical religious leader sharply presents the issue of profane as against divine love. In the 1740's a strongheaded leader, Conrad Beissel, broke with the Dunkards over the question of Sabbath observance and founded the Cloister of Ephrata. This bit of local history is staged in *Ephrata* (1943), a play by Frank Neusbaum and Kathryn M. Popp. It holds closely to the facts of routine and discipline.

The scene is a room in the house of the sisterhood in the Ephrata Cloisters about the year 1743. Seven sisters express their inmost thoughts and feelings freely and daringly toward their sisterhood, their leader, and their God. The chatter is light and unsentimental. We learn, for example, that Father Beissel is stern, forbidding, and unyielding. Then the plot centers on the case of Sister Tabea, intelligent and outspoken, who has fallen in love with a newcomer to the brotherhood, one Daniel. Thereafter her heart speaks and yearns for love; but not without an inner struggle. She swings back and forth between earthly and heavenly love. Finally she decides to ask the father for permission to marry. The ebb and flow of passion between the father and the sister, between Tabea and her lover, and between Daniel and the father make exceedingly good theater. The plot reaches its crest in the final scene of Beissel's prayer to God at the wedding ceremony, after he has failed to make Tabea change her mind. As he speaks, he gathers power. When he reaches the line, "Let her know, dear God, that she may still turn from her weeping, (that) she may clothe herself in white, and have on her no longer the blood-covered garment, except that one which shall clothe her for the cross," the bride goes back to the choir and her Lord. And her groom knows he has lost her forever. The father has won back his follower, and the sisters resume their placid and cloistered existence.

Other plays are motivated by the age-old clash between youngsters trying to make up their minds whether to join or reject the parental faith and elders inured to church submission. When these strict adherents happen to be Mennonites, possibly the oldest Protestant sect in this region, the breach is bound to be wide and deep. In one playlet a hypocritical elder, blind to his own shortcomings in failing to provide for his wife, compels his son to "confess his sin before the congregation." The dramatic irony is intense.[3] In a second play, a Mennonite daughter is warned to give up her carnal ways, for all flesh is grass, and the grass withereth even as the flower fadeth. For such sins as walking on the Sabbath, reading novels, and singing worldly songs, a sinner may be "set back" or "pulled out of meeting." This daughter is torn between filial obedience and love. True to her born instincts she commits blasphemy, is promptly "set back" by her elders and beaten by her father. Then the play takes a theatrical turn which almost invalidates its worth as document. Just when things look black for the maid, she manages, by a sudden stroke of good fortune, to escape with the man who loves her.[4] Over an artificial plot is painted a thin veneer of folkways.

Like the Mennonites, the Dunkers (or Dunkards) are a devout and clannish people. They fear any sinful alliance with "outsiders" who belong to the "world's peeble." Such marriages are bound to lead to a play of cross-purposes. Take the case of the Dunkard youth from Berks County who has just married a "world's woman." She fails to fit into the ways of her husband's family. What is worse, she flatly refuses to wear what they dictate to be proper garb. When two

German spies enter the plot and an explosion breaks her husband's legs, the story goes Broadway. In the end, an argument convinces the runaway wife that she ought to give in and put on the plain dress of the folk. Turning to another example, a wise old grand-pop declares persuasively, "My people would rather stand with their feet on their own ground." In this former Federal Theatre play, *Feet on the Ground* (1936), by H. A. Archibald, the folkways seem faith-fully though somewhat too deliberately set down. Too many traits of character, in the attempt to create fully rounded portraits, seem to submerge character. Besides, nothing is gained by the too-sophisticated chatter of night-club habitués. As one line puts it, "It won't make, ain't?"

These devout Penn-Germans have long been noted for their gloomy superstitions and this branch of their folklore has been the subject of extensive research. A good deal of it bears on the moon, the hex woman, and folk medicine. To quote a few beliefs at random: it is well to plant corn when the moon is in the up sign; witches can kill cattle by feeding them hair; spooks can "verhex" cattle; to cure whooping cough, put nine worms into a bottle or, according to another source, wear the rattle of a rattlesnake.

Especially susceptible to such current beliefs is the credulous farmer whose barn carries the "hexefus" or witch foot, a fertility symbol, and other geometric designs to scare away evil spirits. One such character from a local play is vexed by the question of when to plant corn. Is it good sprouting weather when the corners of the moon point upward or downward? Minor differences ensue when he argues the matter with his farm hand. At any rate, his daughter finds it timely, when the moon points upward, to reject the brush salesman and make up with the loyal hired man. The characters resemble puppets rather than living beings as they come and go uttering such exclamations as *vy, ach,* and *vat*[5].

However harmless the current beliefs in folk medicine may sound in the telling, in actual practice such primitive ideas must clash with science and the law. There are farmers who are also hex doctors. They worship signs and deal in charms and incantations. One such practitioner has become the principal of a play. With the entry of a younger, trained, and cool-headed doctor into the family, the clash of opposite views is inevitable. It comes when a grandson falls ill. Shall it be superstition or medicine? Dire consequences result over a difference of opinion on how to cure the sick child. The opportune removal of the doctor, after he has been shot because he picked up the broomstick placed near a door (a way of testing the child's malady), precipitates the tragedy. It gives the powwow doctor a chance to take over the cure. As expected, he fails; the baby dies and the law steps in. But the self-assured farmer-practitioner walks off to jail with his faith in hexerei unimpaired.[6]

According to local legend, a gate painted blue once indicated that a maid in the house was ripe for marriage. When such a daughter falls in love with a man outside the faith, the fanatical father is made to realize the danger of holding onto narrow conceptions of sin.[7]

A recent composite study of regional manners which appeared on Broadway, *Papa Is All* (1942), by Patterson Greene, also enacts the old struggle of parents against children on the soil of Lancaster. The characters are likeable and vividly conceived, though the outlines of the plot are familiar. It is the story of the tyrant-sire, a compact of "cruelty, fanaticism, greed, and hate," who bullies his family into abject terror. He and his wife are Mennonites while the children exercise their privilege of not adopting the faith until they feel the call to become "plain." The outer details of costume, manners, and speech are carefully pre-scribed. Papa, a burly man in his fifties, wears the traditional beard with upper lip smoothshaven, long black coat, black trousers, and broad-brimmed hat. He doesn't like soldiers, objects to sketching designs of machinery, to driving a car, to flying, going to the movies, and to any kind of enjoyment. His authority is the Bible, which he misuses shamefully. Mama, gentle and meek, wears the brown Mennonite dress, a white cap, and a black bonnet to cover the hair. Both son and daughter strive to achieve their separate am-bitions, but are repressed at every turn. Only one course remains: to get rid of papa. The opportunity comes. But hopeful reports that papa is all ("all in" or dead) prove premature. When he turns up again, he shoots an innocent person and is arrested. To the end he invokes the laws of God. Over a conventional, well-developed plot the Mennonite customs are lightly dabbed. The dialogue, nevertheless, flows smoothly and gracefully.

Elsewhere the playful mood is not excluded. The worthless old man who awakes in his coffin on the way to burial evokes droll amusement. After this miracle the wives of the community serve him devotedly and neglect their husbands. Meanwhile, the peeved males are driven to their wits' end. What shall they do? One of them hits upon a counterhoax. He consents to die and be carried off in a casket. At this point the prophet claims he can restore the body to life. He threatens to pour gasoline over the "corpse" if he does not rise at his command. The end is obvious. The wives, now doubly impressed, renew their labors for the holy man and send their mates home.[8]

Out of the German dialect, with its intermixture of English, has come a shelf of comic poems, tales, and a few good-humored plays. Designed primarily for the local citizenry, these bilingual pieces hold a philological if not dramatic interest for outsiders. In the reading they arouse but mild amusement. Four plays printed in obscure places are extant: a German version of *Rip Van Winkle* (1883) , by E. H. Rauch; *Die Inshurance Bissness* (undated) , by Dr. Ezra Grumbine; and two plays by Clarence Iobst of Emmaus. The first of the two latter pieces bears the foreign title of *En Quart Millich un en Halb Beint Raahm,*[9] first produced in the Emmaus High School in 1928. It is a light farce in conventional design dealing with the marital tangle. In brief, to arouse the dead love of a matter-of-fact husband after twenty-three years of married life, a wife pretends an affair with the milkman. Small-town gossips spread and magnify the story. But in the end all turns out well. The second comedy, *Salz* (1933) , based on a theme in *De Hexa Dokter,* by Charles C. More, presents a middle-aged couple who have neglected farm, home, and church. They blame evil spirits which they hope to ward off by charms. The family is "verhexed." A stranger posing as a doctor suggests a simple cure: a scrubbing brush and a bar of soap, to be used briskly.

A score of similar, light, bilingual pieces, never meant to be distinguished, have been acted out in the local community and college theaters but not released to the outside world. They are meant to be funny. As far as the regional drama is affected, such broad pieces bear only a limited value in that they flash in temporal form local characters, local speech, and scraps of local lore. In this respect they hardly differ from dialect drama in other parts of the world.

In addition to these intimate glimpses into regional character and folkways, the drama of the state has lifted the curtain on one of its pioneer sons, a robust folk figure. Over a century ago colonists migrated westward through the gateway of Pittsburgh Landing, in Pennsylvania, and pushed down the Ohio River into Ohio, Indiana, and up into Michigan and the Great Lakes country. The frontier bred two noticeable types: the quick settlers who decided to stay and build, and the restless movers, lured by rich land and wider prospects. After trying to live on the land, the modest Jonathan (John) Chapman, known by his more familiar name of Johnny Appleseed, felt the call to roam the country on his strange quest. He journeyed about planting apple seeds and fennel and preaching a queer interpretation of the Scriptures. "Fruit is next to religion," he said. Strange stories gathered about this eccentric, unkempt figure as he tramped, with pot on head, over a hundred thousand miles on his mission. After his death in 1847 the man became a legend, a lay saint, a folk hero. Essentially he is blood brother to the Quakers in a deep-felt need to follow the inner light wherever it may lead.

Out of his career have been devised two plays. The first, a rambling account, grounds the action in Pittsburgh of 1800. Jonathan is a nurseryman who sells saplings to pioneers hitting the Western trail. He is friendly with the Indians. Once he is caught in a prairie fire and rescued. After sundry trials, he dies. Like other plays which follow the biographical line, the play lacks compression and a central conflict.[10]

A longer, unpublished play from the pen of E. P.

Conkle, *Johnny Appleseed*, recounts the movements of the tramping pioneer from his eighteenth year, after he and his brother leave their comfortable home in Redham, Massachusetts, for Pittsburgh Landing, up to the end of the journey. At first John, at a border settlement, gives away seedlings to those who pass by. One day the call comes to him; he must scatter seeds and plant trees in the wilderness. Always he is haunted by apples and apple seeds. A romantic note is introduced in the form of his lost love. Even after Johnny finds her, he cannot stay married. She understands him. "You're . . . a poet with a pocket full of apple seeds and head full of apple blossoms," she tells him. In his old age the missionary returns to his ex-wife's daughter. At last the bag is empty and he dies. The figure, on the whole, is drawn tenderly. Now and then the playwright catches the surge of inner feeling and the inexorable drive of a consecrated spirit who spent his life "just goin' round doin' good." As with most chronicle plays, the action spreads over too much ground.

To the extent that these plays and playlets from Penn's state depict recognizably transplanted peoples who have sunk roots into the American ground for more than two and a half centuries, they exhibit a unique strain. The regional sap runs freely. The rooted folk values which have hardly suffered change give these pieces bone and body. Unlike the religious plays from other regions, the didactic streak runs through the characters rather than through the plot structure. No preachment weighs down the tailpiece. The problems resolve themselves plausibly if not logically.

The conditions for dramatic conflict exist in abundance among these plain Pietists. Unique characters emerge. But the net result of published works is less than impressive. No epical or transcendent exploration of the questing spirit, or of the contemplative soul at war with the self or with a set of dogmas, has emerged thus far. Can it be that the cumulative scowl of elders over so many years has chilled the pen of the playmaker?

1. Vernon L. Parrington, *Main Currents in American Thought,* II, 361.

2. See *Quaker Bulletins,* 1934 to 1935, with reference to Pennington Players Religious Society of Friends, New York City.

3. *Mennonite,* by William S. Banks.

4. *A Mennonite Maid,* by Helen R. Martin and Frank Howe, Jr.

5. *The Up Sign,* by M. S. Reifsnyder.

6. *Broomsticks, Amen!* by Elmer Greensfelder.

7. *The Blue Gate,* by Jack Stuart Knapp.

8. *Resurrection Ezra,* by Ronald Elwy Mitchell.

9. See *Yearbook of the Pennsylvania German Folklore Society,* Vol. IV (1939).

10. *Johnny Appleseed,* by Donald Thistle.

IV

The Negro Theme

THE NEGRO has merged with and become part of
the American landscape. After slavery planted him
on an alien soil he quickly took root. In the warm
South his traditions, his temperament, and his culture
found room to expand. Since the Civil War hundreds of the brethren have migrated northward and,
some few, westward. Once settled, the Negro pene-
trated society at many points through his services and
talents and left the impress of a rich, racial heritage.
His songs and dances, his customs and folkways, have
ever since been the object of wide research. Within
this century these studies have yielded clues to his
inner life. Out of such knowledge has come the fuller
realization of his worth as a builder of the republic
and his value as a contributor to the folk arts.

Not until 1910 did the writers of fiction and the
drama discover in the ordinary Negro material for
serious treatment. Delving below the surface, the
writers of plays noted with a kind of rapturous discovery his preoccupations, his sorrows, conflicts, abase-
ment, and self-dramatization. Impressed by his extreme emotionalism and natural self they began to
translate him to the stage, albeit in a distorted form.

Since 1913 a series of plays long and short, written
first by white and later by colored scribes, has assembled types and individuals from the South and
from the North. These plays run the gamut from
primitive pageantry to the sophisticated strut of city
sports in St. Louis and in Harlem. Within this range

are scattered a multitude of observations on topics
racial, historic, social, economic, and domestic. The
treatment varies from that of the case history, which
points an accusing finger, to the more subtle delinea-
tions of complex earthlings allowed to talk and act and
sing naturally as they do in life.

In drama as in life the jungle beat is elemental; the
tom-tom speaks a universal language. Rhythm throbs
in the fiber of the Negro. In African ballet, aided by
mask, pantomime, scenes of hunting feasts in hut and
stockade, in revivalist meetings and mumbo jumbo,
the Negro reverts to primitive levels. Merrymakers in
modern dress burst the bonds of civilized behavior.
In Charleston, South Carolina, during Azalea Week,
Plantation Echoes[1] plays up three moods of the Gullah
Negro: his religious meetings, his burial services, and
his barn dances. Throughout pounds the tom-tom.
The appeal is frankly sensual. Similar entertainment is offered each spring by the Wadmalow Negroes
in the South.

In more dignified style, spectacle may celebrate the
glory of the race. When the need for creating a new
Negro art became conscious, Negro leaders planned
an ambitious spectacle. In 1913 W. E. B. Du Bois
wrote *The Star of Ethiopia* to reveal to the white
world the Negro as a fellow human. Twelve hundred
colored players participated in this brilliant tableau
of Ethiopia and her splendor.

If, to the pictorial tableau are added elements of
ceremonial worship, the effect is not unlike that of
the medieval morality. In fact, for many years such a
Negro play, spontaneously generated, moved from
circuit to circuit across North Carolina. The spectacle
survived by oral tradition. It represented Heaven
with its saints, Earth with its sixteen pilgrims, and

Hell with its imps and devils. Man, surrounded by temptation and subject to punishment and reward, acted out the old allegory. In 1936 appeared a written version, expanded to fit the needs of one hundred and twenty actors of the Negro unit of the Federal Theatre: *Heaven-Bound,* by Laura L. Edwards. Modern lighting, scenic designs, and costumes re-created the old fable of good fighting evil. The setting was elaborately impressive. To the right stood Hell-Mouth from which issued flames—a dreaded exit for sinners. Across the stage marched earthly pilgrims fighting their way from temptation to temptation while a reader (the author herself) narrated the Biblical episodes. St. Peter, St. John, and the archangels, Gabriel and Michael, in resplendent attire, intoned their lines. Central to the whole scene rose the golden stairway upward to the Pearly Gates surrounded by clouds in which sat the choir. More than sixty voices sang spirituals and incidental music. To the left rested a large seven-foot cross from the base of which a white-robed singer at intervals dramatized and sang sacred songs. Then this same singer and twenty old saints chanted and beat tambourines, triangles, and cymbals as they passed through the gray veil of Death while Mercy, draped in flowing white costume, knelt and pleaded as she had done throughout the play. Finally, Victory, lowered to the stage, swallowed up Death in her sheer gown as the choir sang "Steal Away to Jesus."

From the morality to the ritual drama is but a step. Originally introduced by Haitian emigrés to the Gulf coast, voodooism and like practices, with their elaborate secret rites and tense mounting surprises, can supply the pictorial background for open-air showings. The voodoo ritual of the Gullah Negroes of the South Carolina low country trots out primitive beliefs in

"hants" and "plat-eyes" together with the music of
reel songs and ancient spirituals in Gullah dialect.
The same magic strain runs through the services of
backwoods churches. A few spectacular themes for
plays have been suggested by the conflict between the
Baptist Church and the intrusive pagan cult. For
example, through the musical embroidery and frenzied
acting of *Run, Little Children* (1933), by Hall Johnson—part opera, part ballet, part drama—runs an illicit
love story. Scenes shuttle between church observances,
wild hand clapping by the congregation, shoutings and
moanings, words by the preacher, and a few moments
of quiet dialogue. The result is dramatic boogie
woogie.

More tensely projected is the devil worship used to
frighten a sinner. Against a church background unfolds the story of the sinning daughter who "pleasures
herself on the 'tater bank," yet shows no sorrow. For
punishment she is condemned to sit in "de sinnah
cawner." Then the play goes wild. A masked figure
enters, sheathed in flannel underdrawers dyed a brilliant red and trailing a long tail. He jumps to the
platform, waves a pitchfork, and threatens the sinner
with vengeance. But no sign of sorrow is manifest.
Then he tears off the mask. He is her husband! The
woman is petrified. When he tries to strike her, the
pastor restrains him. "Forgibbin' is better dan re-
vengin' in de sight of de Lawd," he says wisely. Suddenly she is filled with remorse; flooded with sorrow
"like de rain f'um Hebben." And she breaks out into
wild song and savage dancing.[3]

Voodoo practitioners, known as conjure doctors,
can bring rain, find lost property, cure jealousy, and
work spells and love charms. He or, more commonly,
she may be called in to cure high steppin' sinners,

bring back an erring wife, or force an unwilling uncle or grandfather to consent to a match. Generally a gaunt and grizzled crone named Aunt Eliza or Aunt Louise mumbles her incantations over the fire, uses grave dust and blood and shawls, and threatens to bring out that most dreaded of spells, the plat-eye! When the charm works, everybody is happy, no matter what the cost. On occasion, Christian theology and black magic unite. "De work ob de sperrits an' de work ob de Lawd gwine jine han's tonight."[4]

The fear of devils, spirits, and hants may be exploited by skeptics for gaining selfish ends. Paul Green's *The Man Who Died at Twelve O'clock* set a pattern somewhat elementary for imitators. A rascally grandpa refuses to give his permission for the marriage of his granddaughter to a local youth. Thereupon the couple decide to wring consent by playing on the superstitions of the old man. The lover, dressed in devil's costume, enters at midnight and scares the old man out of his wits. The man is sure he has died and gone to the lower regions. After a doze he awakens, never knows what really happened, and consents to the marriage.

Similar in outline is the story of the uncle who objects to his niece's marrying because "the sperrits won't let him." Here, too, the lovers feel they must act. By weird magic and impersonation, intended apparently to improve on the prototype, the suitor succeeds in making the uncle relent.[5]

The hocus-pocus of professional cheats may deceive for the moment. "The voodoo man with the gift of tongues," an arrant charlatan, sells gold machines which can change quarters into two-and-a-half-dollar gold pieces. The faker has impressed a young Negro wife before whom, with the aid of an accomplice, he demonstrates the machine. His honeyed words aim to convince the pious, doubting farmer. But the trick of substitution is detected by the Negro's sense of smell, and the cheater vanishes.[6]

A more whimsical piece illustrates the power of a fixation. An old Negro will not and cannot work because he bears the charmed sign of the plow between his shoulder blades. "His daddy was drug all the way down a corn row by a team of horses and died the day before the son was born." Therefore it is hard luck for him to work. Neither the white Baptist preacher from the North nor the wise Southern doctor can induce the wife to let the man do manual labor. Even after she is prevailed upon to look on the imaginary mark, she shouts, "There it is! There it is! Plain as I seen it all my days. The evil's upon me."[7]

Among Negroes may be found the most pious of Christians. But is the ordinary Negro as deeply religious as the pious deacon pictured in the old plays? Is he not more ceremonial than pious; more ritualistic than religious? Certainly, as pictured in several plays, he carries his beliefs lightly, sometimes mockingly, even to the point of blasphemy. At times it almost seems as if Christianity has not been able to blot out his innate skepticism.

Playfully and eloquently the lighter side of Negro faith, the literal folk belief in the Old Testament, is set down in *Green Pastures*, by Marc Connelly. This chronicle play retells eighteen episodes from the Bible in terms of Negro psychology. To these New Orleans folk heaven means a gigantic fish fry, while God is an immensely wise and charitable old preacher who walks the earth in the shape of a man. "Even bein' Gawd ain't a bed of roses," he sighs. Human wickedness is mildly chastised and mercy is represented as coming through suffering. This skillful continuity of scene and spiritual translates the ancient problem of good and evil into simple folk terms. Despite the world-wide success of this modern morality, the fact remains that it is a white man's fabrication rather than a faithful recital of folkways. Five imitations on Biblical subjects have proved less successful, although popular with certain colored groups.

The Negro, too, can shout his skepticism. Mockery and acceptance alternate in *Earth,* by Em Jo Basshe. The inner torment of a blaspheming mother who will not go back to "de Lawd" since they took away her son is set against the fury of a mob of newly baptized. She wonders at "what he (the white God) done gib de black man." After a brief spell of prosperity, during which she has made a turn toward belief, the widow is struck down by a fanatic mob. The point at issue remains obscure and the scheme of ideas is too rigidly drawn. Is irony intended in the fact that black believers strike down those who would deny the supremacy of the white man's God?

Another blaspheming widow, in revulsion against a God who took away her family, is the object of malicious gossip. Her irreverence scandalizes the local preacher. In defiance she removes the scarf from her head and shows a red spot—the curse of the heathen![8]

Southern folklore has brought into prominence one or two Negro heroes. Of these, just one has cast his shadow over the stage. In two plays, the steel-drivin' giant, John Henry, during his fourteen-hour ordeal, never stops driving spikes with his two hammers in competition with a steam drill. He wins the contest, but breaks down under the strain.[9] In a more recent version, a musical play, the fusion of lore and melody fails to come off.[10]

Thus far the characters strung along the lines of ritual and voodooism exhibit more racial than personal traits. They symbolize large forces and sum up typical attributes. These types move briskly, belong to the earth but to no specific area with a specific culture. Not until 1914 did the stage type vanish before the individual possessed of normal and natural instincts. *Three Plays for a Negro Theatre,* by the poet, Ridgely Torrence, ushered in the modern serious play about the Negro. Of these, *Granny Maumee,* produced by the Stage Society of New York, exhibited the tragic side of common Negro lives in a common setting. Blind Granny is bitter against the whites for burning her son. She wants to keep her family clean of the white streak. When her grandchild visits her, Granny prays for a moment's sight—just to behold the child's color. Her prayer is granted, and she sees—a white child! Amid voodoo rites and conjure tricks, she hears her son's voice pleading forgiveness before she dies. In *The Rider of Dreams* the author casts a sympathetic eye upon the Negro dreamer, a carefree fellow saddled to a prim wife. His unscrupulous acts are forgivable. The plaint at the end rings true. "All I wants is room to dream my good dreams an' make my own music."

Ten years later a duplicate portrait appeared in the figure of the happy-go-lucky parasite who lives on his relatives. Not only does he break a husband's banjo, but he turns the man over to the police on a false charge of murder.[11]

Then the note of bitterness, implicit in the indictment of wrongs, begins to ring in the theater. The theme of slavery, never a favorite choice of playwrights, turns up in less than a handful of contemporary plays. Generally the victim is shown struggling to free himself by any justifiable means. One slave who yearns to

be free enlists the aid of supernatural powers to kill
an overseer and escape. After an exciting career, the
Negro finally wins title to a piece of land—a happy
consummation![12] A second slave plans the details of
his escape and deceives his master before fleeing.[13]
More poignant is the suffering of the worried slave
whose children have been sold down the river. Now
she must suffer the horror of seeing her daughter kill
herself rather than mate with the Negro whom the
master has selected for her.[14]

The Negro as victim moved downstage. And the
world saw him as he is: the target of the white man's
ill will. How often had he laughed in public but wept
in private. For his white Christian masters never made
him forget that white is white and black is black. To
maintain white supremacy, the black man must be
kept down. Some of his brethren had grown used to
the idea that, throughout the South, they must cringe
and bow and grin. But a few could not brook discrimination. Especially upon the sensitive spirits and
the children did the burden of suffering fall. Why
must children be made aware of the fact that "our
skins are dark" and why must they shrivel up under
that vile epithet, "Nigger!" To Rachel, who loves
babies and home, motherhood is the loveliest and
holiest goal in life. Ten years previously her father and
half brother had been lynched. Living now in a
Northern city, she and her mother and brother cannot
forget the past. As the whites have cast a curse on
motherhood, she will not marry the man who loves
her. Characters cry out, "Our lives are blasted by the
white man's prejudice." As a play this conscious effort
to dramatize the wrongs inflicted upon the race might
have carried more weight with shorter speeches and
less stilted dialogue.[15]

Inevitably oppression brings resistance. Some folks
will not be stepped on. Ways of striking back are
many. The discharged Negro, returning from the
First World War, has forgotten how to cringe. Did he
not fight for freedom? Therefore, when the soldier
learns that during his absence his dad had been burnt
by his white neighbors, his rage knows no bounds.
No more fear! He rushes out to seek the leader of
the gang.[16] The brooding, resentful brown-skinned
girl meets an equally defiant mate. Together they
plan to go up North. But a crime committed by the
boy at the last minute brings the plot to a violent
close.[17] Similarly, the young girl of nineteen living in
the Yazoo delta of the Mississippi is invited by an
idealistic Negro teacher to flee with him to Chicago.
She consents. But before she goes, she must give herself up to the local planter. Stubbornly she refuses,
and in the scuffle the planter is shot.[18]

Defiance may get by in the North. The aristocratic
Negro gambler, denied admission to a sports arena in
upper New York State, forces an entry, bets on the
black cock, and wins. Haughtily he who feels in his
veins the blood of kings throws back his winnings to
the rude whites.[19]

The sad fact remains that in the South defiance
breeds violence. Woe to the hotheads who dare to defy
the cheating white man. Should the culprit take his
courage in his own hands and refuse to follow the line
that "de only way t' git long in dis country is live on
bended knee"? Here the drama dips into blood and
tears. The initial struggle foretells the end. "I knocked
him down when he called me a liar," whines the
victim. Then the mob closes in, fists fly, and the jig
is up. What makes the climax almost unendurable

is the chain of false and specious reasoning which sends a man to his death.

The plot of the lynch play varies little. Fatalism rules the scene. Generally a dead body is discovered by a Negro on his way home. A sudden fear impels the man to run. Then the trap of circumstantial evidence closes over his head. To heighten the pathos, the young fellow, by chance, may be visiting his relatives in the South, or be a passer-by, or may just have been married. Often what was meant to be light punishment, inflicted for warning, turns out to be disastrous. Even the coincidences fail to mitigate the horror of the lynching.

The mob must satiate its obscene blood lust. The poor victim must be dispatched by rope, faggot, and bullet. No time to reason why, no time to judge the evidence. Act instantly for a trumped-up reason: "to protect the purity of white womanhood." Then cry rape, summon the Klan, burn the cross, set the dogs on the trail, catch him, and string him up! The sadistic strain in the master race is luridly shown up when white onlookers gloat over the gory details of a hanging, as told by one of a party, in an unpublished script.[20]

Lynchings on the stage are as gruesome as in life. Generally the action takes place off stage and is described. As implied in plays, the causes of lynching are many. These include the desire to cover up misdeeds, for fear of consequences, and the will to maintain white supremacy. To cite a few plot cores: a girl, to cover up a secret rendezvous, blurts out thoughtlessly that an innocent, faithful Negro farm laborer has laid hands on her. Of course, she lies.[21] The white son admits, as he enters the house breathlessly, that he has raped a white teacher in a Southern community. But he does not hesitate to lay the blame on a Negro peddler who just happens to enter.[22] A male mulatto who looks white has found a sick girl on the road and generously brought her in his car to a gas station. When she dies, the circumstantial evidence points to him after his questioners discover that he is a "nigger."[23] Finally—the cream of the jest—a white peddler has committed the crime for which a Negro has been lynched. Not a ripple of concern or regret is voiced when the whites in the neighborhood learn of their mistake.[24]

Next to Mississippi, the highest number of lynchings in the South have been committed in the state of Georgia. A bitter play with impassioned speeches shows up white ambition driven to bestiality. A white Southerner has even permitted his daughter to witness the horrible bonfire built when he helped lynch a Negro. "I did my duty," he grumbles when his Northern wife confronts him with the deed. Aptly she counters, "You think you can blot out rape with murder?" The play reaches a crescendo of repulsion when his drunken accomplices cheer the husband as the man who tied the noose, and proclaim him the next governor.[25]

In these plays, where anger runneth over and accusation overshadows character, gradations of personality cannot and must not be expected. The grim issue comes first. The white man's brutality will be starkly balanced against the black man's innocence. Dramatically, such aids as the red sky, the drumbeats, and the screams are in themselves sensational enough to shock the sensibilities of any audience. That is why it is immoral to use a lynching scene unless it caps the climax plausibly and logically.

In lesser acts of cruelty, the white man flaunts his

race pride. It must show itself superior even in death, as in the case of the lowly Negro killed on the railroad tracks. The sheriff's investigation, the identification of the body, and the order to cart it off are all acts carried out in a highhanded manner as if the white man belonged to a deathless world. But the white man's bullying receives a check when the preacher boldly sings out that the "nigger" will be put on the right side of the Lord.[26] Also, there is the Southern plantation overseer who is apathetic to the feelings of his workers. He demands payment of a debt and continuous work in the fields from one laborer whose wife is burning up with fever. The woman dies. Just then the husband enters in a burst of fury and blasphemy. As suddenly he recants, prays, and vows to go "whar Ah can be free."[27]

In this Christian country justice draws the color line. This is starkly illustrated in the case of two Negroes and two "hunkies" trapped two miles from the entrance in a shaft of a West Virginia coal mine. A fifth man is a white policeman, once sent to arrest a Negro on a false charge of murder. Under danger, they speak of their past lives. As the men are huddled awaiting rescue, the policeman confesses he killed the man. Only one man can be saved, and it is the white man.[28]

Two courses remain open to the Negro: he can either resist or he can submit. The case for resistance is sharply brought to focus in two death-defying playlets. In the first, one character argues that it is better to die when he learns that the land he lives on has been bought by the white slayer of his son.[29] In the second, a fighter insists that it is best to perish with your back to the wall, solaced by the thought that others will take up the fight after you are gone.[30]

But when the odds are too strong, resistance is out of the question. Besides, only the few are able to stand up and speak their minds. Prudence, and the necessity of self-preservation, have taught the average Negro to give in. He knows too well that "they got the ups on you to begin with." When a vital principle is at stake, as in the case of the Negro intellectual from the North who has to fight his own race as well as the white, the tragedy deepens tenfold. "We're slaves to prejudice on the part of the whites and to ignorance on our own part," moans the scholar.[31]

More mellow was the older generation in a fight. Bitter trials taught them the necessity of adjusting themselves stoically to acts of injustice. They never forgot an injury. Outwardly faithful and sometimes daringly critical, they waited for the opportunity to hit back. Much quiet wisdom is expressed by an old servant who knows her "yarbs" (herbs) but declines to save the white boy from sleeping sickness because the white master failed to save her grandson from the mob. She lives by the belief that "when yo' gits yo' han' in 'er lion's mouth, pat him en rub him till yo' gits it out." The final bit of counsel is as pitiful as it is practical. "Wuk fo' de good will uv de colored folks en case de time come yo' gwine need it."[32]

Whether the victim of oppression and discrimination resists or yields, the fire of freedom burns like an inner light. It is a precious possession which no man can take away. Two masterful plays touch on this inborn urge. Chained Negroes in a prison camp who labor under the stern discipline of a boss express their distaste of a buckra or "white nigger." They mean, definitely, a fellow prisoner named Tuesday who wants to climb and find out things. This fellow despises voodoo, looks down upon inferior blacks as swamp mud, and feels inspired and ecstatic. He terrifies his cronies by his reckless talk of walking down the road. Suddenly he gets an impulse to break away. He defies the boss and stabs him. Now the gang is free to move ahead. The third scene shows the bedraggled men in a swamp listening to their instigator as he philosophizes. One of them succumbs after his chains are removed. Just then the leader is shot. The action moves along slowly to the rhythm of a poetic and opulent speech interspersed with modified Gullah dialect.[33] Brother to this philosophic Negro is the aged, freedom-loving traveler talking to a colored lad on a dusty road. He has returned to settle down "in duh land I borned in." But he can't. The blood in him is restless. Suffering has taught him that the Negro can't stand up on his feet with his legs spread. Too long has he been talked down to. He feels mean inside. "Muh sperit in me is sick," he moans. To regain his self-respect he resolves to follow the wires to Africa "so I could stretch muh legs and hold muh head high."[34]

Eventually the colored man was persuaded that the only way to solve his problems was to organize, to stand up. No longer must he stoop to plead for mercy, or derive comfort from superstition. Untrue is the notion that the "nigger's place down de bottom." Any submissive brother who repeats like a ritual that "safe is best" or "tain't nothin' we can do" is a miserable worm. Better look to the labor unions for salvation and to militant labor leaders for leadership. Listen to those who point out hopefully that in a democracy men can work together to bring about change. For labor leaders are committed to unity through unionism. The first hurdle to clear, they insist, is the long-standing division between black and white worker. Once this breach is closed, the welfare of the worker as a human being and member of the group can be assured.

The new labor leader, as represented on the stage, bears an aura of dignity. He may be tied to a chain gang and attempt to run away at the risk of a shot in the back. But, unlike the weakling, he will not fly northward. Instead, he stays on the land to organize oppressed workers, knowing full well that he must pay with his life. Realizing, too, that the entry of labor unions in the South has tightened class lines, the union leader, face to face with the white owners, must speak up. He dare not flinch. Big John, a Negro leader from the Carolina tenant tobacco farmers, strives to alter the misfortunes which dog his fellow workers. Compelled to stand up for the rights of the "croppers," who are inarticulate, he kills the white owner. For daring to challenge the white man's privilege of cheating and robbing, the leader is lynched.[35]

Fundamentally the color question is an economic one. The colored laborer must be kept down to be exploited. But once black and white unite in a common cause, the victims of both races can find a solution. In *Stevedore*, by Paul Peters and George Sklar, the economic struggle is simplified. The Negroes of New Orleans are urged to join a white union. The business whites oppose unionism. In the ensuing strife the labor leader is killed. But at the end, the example of active resistance of the blacks, supported by the whites, is novel and heart-warming. The play broke an old dramatic formula and established a new one. In a number of shorter pieces, the identical problem is posed. White and black folks on a farm are evicted. Confronted by the common danger of hunger and necessity, they unite for mutual protection. Finally,

the two united families force the boss man to give in
before they make off.[36]

The call to organize is heard in three plays by the
gifted poet, Langston Hughes. In singing mood, *De
Organizer,* a blues opera in one act (1940), drives
home by means of mass chanting choruses the need to
organize. Poor blacks, like poor whites, crave freedom
and bread. When the organizer calls for unity, the
workers see the point:

> De Union is de only way
> To free ourselves from hell.

A wider message of freedom is conveyed by successive
scenes interspersed with original lyrics in a loose
chronicle play, *Don't You Want To Be Free?* (1938).
A dozen situations unroll from the opening lines of
the Young Man:

> I am a Negro
> Black as the night is black,
> Black like the depths of my Africa.

to the booming refrain of

> Let's get together folks
> And fight, fight, fight.

More unconventional in theme, though dominated
by the same purpose—to unite the two races—is *When
the Jack Hollers* (1936). With fine humor the author
has drawn a community of sharecroppers in the Mississippi delta region in the spring. Tired of cotton
chopping, the Negroes are in a mood to be stirred
biologically whenever the jackass brays. The noise
sets fire to any petticoat, young and old alike. Comic
figures come to life. There is the Reverend Lovelady,
a hypocrite who, in his spare time, sells pictures of

the pugilist Joe Louis. He succeeds in winning back the jack in payment of church dues from a woman who longs to get rid of it. Aunt Billie, a wise old matriarch, is unafraid of whites and skeptical of conjure. Even the Klansmen are represented as merely hungry, pathetic whites. All ends in merriment. The jack hollers, but Aunt Billie outhollers it. This blend of comic and serious strains inferentially points the need of uniting.

These labor plays, important as pleas for interracial unity, do not suffer for lack of individualized characters. Passion and indignation fan into life a spark of individuality. While such persons in minor pieces may seem shadowy, those in the longer plays like *Stevedore* and *When the Jack Hollers* do take on a three-dimensional quality. In addition, folk speech in the hands of a poet can light up character with nobility as well as affix him to a region and do all this within a net of dramatic events.

Three plays on life in Alabama have for their central purpose the simple fact of showing the personal lives of the natives of the Black Belt. Kate Porter Lewis knows her women, be they white or colored. The author laughs at human weaknesses. While the structure she rears seems fragile, the underpinnings are firmly imbedded in human nature. Consider the young widow in *The Scarlet Petticoat* (1940) who, together with her strict mother-in-law, is mourning a husband. The younger woman shows less fervid signs of grief. A flippant neighbor reminds her, "You and her bofe is done overstretched yo' grievin' time." In fact, she wears a scarlet petticoat, unknown to anybody. When a friend, the tombstone dealer, calls to talk business and suggests a double stone, the young widow is horrified. She prefers her own warm bed. At this

"Porgy," by DuBose and Dorothy Heyward

point the dealer dismantles her bed and they both walk off together: he, triumphant, and she, proud and happy in her scarlet petticoat. They will be married.

In *Three Links o' Chain,* the submissive wife whose husband has left her for another woman is studied. She carries on her kitchen work while her children, the three links, prepare to attend the wedding of their father. Beneath a seemingly careless series of events runs an undertone of quiet humor. Eventually the husband returns, disillusioned. He takes up his neglected guitar and waves a new license toward his wife. After this unexpected turn, the couple parade around while their twins hold the veil of their mother-bride.

More formless is *Watermelon Time,* a focus where birth and life meet. Conversation touches on such elemental matters as the delivery of babies, by a practiced mammy, and young 'uns. The watermelon is employed as a symbol for a baby to come. This leads to minor misunderstandings when an actual watermelon is offered to a young girl. The upshot is that these amoral natives grow wise under the stress of experience.

The value of these playlets lies less in the inherent theatrical power than in the nature of their characters, who act naturally, spontaneously, amorally. Feminine wills are caught in the grip of the life force asserting itself through talk of death and birth. Incidental references to guitar-playing troubadours and to "Sad'dy night frolics" touch the wider sector of life in the outskirts of Alabama.

When all is said, the people who struggle with personal problems enlist our deeper sympathies. Human compassion prefers limits. The part-blooded Negro, for example, battling to regain his self-respect in a world of whites committed to prejudice, discrimination, and ostracism, is an object of pity and terror. So, too, are white and black mates tied together in a death struggle for life.

The drama of the last century occasionally dealt with the problem of mixed marriages for the sake of theatrical effect. Only since 1909 has the Negro-white theme been handled with sincerity and power. In that year Edward Sheldon produced *The Nigger*. The play used the framework of current convention and melodrama to drive home the point. The plot tells more than a story. A Southern gentleman who lives in an old-fashioned colonial mansion hates Negroes and believes "white's white and black's black—and mixin' em's damnation." He becomes governor of the state, enforces laws with strict impartiality, and never weakens on principle. One day he learns that his grandmother was a "niggah." Confusion and a thousand hells! After much inner wrestling, he reaches a decision. He will turn the discovery into a personal victory, renounce the girl he loves, and make a public confession. Despite the boyish theatricality and the sudden accession of wisdom at the end, the piece shows how the theme of mixed courtship could be handled with dignity and power.

Fourteen years later Eugene O'Neill, in *All God's Chillun Got Wings* (1923), traced the love life of a white girl and her black partner. The author plays with the theme as if he did not know what to do with it. Mutual antipathy alternates with mutual love as in the cycle of a manic-depressive. Conscious states belie subconscious promptings. To these tortured spirits who attract and repel each other can come no peace except a return to childhood and a renunciation of intelligence. This solution is psychopathic and hardly acceptable to adults.

The father-wife-son relationship against a Georgia setting is exploited sensationally in a more recent theater piece by Langston Hughes and Martin Jones entitled *Mulatto* (1935). A false inherited code will not allow the white father to accept his half-white son as equal. Likewise, the woman who bears his sons is not good enough to be recognized publicly. The double conflict of son against father, of half-black against full-white, propels a series of climaxes toward violence and murder.

The only comparable playlet in this category is *Jute* (1931), by Kathleen Witherspoon, in which is depicted the short career of a young, gay, impulsive mulatto. In answer to her grandmother's fears she boasts, "I ain't no God-fearin' white-folk fearin' niggah. . . . Jute ain't no slave. She born free." When white folks, for no likely reason, inquire into her morals, she parries their questions lightly and blames her acts on her white blood. To which they counter with the pat, racist slur, "One drop o' niggah blood makes a whole niggah." (Thus spake Hitler.) The plot turns improbable towards the end when she is banished by her newly discovered father, the judge. Apparently the author is too anxious to prove her case of social responsibility.

A few minor plays stagger under the burden of color complications between lover and lover. Now a black man is forced to kill his rival to marry the girl, even though she has given birth to a white baby.[37] Then a colored mother is compelled to break up a match between two "lights" because, unknown to each other, they are brother and sister. Pathetic is her assertion that "it's de black women have got to protect their men from de white men by not telling on 'em "[38] Poignant is the plight of the "white-colored" girl in

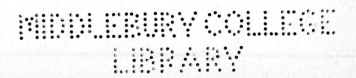

love with a white fellow worker who does not suspect her ancestry. Once he learns the truth, he rejects her. Thereafter she suffers from the thought that she is not good enough for whites or for blacks.[39]

When three blood streams mingle in a society ruled by caste and prejudice, the stigma must be too heavy for human endurance. It is not generally known that, in South Carolina and deeper south, there lives a group known as Brass Ankles. They represent a mixture of Negro, Indian, and white blood—a race apart with characteristics of all three strains. Unaware of their triple ancestry, some of these people consider themselves pure white. When, therefore, in accordance with biological laws, an occasional throwback, generally black, is born into an apparently white family, a crisis is inevitable. Enter love struggling against an inherited code of honor, as in *The Nigger,* and dire consequences may be expected. The problem is theatrically flaunted in *The Brass Ankle* (1931), by DuBose Heyward. A child with Negro-Indian features is born. Wife and husband are forced to meet the event theatrically in this instance. To save the family honor, the wife admits falsely that the father of the child was a Negro. A pistol shot vindicates man and wife. Another weakness of the play lies in the dialogue. Everybody talks too self-consciously and too articulately.

Among the Brass Ankles of another community an old preacher, for daring to raise the standards of his locale, is committed to the flames. His bigoted and benighted neighbors accuse him of the evil eye and lay the blame for their misfortunes upon him. Horrors and sobs mark a violent play.[40]

Thus far, the Negro's relation to his surroundings has been implicit rather than explicit. Wherever he

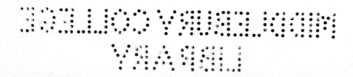

may live, in city or in country, his folk identity is not to be mistaken. The land may modify his earthiness, his habits, his speech. He remains himself. Metropolitan plays dealing with the Negro differ from rural plays in the degree of polish and sophistication. But the same problems of race, of discrimination, and of belief are central to the two species. For instance, in such populated centers as Chicago, New York, and St. Louis millions of Negroes have had to face difficulties unknown to the white residents. Accordingly they have sought panaceas like the Marcus Garvey movement and the Father Divine cult. Not so long ago Chicago numbered scores of devotees of the back-to-Africa movement. To simple minds, settling the Negro on another continent made a dramatic appeal. In *Big White Fog* (1937), by Theodore Ward, the central figure is a baffled Messiah, a visionary, a Don Quixote who would lead his people back to the Promised Land. Aside from having to resist lapses among his own associates, he must meet the rebuffs of his family. Throughout the play he gropes in a big white fog of prejudice. Two subsidiary questions, important though they be, deflect the central theme. The final hope lies in a union of white and black races which must be brought about by socialism. This conclusion admits of little doubt. Nonetheless, upon this platform of dialectics the characters undifferentiated move about for the sake of the argument.

Harlem is the Negro capital of the country. False as well as true leaders have sprung up in this community. During the thirties the church (in Harlem) lost its influence. Therefore Harlemites were ready to follow any leader who promised them bread and faith. Arose a new apostle, Father Divine, with his sham paradise and angels. In *Divine Comedy*, Owen Dodson forged a sensitive medium both poetic and pictorial. Scenes flash from panel to panel. Women air their troubles in church testimonials and find comfort and joy in him. Outbursts on rags and poverty and illness culminate in the antiphonal response:

> Where is Christ?
> Find Him in the Apostle. He's come!

Eventually the Apostle is killed. The changing scenes under changing light supply the pageantry for a message at once reverential and grave. From the scanty excerpts published, the nature of the play may be divined.

St. Louis in the nineties (before the blues song was born) served as a center of Negro sporting life and has long been a cartoonist's fancy. Surface emotions and surface people cross the stage to the plink of mandolins and banjos and to the accompaniment of songs sung by many voices.[41]

As to the slum folk who wallow in squalor and drag out broken lives, they are likely to be puppets of passion. In the Goat Alley of Washington, D.C., a tragedy of promiscuous love rises to a crescendo of horrors. Fury, jealousy, murder, and strangulation supply the theatricalism inherent in the theme of infidelity. The action, however, moves forward under a momentum of inevitability. [42]

When cityfolk invade the country, the dual codes of conduct show up clearly. Some Harlemites carry into a Southern village corruption, crime, and murder. In the end the sterner morality of the elders prevails. In this artificial and over-simplified scheme, dramatic credibility suffers a heavy strain.[43]

More plausible is the reverse move of one rural maid to the city with a colored vaudeville showman, her paramour. Having returned to the farm, she grows disillusioned over her "companion-mate" marriage and agrees to marry her former rural lover.[44]

Among the numerous craftsmen whose plays make up the Negro drama, two in particular, both non-Negroes, have established themselves firmly in repertory: DuBose Heyward and Paul Green. Both writers studied their lowly neighbors objectively, explored their habits, quirks, and failings, and recorded their sentiments, wisdom, and dialect faithfully. The late DuBose Heyward, born in Charleston, South Carolina, possessed a sharp eye for Negro folkways and a remarkable ear for local idiom. His strong theatrical sense created Catfish Row and filled it with a host of vivid personalities who come and go, quarrel and love, scuffle and depart. The canvas of *Porgy* (1927) reaches fullness and balance. In this community of stevedores and fishermen, twenty-four Carolinians reveal themselves in different degree. Of the nine who are more sharply drawn in the foreground, three dominate the scene: Porgy, the crippled beggar; Crown, the burly stevedore; and Bess, the frail wench. These people act spontaneously, naturally, biologically, as their instincts and beliefs prompt. Crap shooting, coke sniffing, a funeral, two murders, the hurricane bell, and double seductions keep the action taut. The speech, sprinkled with Gullah dialect, sounds hearty and authentic. "She de fust pusson I eber see what hipped and busted 'zactly like me." The larger merit of the play lies in the accuracy of the folkways; spirituals, moanings and shoutings, and the mood evoked by fears over the buzzard that lights above the door serve as conjure "for cas' de debbil out of Bess." In such a document of regional life, a chastened treatment might have released universal meanings otherwise lost in a welter of bustle and violence. As in other instances, too much theater debases the drama.

In a later play, *Mamba's Daughters* (1939), the Charleston water front is the backdrop. Hagar, the inarticulate but sensitive mother consumed with excessive mother love, dominates the action. Again the spectacle runs the gamut: seduction, blackmail, murder, and—what is improbable among Negroes—suicide. The frenzied shoutings and clappings in the church alternate with bits of comic byplay. The ending is spuriously contrived. Granting the tenderness of the opening scene and the naturalness of certain individuals, the contrast of personalities is too strongly highlighted: Lissa's purity against Gilly's villainy; dull mother against shrewd grandmother; and the exalted saintliness of the white overseer against the vulgarity of the cruder whites. Nevertheless the racy, theatrical speech springs directly from the folk.

If Heyward was the local colorist of the Carolina Negro theater, Paul Green is the poet-historian. He is keenly aware of place and circumstances geographic, climatic, and economic; the strong contrast of poverty and plenty, of culture and barbarism, "the starveling sharecropper and the machinery plantation," in the South.[45] More strictly than most playwrights he looks upon himself as the historian of a locality, in particular the one-hundred-and-twenty-five-mile stretch inland along the coastal plains of North Carolina where roughly one-third of the population is Negro. His best works deal with Negro types studied in and around the town of Lillington. Some of his early genre studies are in the style of modern painters like Thomas Hart Benton and Joe Jones.

The career of Paul Green has been an adventure in regional writing. At seventeen, as a student at the

University of North Carolina, he wrote his first play under the direction of Professor Koch. Along with others he came under the spell of the Irish Players from Dublin. His first offering, *The Last of the Lowries* (1920), shows traces of borrowings from *Riders to the Sea*. In that little masterpiece *No 'Count Boy* (1923), there is more than a flash of Irish fantasy. The humdrum relationship between the dreamy maid and the sluggish beau is shattered by the intrusion of a dreamer who tells strange tales of far-off places and sings wild songs which strike at human roots. The dreamy misfit, inhospitably fixed upon this prosaic planet, is a universal figure.

Resolved to create an American folk drama, the playmaker dressed up other foreign models in native clothes. Ibsen's *Brand* must have suggested *The Lord's Will* (1921) with its Negro counterpart, the preacher and tenant-farmer obsessed by religion and "always dribblin' gospel from his jaws instead of pickin' cotton." As a result, his wife and child die.

In these apprentice pieces, skillful re-creations as they are, the central problems are too sharply outlined, the characters carved strongly according to type, and the dialogue too artfully employed.

Followed six plays for the Negro theater under the title of *Lonesome Road* (1926). These portraits of common folk who live next to the earth and are tricked by human destiny show sharp lineaments. A white dress becomes the symbol of tragedy when presented as a gift by a white boy to a mulatto girl. Years before, a similar dress had been sent to the mother. But prudence counsels that the dress be burnt instead of worn. Why? The maid is kin to the white man whose son she loves. Dark threads in human lives complicated by color and kinship knot into the final line.

"I knows yo' feelin's chile, but you've gut to smother 'em in. You's gut to smother 'em in." A harassed laundress refuses to bed with her delinquent husband. Climaxing a train of miseries, she kills her man with a hot iron. Another disgusted mother hurls a withering blast against the lewdness of the young. "You rutting bitches, coupling like goats." Two mulatto girls anxious to gain the favor of a white man employ totally different means. One is a "bag of gluttony"; the other is an elegant female version of the later Abe McCranie who is eager to educate black folks. But the idealist fails to receive any encouragement from her white admirer.

The germ of a later play lies in *Your Fiery Furnace* (1923). Filled with consuming ambition to better his race, a father clashes sharply with his no-'count son who admits that "the nigger belongs at de bottom doin' de dirty work foh de white man, dat's it." In the end the father is handed over to the K.K.K. by his own son. Two other fragments went into the making of the matured *In Abraham's Bosom* (1925), a biography in seven scenes which unfolds the career of a Negro Moses who never saw the Promised Land. Abraham McCranie, half white and half black, wants to beat down ignorance and raise the condition of the black man. "Ignorance means sin and sin means destruction." For his brethren in the North Carolina of 1885 he strives to bring down justice from heaven. Like Job he is repeatedly struck down by misfortune. He fails as a teacher, and is fired for sassing a white man. Still he refuses to believe that the white man is better than the black. He dreams of a Negro college, a "light on a hill." In a scuffle, he kills his white half brother. Ironically, his no-'count son has learned by experience what Abe never would see. "We belongs

down wit de pick and de sludge hammer and de tee-
arn and de steam shovel, and de heavy things—at de
bottom doin' de dirty work foh de white man, dat's
it. And he ain't gwine stand foh us to be educated
out'n it nuther. He's gwine keep us dere. It pays him
to." Abe is finally shot; and peace comes to his battered
soul. The will was too strong for the frail body.

Incidentally, this play illustrates Paul Green's attitude toward technique. "I haven't any dramatic technique. I merely tell a story episode by episode." The
total effect is that of a hail of shots instead of one
sustained salvo. As to dialogue, too many addresses
and prayers maintained at high pitch create a condition
midway between Biblical exhortation and political
oratory.

Fantasy is Green's strongest gift. In several playlets
the action inheres in a mounting wave of fears which
dash boldly against mundane reality in a medley of
hallucinations. Phantom succeeds phantom. Horror
springs from such homely images as a black dog, or an
iron-faced man. The immediate story of *In Aunt
Mahaly's Cabin* (1925) concerns two Negro murderers
in a swamp evading capture by a sheriff and his deputy.
More eerie by far, with a touch of voodooism and
diablerie, is *Supper for the Dead* (1927), the story
of a Negro conjure woman's success as she operates with
her snaky twin daughters, aged sixty, to establish a
man's guilt. By a weird jumble of incantations she
makes the father confess that he raped his own daughter
and then drowned her. The dialect is clipped and
tense. In *Blue Thunder* (1928), fantasy becomes
playful. Three mulattos decree that the Great Popper,
a powerful, pantherlike fellow, must not leave his
cabin. Their farewell chant in cryptic couplets causes
sticks, pots, pans—as well as blankets and pillows—to

dance. In little time the jaunty braggart is destroyed.
Then the women pick his pockets for money and pull
the diamond out of his tooth. Enter a buzzard, the
dreaded omen, driven by a little black man. In these
ghostly sketches the weird has been trapped. Our
suspension of disbelief is complete.

But the pull of earth drew the author back to
ordinary folks. The play of attraction and repulsion,
of love and hate, of energies struggling for release
against the iron clutch of destiny, found full vent in
symphonic dramas. *Potter's Field* (1931), renamed in
a later version, *Roll, Sweet Chariot* (1935), crowds
the scene with varied figures. Enlivened by folk and
choral song, life in a boardinghouse of a Southern
village runs the gamut of love, lust, ecstasy, deception,
crime, vulgarity, and depravity. The final scene showing convicts digging to a monotonous chant in which
the flash of retribution answers the flare of open rebellion prefigures *Hymn to the Rising Sun* (1936).

Paul Green, in his Negro plays, copies life, not the
theater. The artifice of theatricality which Eugene
O'Neill and DuBose Heyward seemed unable to avoid
he has successfully shunted. His concern with people
rather than with plots may tend to weaken story power.
But, in compensation, the air of casual progression
he sometimes achieves resembles life itself. Above all,
his distraught men and resigned women bear no likeness to characters invented by loungers in the green-
room. (The "white" plays of Paul Green receive attention in the next chapter.)

As long as good plays are written, few will ask
whether they are done by white or black. For the sake
of the record, however, one cannot help noting differences in depth and point of view. Naturally the
Negro understands his personal status and race psy-

chology better than any white man. Beneath the
hilarity and heartiness of his people the Negro detects
a streak of melancholy. Himself an object of discrimination, he is likely to overstate his case in the
theater at the expense of credibility of character. He
magnifies and minifies. The white man, less on the
defensive, less eager to vindicate his honor, and less
pointed in propaganda, possesses the detachment necessary for writing balanced plays. As outsider, he can
often sense tragedy where the colored man fails. In
craftsmanship, too, it must be admitted that the white
playwright has the edge. An impartial survey of the
longer plays points to the conclusion that thus far
Ridgely Torrence, DuBose Heyward, and Paul Green
have written the outstanding plays about the Negro.

With regard to the theater, prominent literary leaders like Alain Locke and Sterling Brown, Montgomery
Gregory and Randolph Edmonds, as well as white
directors like Rowena and Russell Jelliffe, have toiled
for years to build an authentic Negro theater and
drama. Since 1921, enthusiastic acting units throughout the country have provided opportunities for play
production. Negro theaters, college troupes, and such
companies as The Howard Players, The Hampton
Players, the celebrated Gilpin Players of the Karamu
Theater[46] at Cleveland, the Skyloft Players of Chicago,
and the American Negro Theater of New York have
been responsible for sporadic revivals of interest in a
native Negro theater. In 1939 there were 390 theaters
serving Negroes in the United States. Since 1930
dramatic activity in the South has been unified by two
organizations. The Negro Intercollegiate Drama Association, founded by Randolph Edmonds, unites
seven colleges, while the Intercollegiate Dramatic
Association, founded in 1933, in North Carolina,

covers thirteen colleges of the state. In addition, the Southern Association of Drama and Speech Arts, also founded by Edmonds in 1936, has a listed membership of most of the important colleges in the South. Meanwhile an audience has been trained to accept the modern Negro on the stage.[47]

As actor in life and on the stage the Negro is unique. He often dramatizes everyday situations as naturally and spontaneously as he dances. In fact, his very existence is one long drama. Given space, the freedom to act, and the opportunity to enjoy the same rights as the white man, he will add vastly to our cultural repository and help to create a real regional drama. Once the black man is recognized as compounded of the same protoplasm as the white, the playmaker will be bound to stage the Negro, not as a problem in caste or color or race, but as a humble dweller among men struggling to be himself.

1. Virginia G. Tupper, "Plantation Echoes," *Etude*, March, 1937.

2. Gullah is supposed to refer to a region in Africa from which black folks were originally taken to be sold as slaves to plantation owners of the Carolina coast.

3. *Got No Sorrow*, by Caroline Hart Crum.

4. *Washed in de Blood*, by Rietta Winn Bailey.

5. *The Seer*, by James W. Butcher, Jr.

6. *The Gold Machine*, by Eugene Selnick.

7. *Marked for Rest*, by Turner Rose.

8. *Two Gods*, by Doris D. Price.

9. *The Natural Man*, by Theodore Browne.

10. *John Henry*, by Roark Bradford.

11. *The Broken Banjo*, by Willis Richardson.

12. *John Henry*, by Frank B. Wells.

13. *The Flight of the Natives*, by Willis Richardson.

14. *Breeders*, by Randolph Edmonds.

15. *Rachel*, by Angelina W. Grimké.

16. *Aftermath*, by Mary Burrill.

17. *Go Down Moses*, by Adolph Levy.

18. *Frances*, by G. D. Lipscomb.

19. *Blood o' Kings*, by Jane Dransfield.

20. *The Hanging,* by Chad Walsh.
21. *Country Sunday,* by Walter Spearman.
22. *The Forfeit,* by Corrie C. Howell.
23. *No Hidin' Place,* by Wayne Gregory.
24. *Judge Lynch,* by John W. Rogers, Jr.
25. *The Noose,* by Tracy D. Mygatt.
26. *Singing Piedmont,* by Anthony Buttitta.
27. *Bleeding Hearts,* by Randolph Edmonds.
28. *Black Damp,* by John F. Matheus.
29. *Death Comes Creepin' in the Room,* by Grant Moss.
30. *Sick and Tiahd,* by Theodore Ward.
31. *The Slave,* by Elizabeth H. Yates.
32. *The Lion's Mouth,* by Harriet L. Kennedy.
33. *Swamp Mud,* by Harold Courlander.
34. *Home to Langford County,* by Harold Courlander.
35. *New Nigger* (or *Big John*), by Fred Howard.
36. *Mighty Wind A-Blowin',* by Alice H. Ware.
37. *Sugar Cane,* by Frank H. Wilson.
38. *Blue Blood,* by Georgia Douglas Johnson.
39. *Chloe,* by Jack Stuart Knapp.
40. *Fire of the Lord,* by Frank Durham.
41. *St. Louis Woman,* by Countee Cullen and Arna Bontemps.
42. *Goat Alley,* by Ernest Howard Culbertson.
43. *Jericho,* by H. L. Fishel.
44. *Companion-Mate Maggie,* by Helen Dortch.
45. From preface to *Out of the South* (New York, 1939), p. xii.
46. Swahili for "center of the community."
47. It has been estimated that there are fifty dramatic staffs in the 120 Negro colleges of this country.

V

The White South

VIEWED broadly, the crescent of states known as the South is no simple, homogeneous entity. Virginia, Carolina, Georgia, and Alabama are hardly of a piece. In point of fact the component parts differ in origin, history, and composition. From the beginning the contradictory forces liberated by the system of Negro slavery ran side by side with unifying forces. Along the coastal plain (as distinguished from the mountainous regions) the need of the early colonists to adapt themselves to a different climate, a flat terrain, and a new economy made for common experiences, common problems, and even common folkways. Having brought with them from the Old World a stock of songs and ballads like "Barbara Allen" and the rest, they found a common bond in their pleasures. The net result was a blend of loosely knit cultures.

Once the Southern States became conscious of boundaries, the natives reverted to a natural instinct to express their local pride in soil and ancestry by scenery, costume, and words. Backward they looked to early explorers, settlers, and adventurers, and joyfully commemorated the deed and the hero. From *Raleigh, the Shepherd of the Ocean,* written by Frederick H. Koch, to the recent *The Common Glory,* by Paul Green, the procession of local historic masques and pageant-dramas has been intermittent but impressive. When historic subjects have failed, the homage to flowers, oranges, peach blossoms, strawberries, apple blossoms, dogwood, cotton, tobacco,

Photo courtesy Wootten-Moulton
The Playmakers Theatre at Chapel Hill, North Carolina

as well as to such abstractions as Education, Youth, and Culture, has been uninterrupted.

Among pageant masters, Paul Green of Chapel Hill, North Carolina, has welded the visual arts into mammoth symphonic dramas on historic themes. *The Lost Colony,* an annual event on Roanoke Island since 1937, unfolds a thread of history in episodes related by a narrator, actors, and a chorus. The story follows the facts. Three hundred and fifty years ago, a band of British settlers landed on the island. They fought with the Indians, suffered agonies, and eventually were forced to flee into the wilderness when a Spanish ship anchored in the harbor. First the Indians, then the whites, and later the British court pass in review. Much is made of the birth of the first white child in America: Virginia Dare. The final chorus chants the hope that the pioneer dream still lives.

Green's second symphonic drama depicting the struggles of the colonists, *The Highland Call* (1939) commemorates, in five scenes, the bicentennial of the Scottish settlement in the upper Cape Fear River Valley of southeastern North Carolina. With the aid of poetry, music, and the dance, this drama re-enacts the conflicts of Loyalists and Whigs, and portrays the Jacobite leader, Flora Macdonald. Annually the citizens of Fayetteville assist in staging this impressive spectacle.

After these murals, historic plays on our first theme, the Indian, seem but miniatures. Pocahontas was long a favorite heroine in the South. Of the numerous plays which dramatize her story, the version which strikes close to our common humanity is *Pocahontas and the Elders* (1933), by Virgil Geddes. The well-known incidents of the rescue of Captain John Smith by the Indian chieftain's daughter, her marriage to

John Rolfe, and her sailing to England are developed from the viewpoint of modern psychology. Dealings between white and red men, and the political wrangling by whites seem soundly motivated. The artificial manners of the English court, set against the natural ways of the Indian, make good drama. But Pocahontas does not escape a touch of sentimental reverence. She understands the language of the heart while John Smith craves for naught but power. Ostensibly the author is set on viewing his characters not as members of a race but as human characters ruled by convention and shaped by circumstances.

Another Indian play presents a few strands of history in the camp of the Cherokees, a powerful and superior tribe which once claimed territory in six states from the Ohio River southeast to the Atlantic. They were friendly with the whites. Without drawing too heavily upon native customs, the play presents, through tribal chatter, a veneer of information on the magic, superstition, drinks, medicine, and spells of the tribe. Beyond that, the aim of the author is to compare the marital codes of Indian and white. But the plot falls into stereotypes. The bad Indian wants the white girl for his squaw, and the jealous War Woman, who acts as judge, condemns the white girl to be burnt. Luckily the traditional hatred of the Cherokees for the Senecas enables the hero to free his bride. Conventional rhetoric and ditties opening with the line, "Paleface come in big canoe" remind one of old paint and feathers.[1]

The same inveterate tendency which idealized the Indian gilded the landscape and resident of the "white" South. In the last century song and story chanted of the frail beauties of the big house, the cabin in the cotton, magnolia and moonlight, honeysuckle and crinoline. Fiction wove a halo about the head of the pure maiden, the chivalrous hero, and the docile darkies singing in the cornfield. God's noblest creation was the Southern family. Any criticism was taboo. Even when the local-color school, initiated in the 1880's by a Southern journalist, toned down the sham-exotic, the fine-pretty, in favor of a franker delineation of the common man, the sentimental strain did not die. While Joel Chandler Harris in his tales of the Georgia cracker aimed to create frank, local types, his contemporaries from Virginia, Kentucky, Alabama, and Louisiana continued to daub the residents of their respective locales with the familiar brush. Into this century their followers continued to show the Southern belle standing prettily under the portico of the ancestral mansion, amid the wisteria blossoms, awaiting her renegade brother form the North while faithful old Chloe in the background weeps for sheer joy.

After 1900 poetic plays toyed with classical themes. Their makers carried on the genteel literary tradition which has always marked the aristocracy. It was natural for writers steeped in the classics, and members of a class inured to drinking and gambling and wenching, to ape the Greeks and the Elizabethans. Though they chose the dramatic medium, they manufactured elegant little trifles couched in elevated blank verse adorned with pseudoclassical tropes. To this class belong the literary plays of Olive Tilford Dargan who, in 1903, wrote polite sketches on the themes of Semiramis, Maximilian, and Carlotta of Mexico; those of George Henry Miles who spoke the sorrows of Mohammed and De Soto in Shakespearean cadences; and Cale Young Rice who versified on Petrarch and Charles di Tocca.

The popular theater showed far more lustiness. Melodrama may thunder in the index and sound silly and artificial; but it does not preclude flashes of insight into character and even an occasional handling of lowly themes. One contemporary playlet of po' white trash of Georgia in 1900 sets the scene on the edge of the Oloochee Swamp. Here and there a few surface tints look like the real thing. But closer examination of *Po' White Trash*, by Evelyn G. Sutherland, reveals the shoddy fiber. The soft banjo playing, the talk about the boy who can't kill a 'coon because he saw his eyes, the lad who takes the snake bite to save the girl, and the papers to vindicate somebody's honor are all old stuff. Also the lush dialect and jerky action keep the play dated. Yet, one figure of vitality was to reappear in later regional plays: the country girl who dips her brush in snuff and rubs it on her gums.

Not until the First World War was the drama to cut new furrows. It was a college professor who upturned new soil for new plantings. In 1918, after Professor Frederick H. Koch came to Chapel Hill, North Carolina, he organized a course in creative writing called English 31. He impressed on his students the cardinal principle of discovering the dramatic in the history, the legends and lore of their own locality, and, above all, in the experience of the near-at-hand. Accordingly, he urged his apprentices in playmaking to listen to old family tales, to observe simple folk, and to write of what they knew. In no little time he had fired the kinetic imagination of his students. Bravely these Playmakers, as they were called, set about uncovering fresh thematic material. The experimenters searched familiar nooks for situation, character, and dialect. Together with their instructor they believed

that "the locality, if it be truly interpreted, is the only
universal." The result was a respectable body of folk
or regional dramas.

Truthfully and even skillfully these undergraduates
of the University of North Carolina began to dramatize
what they knew and heard and saw. Their stage became the whole of rural and semirural America. Aided
by an experimental Playmakers' Theatre, dedicated
in 1921 to a native drama, and by group criticism,
they eliminated the artificial and the faraway. After
avoiding the usual pitfalls of beginners, they succeeded
in turning out one-act plays which showed qualities
of dignity and power, of beauty and sincerity. Thereafter the Carolina "folk-play," as it was named, provided a model for imitators.

Their influence spread across the land. Notable
within the state has been the yearly drama festival at
Chapel Hill where plays original and borrowed are
presented by high schools and colleges. Since 1920,
a touring company of the Carolina Playmakers, traveling by show bus, has carried folk theater to the
northern border, south to Florida, and west to Texas.
At the same time extension work, since 1918, has been
conducted by the Bureau of Community Drama in
the Eastern Division to assist those wishing to promote
community expression. In short, in twenty-five years
of playmaking, more than five hundred original one-
act and a considerable number of full-length plays
have been produced.[2] Besides, some nine volumes of
plays have been published.[3] Also, the University has
furnished scores of expert play directors for the nation
and published an interesting quarterly, *The Carolina
Play-Book*.

The first fruits were derivative. The example of
Synge of the Irish drama left its mark on plot and

character and dialogue. Reminiscent of Celtic humor
is *Cottie Mourns*,[4] the story of a widow who, at the
coffin of her husband, bullies a fourth suitor into
marriage. At mention of the word "heifer-steer,"
the dead man suddenly sits up and protests. In *The
Last of the Lowries,* the final passage, spoken by a
grief-stricken mother, recalls the mournful rhythm
of *Riders to the Sea.* "That's all that's left o' them I
loved . . . a bundle o' clothes to show for my man an'
four grown men . . . and you'll all sleep quiet at the
last. But they're all gone, and what call have I got to be
livin' more." Into a number of other pieces at this
time there entered the idealized Irish vagabond dis-
guised as a native.

Somewhat lurid, too, were these first plays. The
vast world of the supernatural supplied the material.
Such wild trappings as stormy nights, madness, witches,
outlaws, and pirates made an easy appeal to buried
layers in the human mind. The belief in witches,
which folklorists claim is deep-rooted in the human
psyche, was exploited in three witch plays. The skele-
ton of these plots reduces to ashes in the telling. It is
the horror conveyed by speech and background which
gives to these early pieces their blue flicker. In each
appears a witch out of the night. In *When Witches
Ride*[5] she falls asleep, dies, wakes up, and passes on
her spell to one of several men playing cards. In
Trista,[6] an eighteenth-century witch disappears at
mention of the word "baptism." In *The Old Man of
Edenton*[7] the ghost of a leper wife is brought back by
a witchman and an African slave.

Using the worn-out properties of Gothic horror,
Thomas Wolfe, one of the early Playmakers, put together a queer character against a supernatural setting
in *The Third Night.* Murder, continuous rain, the

miser's hoard, the return of the murdered man, a sil-
houette, a ghostly chuckle, and other adolescent devices betray a love for the macabre for its own sake.

The treatment of local history was sensational. The
subject of the Lowrie gang, a famous band of outlaws of mixed blood, partly Croatan Indian, became
the subject of four plays. Actually, during the Civil
War, many of these Croatans resisted efforts by the
government of the Confederacy to conscript them for
labor on the forts of Cape Fear. Once they killed an
officer and fled into the Scuffletown Swamp. There
they turned outlaws, spread terror, and robbed and
murdered wayfarers. The last of the Lowrie gang
was shot in 1874. Thomas Wolfe's *The Return of
Buck Gavin* pictures a burly mountain outlaw. Paul
Green's *The Last of the Lowries* narrates the visit to
his home of an outlaw eager to see his mother again.
But he pays with his life. In *Scuffletown Outlaws*[8],
a semi-Indian chief smoldering with resentment against
the whites for taking his land and degrading his people
suffers blow after blow silently until goaded to final
action. *Swamp Outlaw*[9] toys with the theory that the
Croatans may have been the descendants of the lost
colonists from Roanoke. The leading character, Henry
Berrie Lowrie, is conscious of his heritage of white
blood and bitter because his white contemporaries of
1864 feel no kinship with his people. In this last play
a hoodoo Negro chant adds a touch of local realism.

Brother to the outlaw is the pirate. Along the
coastal towns of Carolina piracy was quite common.
The elements of taproom talk, a swaggering sea captain, a half-naked fellow staggering in to blurt out
the news that "the ship were lost," a riot, and the seiz-
ing of pistols keep the action spinning. The hearty
speech, presumably put down as authentic, gives the

play an appearance of great historic verisimilitude.[10]

From legends of past pirates who used to lure ships to shore by swinging lanterns to and fro, one playmaker chose his subject. Off Nags Head and Ocracoke Island live the "bankers" or fisherfolk bitten by winds, unhurried, and given to provincial dialect. Against this setting an old demented woman had been rescued from an induced shipwreck fifty years before. As the bell rings for her, she goes out in a storm to be drowned. The daughter of Aaron Burr is off to see her father.[11]

From wild, legendary plots the Playmakers turned to character studies. But the figures stalk stiffly and exhibit strong, single streaks and an outward liveliness credible on the stage. To cite a few examples: there is the swain who has difficulty finding privacy in order to propose.[12] The stingiest man in the county, a paralytic, has been saving money for his absent son. But when the bank collapses, all is lost.[13] A spiritless husband is cured of his timidity by drinking a medicine sold to him by a traveling faker. Now he can assert his power over his shrewish wife.[14]

Finally the Carolina scribes inspected the apple and found the worm. They looked, saw, and despaired. After this they did not hesitate to attack social problems frontally or laterally. In fact, they were the first to find material for drama in the commonplace struggles of the cotton and tobacco farmers, the mill workers, and the sharecroppers. Within the frame of neat plots they introduced a number of earth-weary bodies. There was Peggy, eighteen and pretty, daughter of an overworked drudge. Her mother, a familiar regional character who dips snuff and dangles a snuff brush from her mouth, listens to Peggy asserting her wish to marry for love. In an outburst of

temper at her boldness, her father dies. But if she
and her mother are to stay on the farm, she cannot
follow the promptings of her heart. She is therefore
compelled to marry the farm hand.[15] Made of cruder
clay is the tenant farmer so inured to the soil that he
cannot understand his wife's love of finery or her
want of common decencies. After a time the continued
denial of simple necessities and human cravings brings
on a domestic break. And dumbly the dull-witted
peasant watches his irate wife leave the house.[16] Pervasive is the bitterness caused by poverty and ignorance. To one family, farming is "nothing but work
and poverty . . . and dirt!" Besides, they mumble,
"them as is pore ain't never goin' to be nothin' but
pore." The same defeatism makes them distrust education in the face of their children's longing to get
ahead. They see no way out of their misery.[17]

Stripped of romance, the plantation can turn out
to be a cruel incumbrance. A false attachment to the
ancestral home can cause misery for the submissive
young.[18]

From the group of anonymous scribes who helped
build the foundations of a folk regional drama, four
Playmakers have attained distinction: Loretto C.
Bailey, Bernice K. Harris, Kate Porter Lewis, and
Paul Green. All four have studied and loved the soil
of their native habitat and each has chosen to portray
one segment of humanity. Loretto C. Bailey, born in
Winston-Salem, prefers the family unit as a subject
of dramatic scrutiny. For three generations she traces
the lives of the Meadows family from the strictly pious
grandmother to the hard-working, mill-employed
mother, and down to the flippant, self-willed granddaughter. In *Job's Kinfolks* (1928) the mother, to
avoid arrest for her daughter's misconduct, gives the

girl in marriage to the humdrum neighbor, although she knows well what this union will mean. *Black Water* (1929), a sequel, shows the same daughter tied to the dolt and trying hard to break away from the intolerable union. Recklessly she flings defiance to the world. "I've got to take whatever I want." In short, life to this family is but a stream of black, muddy water. In these sketches the women are drawn with rare understanding. The grandmother is a perfect summation of old age with its cautions and fears; the mother, a model of resignation; and the granddaughter, a typical rebel.

Cloey (1931), by the same author, presents a study in character. The old Greek flaw in this case is ineffectual fear, which ends in meek surrender. A young fellow falls into the coils of a forceful, domineering matron who had been married three times. He loves her niece, but is too weak to resist the power of the older woman. Despite the tender talk between the young couple and a momentary rallying of courage, he yields to the stronger. The hurt, lonely niece can only reel from the blow.

On a wider canvas are arrayed some Southern mill workers on strike. The story follows the facts of the attempt to organize the textile workers of Gastonia in April of 1929. In this case the organizer is a woman from a mountain cabin. She calls a strike. But she knows that in any fight for civil rights the radicals or the "nigger-lovers" have always been beaten by poverty, eviction, hunger, and death. The strikers are dragged off to jail and the leader is shot. The funeral makes a bright spot. Back and forth, as point to counterpoint, weave the opposing strains of orthodox funeral chant and rousing strike song. In this plea for workers' rights, *Strike Song* (1931), the men

and women are not reduced to ciphers but manage
to retain their town and rural identities. Social criticism is shot through with womanly pity.

Far less militant is Bernice K. Harris from Seaboard,
North Carolina. She excels as a dramatic reporter
who transcribes literally what she sees and hears.
There are few overtones in *Folk Plays of Eastern
Carolina* (1940). The simple feminine facts and quiet
traits of character attract her eye. Three crabbed and
querulous old virgins indulge their maternal cravings
over a doll while waiting for the cavalier to come. In
another play, the typical, overworked farm girl who is
tied to two selfish aunts wins her man by the friendly
intervention of an earthquake. More sharply etched is
the droll person of Ca'line, the headstrong, uppity
woman on a visit from the "country-home" to be
married. Other pieces show subdued anger, satire,
and caricature. The stiff-necked mother, just evicted,
refuses relief in money while her children have learned
readily to dissemble and beg slyly. Social criticism
is implicit in the playlet of the sharecropper who is
forced to take shelter in a church house where he
guards his three jewels, his children. In the main
these characters are so many profiles or silhouettes
done deftly.

Kate Porter Lewis, a recent Playmaker who wrote
Alabama Folk Plays (1943), was born in Greenville,
Alabama in the back country of the deep South. She
has written about half a dozen strong plays. Two of
them deal poignantly with the tenant farmers in a
remote section of southern Alabama. She etches with
a fine needle the lowly farm girl desperately
clinging to her dreamworld. In *Party Dress*, the
maiden, as she irons her white party costume,
dreams of her first love, her dance of the last year's

spring gatherin', and her town beau. Against this
fragile dreamer is pitted the dry, crabbed, sullen sister-
in-law who, with icy sarcasm, blasts the fairest hopes.
In despair the girl leaves her party dress and dreams
behind her and runs off to marry the village oaf who
wants her to manage his house and store. So perishes
the romantic strain in a world committed to bread and
toil. The sequel, *The Ivory Shawl,* presents the same
girl years later, grown to womanhood and herself the
mother of a girl who has just been graduated from
the local high school. The daughter has won a two-
year scholarship to State Normal School. Can she go?
Her struggles with her father are tense and cruel.
"Well, you ain't a-goin'," he roars as he rips the new
diploma from the wall and throws it on the coals. To
him only one career is open to girls: marriage. For
a moment all is lost, and the girl is resigned to marry.
Meanwhile, her weary-eyed and half-numbed mother
looks on. When she hands over a hand-embroidered
shawl of ivory silk found in an old trunk, the mother
awakens. Her own past rises up in reproach. No, the
girl must not repeat her own tragedy and throw herself away. She is too good. That night she leaves for
college. The dramatic action of these pieces is entirely inward. These creatures seem molded from
warm, palpitating flesh. Anguish gives breadth and
edge and firmness to these human targets under steady
fire.

Most prominent of Carolina playwrights is Paul
Green whose Negro plays were appraised in the pre-
vious chapter. From the beginning he made the
coastal plain of North Carolina his laboratory. Its
rocks and pines and sand hills, as well as its history,
became his world to explore. Within this region he
found a breed of men and women whom he trans-

scribed to the stage. There, in a series of sketches, he tried to unravel the secret of their personalities. "I too try to tell the story of my people as human beings, and in the world of the drama, people are people," he wrote.

By the time he concentrated on his "white" plays, his theater had begun to widen. He had moved beyond the tight formula of the one-act play to the longer form. With this change, his characters, too, began to roam in space, to lose their individual sharpness, and to turn philosophic. Complex abstractions, conceived in experimental freedom and wedded to musical formlessness, set out in quest of answers. They meditated deeply and discoursed wisely. Stripped of local mannerisms, they became symbols of a spurious universality. The result was that the intense and abounding vitality of an Abe McCranie or of an Old Queenie gave way to pale metaphysics, to pseudo sublimity, and to formularies of nineteenth-century philosophy.

The themes of the white plays follow three recognizable lines: (1) religious experience of sin and guilt, (2) decay of long-rooted stock, and (3) wrath at penal brutality. Humble white folks appear in a preliminary sketch, *Saturday Night* (1928). Here some sharecroppers and tenant farmers play, sing, and dance. Simple animal delights and human situations call up little vexing questions about nature and the soul. Spiritual strivings from the mud point to the query, "What is the soul of man?" This genre picture was later enlarged to *Potter's Field* (1931). A more ambitious piece which develops a similar theme was suggested by that storehouse of wisdom, the books of Job and Ecclesiastes. The sin of heresy in an orthodox community, the struggle of conscience against imputed wrongdoing, the joy of nature against the gloom of Calvinism come to grips in *The Field God* (1927; revised, 1940). In this drama of "man's work, his faith, and love" Green aimed to revise the story of Job by the grace of Ibsen. In his own words, he hoped to illustrate the affirmation of the will through the destruction of the will.[19] Reduced to human terms, the conflict centers on the infidel husband, a blaspheming Job tied to an ailing and pious wife. Troubles come fast. The wife dies from shock when she senses love going on behind her back. Her successor drives a suitor to kill himself. Things get worse. The child dies and the church intervenes. Agonies of remorse overwhelm the second wife, who succumbs to a sense of morbid guilt. "She put a curse on us and we fed our lust on top of the grave," she wails. But the unrepentant husband who wrestles with the question of sin reaffirms his belief. "We are God . . . man is God." On the whole the thesis is driven hard, explanations are overdone, and the tail is too heavy for the kite.

In gayer mood the one-act play *Unto Such Glory* (1927) treats the subject of religious worship employed as sex lure and sex outlet. In the name of religion a pious hypocrite aims to steal another man's wife. But the wronged husband, suddenly inspired by a self-induced spell of visions, routs the revivalist preacher. Trick meets trick, and the tables are turned.

Folk fantasies also treat the question of sin and guilt. As in certain plays of Yeats and Hauptmann, *Tread the Green Grass* (1929) crosses the dreamworld with the real world. In a strictly Baptist South, paganism and Christianity are bound to clash, and free love to collide with duty. On the imaginative plane Davies, the Ariel of the woods, woos the dainty Tina, "the poor heart lost in darkness." While paganism is in the ascendant, the countryside sings and shines in glory. But once the free spirit is banned, the cross wins. "All was wrong," wails the lovely spirit.

Mood and theme are jumbled in the experimental *Shroud My Body Down* (1935), a study in guilt "conceived in poetry and music." A morbid introvert shoots his own son. We never know why. Inbreeding and decadent stock may have something to do with his strange malady. Lora, child of impulse and beauty, is in love with her brother and Jesus. The wisdom of the folk is expressed Poloniuswise by an old man. Through a kind of pseudo poetry runs a metaphysical thread. And amid the confused chatter is a striving for—what? Bits from Celtic, Greek, and Teutonic sources fail to evoke a whole mood or establish esthetic unity. Theme flows into theme and vanishes. The effect intended, a flow of melodic line, merely runs to formlessness.

Gone is the old South and, with it, a world once considered unalterable. Economic causes have been responsible. As a result, the inrooted devotion of old families to the homestead has run to seed. In *The House of Connelly* (1931) everything exudes decay, and there is "the rot of death in the air." The Connellys are shabby and solitary aristocrats who cling to an old way of life in their onetime mansion set on two thousand acres of "purty land." Then along comes Pansy, landhungry and bubbling with life, who unites with the son of the house to remake the farm. Slowly the elders drift away one by one. Uncle Bob, the last survivor of the old order, shoots himself because "we're all rotten." The new generation sweeps out the old with a new broom. This bare outline of events hardly suggests the breadth of treatment. By far, however, the most subtle portraits etched by Paul Green are the two Negro crones, Big Sis and Big Sue, who act as chorus. Cunning, sensitive, divining, they snicker at the goings on in the big house. The witches in *Macbeth* are no less skillfully drawn than these two weird sisters. The tendency to sermonize at the end and to fall into oratory mars the dramatic effectiveness of an otherwise perfect play.

An offshoot from the same decaying limb is *The Southern Cross* (1938). This time the old mansion has fallen into decay. Clara dreams of escape to Texas with a young adventurer. But public exercises on Memorial Day bring her back to a sense of ancestral glory and duty. She stays on.

Former shots at the chain gang and escaped convicts gather into one burst of wrath in *Hymn to the Rising Sun* (1936). The events are stark and the picture of whimpering and crawling convicts being bullied by white guards is sharply drawn. Ironic indeed is the long harangue on patriotism delivered on this Fourth of July, followed by a casual dropping dead of a prisoner who had been imprisoned in a box. The play stops short of the limits of horror and repulsion, of cruelty and sadism. When the convicts sing as the sun rises, the peak of irony is capped. Where now is the soul of man?

To sum up: Paul Green senses the tragic rhythm of life. Puzzled by questions of faith and reason, of affirmation and denial, he is torn between Voltaire and the Bible. He talks much of God. His is essentially a religious mind rooted in the soil and searching for ultimates. As craftsman he marshals his incidents along a straight line. But the plot line often bears singular characters who express themselves darkly in poetry half-folk, half-literary. Mainly his concern is with the glowing inner core, the flaming center, the spiritual essence within the human shell.

"The Field God," by Paul Green

Paul Green, the experimentalist, is often abashed by the inadequacy of words bound by the dramatic form, and has therefore sought the aid of music. Folk songs, ballads, lullabies performed on a stringed gourd, a banjo, a mouth organ, a spinet, may complement a mood or strive to express the inexpressible. He has even written a number of such ditties. Of late years he has advanced for others to solve the ever-recurrent puzzle of marrying poetry to music on the stage, as in the pageant-drama. This estimate of the poet-playwright rests, of necessity, on his regional plays alone.

An industrialized economy has completely changed the face of the South and with it, the people. From the report to the President on *Economic Conditions of the South,* prepared in 1938, the nation learned a number of pertinent facts. One half of the South's farmers are tenants: roughly, nine million; while another two million belong to wage-earning families on farms. Large plantations worked by machinery have created a class of day laborers subject to hire and fire. Two and a half million houses are substandard. Poverty is widespread and industrial wages are the lowest in the United States. Illiteracy is higher than in any other section of the country.

Nobody can fail to be impressed by these facts, not even the playwright. Heir to the old lies, he must repudiate them or be out of touch with his times. Fictionists and dramatists of late years have noted the baneful effects of a changing society upon the cropper, the tenant, the farmer, the moonshiner, and the mountaineer. With stinging fury and unmitigated sincerity some writers have rendered faithful portraits of the drab, the sordid, and the unspectacular. On occasion a backward glance at the old order with its faded splendor will merely emphasize the new. Clearly presented in *'Lijah* (1926), by Edgar V. Smith, is the aristocratic judge rooted in the soil of Alabama. He moves like a ghost among the living. Inured to ancient ways on the plantation and handicapped by poverty, the old gentleman cannot expand in the lordly manner of his forebears. He therefore invents a Negro servant. Yankee businessmen who come to bargain with him over a hill of mica are so awed by his gentility that they offer him a good price if he will sell. He accepts with dignity unhurt. Characters are sketched with sureness and restraint. These include a Negro mammy shrewd and clever, and, above all, the imaginary 'Lijah who, though never seen on the stage, almost comes alive.

Down the Southern coastal plain rural life is bitter and degraded. Under the impact of penury and want too terrible for words, characters decay and degenerate into fiberless sponges that walk like human bipeds. Starkly twisted to brutish shapes, these starved bodies and misshapen minds drag out warped lives on the byroads of Georgia. *Tobacco Road,* by Jack Kirkland and Erskine Caldwell, shows Jeeter Lester and his brood in their tumble-down shack on the worn-out sand hills. One by one they cast off until the father is left alone. The concentration of lust and depravity produces an effect that approaches caricature and exceeds the limits of pity and belief.

Florida as background to the drama presents a composite picture. In its brief history the state has changed flags four times and passed through various cultural stages: Indian, Spanish missionary, pioneer, and Negro. Under the influence of the Spanish fathers, the Indians turned to Christianity. Meanwhile, the shiftless cracker backwoodsmen, of the same stock as the folk of the Appalachian Mountains, acquired and handed down a body of folkways, while the Negro carried down voodoo ceremonials and frenzied dancing. In recent years, out of the sawmill camps have come scores of ballads and work songs. Taken together, the result of so many cultures side by side has been a medley rather than a fusion of strains. About a handful of pageants and plays testify to this fact.

Legends of trouble between Spanish traders and Seminole Indians abound. One of these takes dramatic form in a tale of revenge. The daughter of a highborn Indian chieftain has been seduced by the Don Juan trader. For this indiscretion the price is total massacre of the Spanish residents.[20]

The Spanish missionary influence has remained relatively strong. Narrow notions of sin, of race pollution, and of honor combine to destroy the happiness of a swamp exile who lives out of wedlock with a native maid. This tourist guide is subject to wayward gusts of passion. When he returns to a former love, misfortunes rain upon his deserted mistress. The church casts her out. At the climactic moment, her man returns, repentant. City people are pictured as shallow while rural folk are sketched as noble. A stencil character is the old grandma who maintains that "education in wickedness." Despite the obvious improbabilities in the plot, the "cracker" dialect is handled delicately and credibly.[21]

Less bound is the theme of the farmer who must make his peace with nature or fight. Tremendous can be the havoc wrought by the Florida hurricane, high water, and mosquitoes. It takes optimism and courage to stand up under repeated blows. To some settlers the lure of the tropics cannot be destroyed by damage to crops. Only the resigned words of an older farmer instill hope in the disheartened, younger farm owner.[22]

On a larger scale, hurricanes and a church service and cracker ignorance unite to form a melodrama with a nub of realism. Elemental types set in the scum of the Everglades represent native obduracy. By will and daring in the persons of some Western settlers, local prejudices, Negro hate, church hypocrisy, and feuding are finally overcome.[23]

Heterogeneous as is the coastal South, so are its dramatic resources. Nevertheless the pattern is fairly uniform. From Chapel Hill there has flowed a stream of folk dramas ranging from theatrical *études* to deeper regional studies. Tributaries have yielded a mound of actable plays to the nation. Whatever influence the Carolina scribes have exerted in the creation of a people's drama can be discerned in the variety and naturalness of themes which deal with life in the back-woods or smalltown areas. Paul Green remains their most productive and most distinguished playmaker.

Although the states of Louisiana and Mississippi, on the Gulf of Mexico, technically belong to the South, their regional base is different enough to warrant treatment in a separate chapter.

1. *Tangled Trails*, by Eugene H. Blake.

2. Robert Finch, "Playmaking in North Carolina," an investigation conducted in 1940 and now on file in the office of the Department of Drama at the University of North Carolina, Chapel Hill.

3. *Carolina Play-Book*, March-June, 1943, contains supplementary material.

4. By Patricia McMullan.

5. By Elizabeth Lay Green.

6. By Elizabeth Lay Green.

7. By Paul Green.

8. By William N. Cox.

9. By Clare Johnson Marley.

10. *The Loyal Venture*, by Wilkeson O'Connell.

11. *Off Nags Head or The Bell Buoy*, by Dougald MacMillan.

12. *In Dixon's Kitchen*, by Wilbur Stout.

13. *Old Wash Lucas*, by Paul Green.

14. *Quare Medicine*, by Paul Green.

15. *Peggy*, by Harold Williamson.

16. *Fixin's*, by Erma and Paul Green.

17. *Hunger*, by Ella Mae Daniel.

18. *Glendale Plantation*, by Tom Loy.

19. Spoken at a Regional Theater Festival, April 6, 1940, at the Playmakers' Theatre, University of North Carolina.

20. *Trafficante*, by Maxeda von Hesse.

21. *The Swamp Bird*, by Cale Young Rice.

22. *Hurricane*, by Natalie Grimes Lawrence.

23. *The Big Blow*, by Theodore Pratt.

VI

Mountain Plays

HIGHLANDERS are wont to exhibit traits which lie dormant in the subconscious. Like most primitive in-groups they inbreed, fear out-groups, adhere to settled moral codes and folkways, and speak an ancient speech. Nowhere are these reversions so aptly illustrated as among the cabin folk who live in isolated pockets along the creek beds and ropewalks in the southern Appalachians. Toughened by winds and storms and badgered by the ornery cussedness of man, these gaunt men and stoic women bear the marks of their region.

For amusement the natives fall back upon old "ballits," old ditties, and old jigs. At the "Big Meet-in'" and the "Singin' Gatherin'" they give vent to group emotions in play. But the pattern is generally obsolete. Witness a revival in two districts of an old morality and of classic mummer plays at Christmas time.

Within these hollows, legendry has furnished a few themes for the drama. For example, in mining towns of the Blue Ridge Mountains southward from the Maryland border to Georgia, there circulate ballads of the popular folk hero, John Henry. One version of the crucial contest of hammer against steam-driven rock drill associates the giant with the building of the Big Bend Tunnel. But two flimsy sketches on John Henry fail to give him any semblance of vitality.[1]

The drama is more at home with living persons. Two plays reveal different viewpoints of the man who was to become a legend soon after his death following his daring raid at Harper's Ferry on October 16, 1859. The life of John Brown was a covenant and a consecration. In the year of his execution appeared a hollow invention held together by long outbursts, speeches, and soliloquies. The plot turns on the leader's strong will, the sacrifice of his three sons, and his talks to reporters and visitors in his cell. One of them, addressing the martyr, condemns the cause but admires the man. Halfhearted justifications expressed in *Ossawattomie Brown* (1859) seemingly voice the views of the author, Mrs. Kate Lucy E. Swayze and her class.

A recent playlet strikes closer to the heart of the prophet. John Brown sits talking to reporters in his cell. He calls himself an instrument of Jehovah, akin to Moses who freed the children of Israel. Like all martyrs he feels that "persons are nothing compared to the Cause"; that slavery is wrong against God and humanity. Calmly he bears the accusations of fanatics while his faith remains unshaken. "God uses us and then passes on." As he prays for a sign, a lamb—the sacrificial lamb—passes his window.[2]

One contemporary sketch projects a living regional character, the stoic mountaineer. The features are vividly drawn. This woman has "sinful honin's" (impulses) to kick, stomp, throw a flatiron, and even kill her family. So long has she been absorbed into her family that she has lost her selfhood. She complains to an old "granny-woman," who advises her to play sick. The trick works. Though the plot moves slowly, the persons are real.[3]

In the Great Smokies, astride western North Carolina and eastern Tennessee, and roughly between the cities of Asheville and Knoxville, natives still act out English "ballits" and old play-party games. The old fiddler fiddles at frolics, and in the hill counties young and old take part in hoedown corn dances. Primitive pageantry is still witnessed in these mountains. For example, every Christmas an outdoor miracle play, *Twelfth Night,* re-enacts the Christ story in verse chant. Mainly a throng of singing Biblical characters pass by on their way to the Babe in the manger while other travelers on muleback ride to the barn and back.

Long has the local historian repeated a legend of Lincoln's mother which came to rest in a semifolk play. It appears that the young Nancy Hanks had been hired out to a neighbor, Abraham Enloe. As she matured, her comely face and figure attracted the eye of her master. Suspected illicit relations between the two anger the Bible-reading, invalid wife. By craft she induces a shiftless visitor, Tom Lincoln, to take the woman for his wife. Then the play turns oracular. Like the bondwoman in the Bible, Nancy walked off conscious that she was bearing the seed of one who would make a nation. The fable is clear; the leave-taking, theatrical.[4]

Translated into the moden triangle of ailing wife, serving maid, and husband all bound up in intimacy, yet justified by circumstances and condoned by the wife, the Hagar motif from the Bible may be expected to arouse the anger of the church in rural communities. One such dramatized story bears the imprint of sincerity and intensity. "Abram's wife took Hagar her maid, the Egyptian . . . and gave her to her husband Abram to be his wife." But the opposition of the church breaks down the willingness of the wife. The plot pulses along in authentic Biblical speech rhythms as spoken by mountain folk.[5]

The weather-beaten mountaineer, face to face with a hard environment, comes upon the stage with all his doggedness and prejudices. He acts true to form. Apparently the motive power for many of his decisions is bound up with larnin', lovin', feudin', and moonshinin'.

In the matter of learning, parental wrongheadedness can work havoc. It must be battered down before the young can win a measure of freedom. When opportunities for education are limited, the craving for getting it grows strong. Children plead with their elders to allow them to go to school. In cabins scattered along the hollows, how often is heard the common wail, "I'm a-hankerin' ter larn. I ain't never goin' ter git no larnin' iffen I stick here in these mountains." The obstacles to learning may be sundry: parents, poverty, love. Frequently the pappy, one of the "poor mountain trash," insists "What was good enough for me is good enough for my children"; or, "Indeed, a body can make on without book-larnin'." Too blind to see the value of "eddication," the old codger remains sunk in lethargy until a crisis or accident opens his eyes. It may be the danger of substituting the liniment bottle for the cough medicine when nobody can read the labels.[6] It may be the loud insistence of a relative or outsider, or the pleading of a country nurse or teacher. In a moment of weakness the father may give in halfheartedly and allow his son or daughter to attend the mission school. The mother generally sides with the child. On the other hand a parent may plead poverty to carry his point, and the child's yearning will remain unfulfilled. To the mentally starved youngsters the teacher becomes an angelic vision, the symbol of a better life.

At times elders may agree on the need of education. "We'll have one that kin read and write, praise God." What better way to overcome "cussin' and damnation" than to train a boy to be a preacher. But circumstances interpose. The debt collector intrudes and the sky-high dreams of a saving grandmother crash to the ground. The struggle may end on a futile note. "Ain't no use ter want nothin' on the farm!"[7]

Education and love may demand equal claims. Like others of his kind, one ambitious youngster, although ready to leave the mountains for a school, suffers a check when the feminine lure of a beloved proves too strong.

The resulting ignorance is responsible for the granite streak of fanaticism formerly expressed in feudin'. Of late the younger generation has questioned the utility of family grudges. Especially when love enters does feudin' vanish. Romeo still woos his Juliet. In spite of standing wars or "troubles" (as natives refer to feuds), an occasional marriage between a boy and girl of hostile families is not uncommon. The groom must overcome opposition even if he has to use a shotgun. To cite a few instances, mention is made of the following plots. One feudist runs off with the daughter of the other house after covering the girl's father with a gun and delivering a final plea for peace. "They ain't no use of us bein' bad friends 'cause our granpaw fit over a hawg."[8] A similar message is spoken at a wedding consummated under duress and against the wishes of the bride as well as of her father. These two believe their enemy should be killed "cause . . . his folks killed my folks." During the ceremony the old man is covered with a gun. Then the groom and father-in-law wrestle. After the preacher declares that "down underneath we're all alike" opposition breaks down.[9]

The shotgun splicin' can afford moments of sardonic merriment and throw light upon the mountain code. The mountaineer marries as often as he must, for on the farm a woman is essential to a man's happiness. Humor is implicit in the situation of the petty official mourning the death of his third wife and resolving suddenly to take a fourth, the brainless but kindly neighbor. In this instance he is forced to cover his daughter with a gun because she objects loudly as the priest reads the services.[10] Elsewhere the shotgun comes into play when a jack-leg preacher insists on marrying his sister to one of two reluctant candidates.[11]

In the mountains strangers are suspect. Each is readily mistaken for that detestable violator of civil rights, the "revenooer." In local plays he is pictured as the villain of the piece. One such snooper, after creating a scandal by stealing the daughter of an enraged moonshiner, turns out to be a harmless magazine writer.[12] In another hollow an officer bent on investigating a camp of moonshiners talks to several of the men. He denies his identity, begs to be put out of this weary world, and, by clever moves, escapes.[13]

But when a willful daughter takes matters into her own hands, she upsets the local regulations and scandalizes her neighbors. One such headstrong maid, ripe for love, woos a captured stranger and, to everybody's astonishment, gains her own personal ends.[14]

The mountain code rules against outbursts of lust. It points with scorn at the sinner caught in the toils of the temptress as sung in the ballad of "The Woman from Merry River." In the play of the same name,[15] the black-haired, voluptuous maid in silk dress and bare feet lures the unhappy mountain lad, and they dance wildly and run off. In the wicked town saloon he, his Jezebel, and a flirtatious stranger enter into a three-cornered brawl. Back in the mountain cabin, with aberrant fancy checked, he makes up with his former love.

Among the mountain types bred by primitive living in the hollows stands the patriarch whose authority rests on the Bible. Natives call on him to settle private disputes and they accept his judgments without question. Aged seventy-five and cultured, one of these inspired jurists in the Alleghenies is obliged to try his own younger son for the murder of an elder brother. Judgment is pronounced. The son must give himself up on the following evening, and the girl who instigated the crime must leave the mountains. Though closely knit, the action is conventional. The flow of feeling is warm and the portrait of the old judge impressive and plausible.[16]

Most renowned of mountain characters is the Widow Cagle from the hills near Asheville. Her creator, Lula Vollmer, who knows her mountain folks intimately, has rounded the flimsy outlines sketched in by others and endowed her folks with vitality. The set properties are present: the sheriff, the fear of "furriners," feuds, hatred of the law, and the readiness to kill. But with a difference. The people in *Sun-Up* (1923) live and suffer and talk like the folks of the soil. Isolation accounts for their folk wisdom and folk beliefs, which are neatly interpolated in the text. "That's what the mountain folks need—larnin'." "Ye kin fill a youngun's brain all ye want to, but hit's a-goin' to run out if thar's a hole in the stomach." As for war, "hit air murder, and the law air back of hit." Mrs. Cagle, a rugged, positive matron who smokes a corncob pipe, says, "I've heard tell of Asheville, but I ain't never bin there." Like her neighbors she is ready to kill the son of the man who murdered her husband when he seeks shelter in her cabin. But inner voices plead for mercy and she desists. Suffering has brought faith. The slow, sad music of the hinterland flows from this play.

Laid in a lumber camp, *The Dunce Boy* (1925, unpublished) by the same author, is motivated by the constant buzz of the sawmill. Briefly, it deals with a half-witted son of nineteen who has been tenderly reared by his mother and protected against the cruel outbursts of an illiterate father. She senses and fears the onrush of sexual awareness in the dim brain. Innocently the boy worships the schoolteacher but dares not, must not touch her. When the secretly wedded woman is touched by her husband, the idiot kills the man in fury. There are hints of Celtic borrowings in the portrait of the half-wit. "I hear music, I see cloud, see stars, big moon."

A later series of loose sketches taken on tour across the nation, *Moonshine and Honeysuckle* (1934), less successfully attacks the topic of feuding. The local Romeo refuses to kill; he detests the "maggots o' men a-squirmin' in hate." When he marries the native Juliet, will the war of the families cease? Despite the obvious message, the coming and going and shooting by stereotypes is confusing. The local mannerisms are too quaint and the speech of the hill folk sounds labored.

In *The Hill Between* (1937) the Carolinian playwright invokes a mellower mood. City and mountain codes are contrasted through the relations of a former mountain boy, now a New York physician, and his pampered city-bred wife. Returning to his native soil he feels that the hill between him and his people can be removed if he wills it. Despite his wife's opposition, he succeeds in doing so. The quiet satisfaction of the mountaineers expressed in the phrase, "I air content," and the strong dignity won through self-denial by those who have learned that "the strength to live without love air greater than love," and "I reckon learnin' don't have nothin' to do with happiness" sum up the best in regional character. Here and there a portrait is overdrawn, as in the instance of the city wife with her snobbish airs. City pleasures are pictured as those of café society. Unfortunately, the ending (as revised by the publisher) is forced and oratorical.

A kindred doctor appears in a playlet by another hand: the northern missionary who comes South to fight poverty and prejudice. But hostile forces restrict him.[17]

More theatrical are the portraits etched in *"Hell-Bent for Heaven* (1924), by Hatcher Hughes. Villainy with a capital V snarls in the hollows! A religious pretender who poses as a man of peace breeds trouble and stirs up feuds. This mountain Iago-and-Tartuffe vainly loves a mountain girl. So hell-bent for revenge is he that he breaks a dam with dynamite to drown a rival. Ironically, the final scene shows the trapped sinner praying to God, then denying God, as the water in the cabin rises. Thunder and lightning and flood furnish spectacular obbligato to the action. *Ruint* (1925), Hughes' second offering, plays lightly on old prejudices connected with the mountain code of conduct. Any infringement, real or fancied, like the kiss that does not lead to marriage, must be avenged by tar and feathers and threats of hanging. The character types are wooden; the humor, pumped; and the speech, though clipped and authentic, is neither imaginative nor racy. Folk flavor is lost in factitious theatricalism obviously meant to be satiric.

Humbler mountaineers touched with humor are outlined in three studies from the pen of Fred Koch, Jr. Drawn from life is the rustic who sets booby traps to bog down luxurious touring cars. He pulls them out for a fee.[18] Another pocket of these mountains serves as background for a satire on machine politics. Voters who cast absentee ballots for a chosen party are paid sums averaging ten dollars. The local leaders attempt to induce an idiot to sign a ballot. Driven to extremes, they go so far as to get a dog to vote for the "Dimmercrats."[19]

The ingrown habits of mountaineers are likely to suffer strain under pressure. When the outside world batters against the ridges, the folks must act in their own way. They hear that a new highway is to be constructed in Cable Cove. One of the originators forecasts wonderful days to come. For this reason he will not sell his bottom land for a newly proposed power lake. Things reach an acute stage after the road is opened the tourists invade the coves. Driven to despair, "paw" will sell his land gladly in return for "a great, big, quiet lake." The figures are sharply though flatly drawn, and the dialogue reads like a literal transcript. In the course of the story, cityfolk and their music, dancing, and speech are unfairly lampooned.[20]

The mountain plays thus far recorded seem pale when set down against a three-act play astir with indignation. *Let Freedom Ring* (1936), based upon a novel by Grace Lumpkin and dramatized by Albert Bein, draws a sad picture of mountaineers dislodged from their hills and cabins. They move from a life of poverty they have known, where "ye were free men so long as ye had yer own potato patch and house and gun," to a strangely new manner of living in the cotton mills of a town far away. Here they must adapt themselves to the machine and its evils: the speed-up, long hours, and low wages. This panorama of mountain folk with their dander up narrows to four characters:

the grandpappy, the two brothers of opposite views, and the long-suffering mother. These victims of the millowners, cheated by company stores and terrorized by thugs and sheriffs, move with dignity and bewilderment. Throughout the recital of their woes, the mountaineers yearn for their hollows. In time they become tied to a ruthless system of mill-town life. The play points a fine plea for workers' rights.

In the coves of the Cumberlands, across east Kentucky and east Tennessee, the poor, ornery, backwoods people find pleasure in the summer's outstanding event, the "Big Meeting": "two weeks of fiery sermons, sweet music, prayer shouting, conversion, baptism, dinner on the ground, visiting, and courting."[21] At other times men on the Liars' Bench swap stories and invent fantastic yarns. One of the myths, still repeated, concerns the exploits of the Tennessee congressman and fabulous hunter, Davy Crockett. At the heyday of his fame the great hunter claimed to have shot, in a season, 105 bears and to have slain six deer in a day.[22] After this, his fame spread westward. Two plays which deal with this folk figure deserve note. The first of these still clings to the stage picture of the mountaineer or backwoodsman which once appeared in our national drama. In fact, up to 1825, he could be identified by his coonskin cap and long rifle. Best known among the early stage frontiersmen was Nimrod Wildfire, unpolished and generous, who appeared in *Lion of the West* (1831), by James Kirke Paulding. Often this bustling hunter was a point of contention between restless pioneers and stay-at-homes.

The well-known frontier melodrama, *Davy Crockett; or, Be Sure You're Right, Then Go Ahead* (1872), by Frank H. Murdoch, played in many cities

"Sun-up," by Lula Vollmer

from 1873 to 1906. It was progressively and substantially revised by Frank Mayo who, during a successful English tour, performed in the title role more than two thousand times. The famous yarn spinner, a youth of "natural-born sense," springs from the ground. The worn-out theatrical properties are evident. Davy calls himself an ignorant backwoodsman. He dares to love the "scholared and dainty" friend of his boyhood who has returned from abroad with a guardian, a beau, and a snobbish uncle. She understands the heart of Davy and loves his people. "I love their honest simplicity, rugged though it be. It refreshes me like a draught of pure spring water, or a breath from this fresh mountain air." The snow scene, in which Davy saves the life of the freezing and terrified girl from the howling wolves by barring the door of his hut with his strong arm, must have called forth loud cheers from the gallery. Davy emulates the brave young Lochinvar by running off with the girl. The last scene bustles with a hasty marriage under duress, and the exposure of the guardian as a criminal and forger —to the final strains of "Home, Sweet Home." How the simple-minded Davy shines against the black-hearted villainy of the rotten aristocrats! The formula is too transparent today.

A later dramatization sets the coonskin hero in a backwoods tavern while a square dance is on. There is talk of General Jackson: pungent and boastful talk. "I'm that same Davy Crockett, half-horse and half-alligator!" Then a burst of rakehell, pompous oratory. "I can whup my weight in wild-cats an' if any gentleman cares (for a ten-dollar bill), a panther throwed in! I can hug a b'ar too close for comfort, an' eat any man that's for old Andy Jackson." The crowd enjoys his prowess, his speech, his yarns. Soon after this scene, Davy leaves for Texas to fight for freedom. The death of Davy and of a young Irish companion are eloquently foretold by two wives in a poetic finale. The shrill swashbuckling of Davy is counterbalanced by the subdued double lament at the end.[23]

Tennessee calls up memories of "Swanee River," "Old Black Joe," and of their creator, Stephen Foster, a semifolk figure. Any play based on his life must necessarily stress romance and melody. Though set in the Pittsburgh of 1850, delectable associations of the whole region come to life. *Stephen Foster* (1926), by Earl Hobson Smith, a loose chronicle play with music, has been popular in the Cumberlands. Another play, written by another hand and based on the songs of the composer, has likewise been performed.[24]

Yet all is not honey in these hollows. Hate more than love overpowers these people, not to mention clannish notions about domestic relations. Harsh elders often throttle the natural instincts of the young. Consider the daughter married to a feudist's son and gone to live in the city. One day she returns to mollify her stern mother. After a spell the hard matron accepts the new babe and relents.[25] Consider too the secretly wedded daughter who goes out to the woods to meet her husband after he signals by imitating the notes of the whippoorwill. At this point the puzzled father rushes out to kill the "bird." Instead, the girl is brought in dead.[26]

Contrariwise a grandmother, remembering the old feuds in which she lost six sons and a husband, tries to induce her grandson to stop feuding. Yet he insists on going out to resume the old shootings in order to retrieve the family honor. When he kills, the old woman cannot help rejoicing.[27]

Conventional in design as these hate pieces may be,

variation in character is achieved, a degree of pathos sustained, and a sense of region successfully conveyed. The sharply etched women exchange a speech that is racy and redolent of earth.

The deeper one penetrates the Cumberland Gap, the more provincial and pronounced are the human types. These landlocked folk exhibit those qualities which go with isolation. To them the Devil is real and witches ride by night. Their dialect shows ancient British origins. Their pleasures have hardly changed with the centuries. The old-time rhymester plays jig tunes on his dulcimer while mountain folk dance the hoedown corn dance and breakdowns with or without a fiddle. Most notable of social events is the annual "Singin' Gatherin'" held in June. "Ballits," declaimed by two, as well as the crude old play jigs, wherein give-and-take dialogue is carried on by a boy and a girl, can still be heard.

Up to the year 1938 revivals of an old mummer play featuring the droll Turkish Knight, and an old Christmas entertainment showing the clown, Pickle Herring, were done in doggerel. Likewise, a Plough Monday Play (with corruptions in the text), showing scenes of combat and cure, of figures dropping dead and jumping up to symbolize the seasons, has actually been performed on American soil.[28]

These classic folk plays of another day and continent are far removed from the crop of stage puppets yielded by the rich loam of Kentucky in the late nineties. In that old idyl of the mountains and the Bluegrass, *In Old Kentucky* (1893), by Charles T. Dazey, characters are modeled after certain New England types. Most significant is Madge, the illiterate flower of the "mountings," a child of nature who confidently holds her own against the proud, patronizing city swells.

However patent the imitation, she never takes on fullness or catches the vitality of a Jonathan. The note of sectional pride in the toast to the "bright-eyed, cherry-lipped, rose-cheeked girls of old Kentucky" may be forgiven.

Crude as such melodrama was, it had more life than the pale, poetic drama of the early 1900's. Current plays by Kentucky scribes might have been penned in London. There is no attempt to create native character in a familiar setting. The gentle piping, the calm pastoral mood in the early plays of a Cale Young Rice merely revived Elizabethan echoes. In the story of the shepherd of the hills secretly anointed by the prophet Samuel, the versifier timidly approached a rural subject.

Suddenly, in 1912, a pioneer swung open a gate that led to folk pastures in the North. Eight years later the same Percy MacKaye, with his wife, visited the Kentucky Mountains on a mission of "creative research." Resolved "to interpret certain native American backgrounds of our national life," the two rode for fifteen hundred miles on horseback along the Appalachian trail. The poet who had become an advocate of the folk theater, as established by the Irish, strained every nerve to capture and record the idiom of the mountaineer, his "noble illiteracy," his folkways. On his return to the North he concocted *This Fine-Pretty World*, which was produced in New York in 1923. This jumbled tale of the rich uncle and the poor nephew, of a husband's desire to put away his wife and marry the maiden, of adultery and charges of "deefamation," of a babe delivered in a sack, of a kidnapping, trial, public repentance, and jail sentence, are all tied up into one ludicrous knot. There is too much Bible-quoting, lengthy oratory, and puffed-up imagery. The

North took the play to its bosom. Eulogies over the rhythm, color, and fantasy by fifty contemporaries did not stave off oblivion. This overwritten play today remains a museum piece.

A year later the same pen wrote *Kentucky Mountain Fantasies* in the one-act form. Only one of these sketches is strictly a fantasy. The characters are the rustics the author had met. *Napoleon Crossing the Rockies* tells of an old couple in a cabin near "these God-forsook creeks" who are induced to sell their cabin to a lumber company. The curtain falls on the fiddler playing a tune and the old woman hugging a gift of beads. The dialect is full of such gems as "I creened over and plumb changed the ends of me. . . . When I first unwiddered ye in wedlock. . . . We's bit by the torch o' carkin' sorrer." A bit of quiet drollery marks *The Funeralizing of Crickneck*. Here the country preacher who courts the widow speaks the funeral oration years after the husband has disappeared. On the very day of the sermon, the husband, an ex-convict, sneaks back, secretly changes his jail clothes, and escapes with his own money. Once the loss is discovered, the match is off. Knowing all this, the reader is doubly amused at the pompous tribute, "He were a friend of unwashed hands. He were a walkin' text of the Ten Commandments. He were a livin' parable of the Sarmin on the Mountain." In *Timber,* the third playlet, the spirit world appears. The Devil in goggles succeeds in luring to town the son who "cain't be hurted by nothin' made outen wood." The speech takes on familiar Celtic inflection. "And his both gret laigs mashed red-bloody by the log-slide and him now layin' his len'th in the blind ground with the others."

MacKaye made the common error of accenting the

quaint and of overloading rural dialect. He evidently aimed to carve a backwoods dialect, as Synge had done, out of the musical idiom of the fisherfolk for the Abbey Theatre of Dublin. He did not succeed. One of his own lines hits back at him. "He talks a queer down-crick lingo."

Modern playmakers of Kentucky have used a less pretentious style with less spectacular material. In *The Mountain,* by Carty Ranck, feud, moonshine, bloodshed, larnin', revenge, and love are strung on a well-defined plot. Two codes fight for survival; past and present are personalized in the struggle of the father against the son. The old gospel of blood revenge is countered by the new belief in justice. Personalities are sharply contrasted. The main weakness of the play lies in a lack of pathos and power. It is singularly pale and bloodless.

More argumentative is the one-act play which expands the theme of blindness. The tall, gaunt, and blind matriarch who has laid away her man and seven sons is a well-known stage type. She is unorthodox in one respect: she scoffs at folks who get religion without joy, at long-haired preachers with their *shalts* and *shalt nots;* and she even blasphemes the God of vengeance. The action is submerged in the didactic discourse. The old woman is merely a peg for ideas on right living. Related matters on the care of babies, the sad lot of the mountain woman, the value of medicine, medical care, and science are developed. The moral is pointed: only knowledge will reclaim the impoverished mountaineer.[29]

Aside from the false starts, deflections, and experiments, the mountain plays of recent years have reached the stature of regional drama. They reflect the folk. Highland plays seem to fall into the patterns of situation and character. The tight formula embodying the normal pursuits of the ordinary Appalachian lends itself to repetition and even to ridicule—as in the shotgun marriage, lovin' and feudin', contempt for law, and fear of revenue officers. Characters, too, bear a likeness: the hard-headed pappy, the tight-lipped mammy, and the earnest young ones crying for larnin'. Ready-made as the plots may be, gifted playbuilders like Lula Vollmer and Albert Bein have filled the mold with living flesh and human impulse made visible and memorable in the lore and idiom nurtured by generations of landlocked existence. In the better plays of the region, the tang of the sod, the whimper of hurt mortals, and the pathos inherent in restricted lives reared in the remote hollows and ridges of the Southland come to fullness.

1. *The Natural Man*, by Theodore Browne, and *John Henry*, by Roark Bradford.

2. *John Brown*, by Phyllis Winn Jackson.

3. *For Better or Worse*, by Susie Smith Sinclair.

4. *Nancy Hanks, Bondwoman*, by Janie Malloy Britt.

5. *Abram's Wife*, by Mary Hoyt Reese.

6. *Larnin'*, by Alla Webb.

7. *Stockin' Money*, by Eloise Earle Dean.

8. *Mountain Laurel*, by Curtis Cooksey.

9. *A Mountain Wedding*, by Pearl Franklin.

10. *Funeral Flowers for the Bride*, by Beverley du Bose Hamer.

11. *A Shotgun Splicin'*, by Gertrude Wilson Coffin.

12. *Dod Gast Ye Both*, by Hubert Heffner.

13. *Moonshine*, by Arthur Hopkins.

14. *Muley*, by Chase Webb.

15. By Chase Webb.

16. *The Patriarch*, by Boyd Smith.

17. *The Doctor Decides*, by Fred Eastman.

18. *Wash Carver's Mouse Trap*.

19. *These Doggone Elections*.

20. "Smoky Mountain Road" (unpublished).

21. Writers' Program, W.P.A., *Tennessee; a Guide to the State* (New York, 1939), p. 138.

22. Dixon Wecter, *The Hero in America; a Chronicle of Hero-Worship* (New York, 1941), p. 193.

23. *Davy Crockett*, by John Philip Milhous.

24. *Carry Me Long*, by Rollo Wayne.

25. *The Tie That Binds*, by O. F. Cornelius.

26. *The Whippoorwill*, by O. F. Cornelius.

27. *On Vengeance Height*, by Allan Davis.

28. Marie Campbell, "Survivals of Old Folk Drama in the Kentucky Mountains," *Journal of American Folklore*, LI (January, 1938), 10-24.

29. *Blindness*, adapted from stories of Lucy Furman by Besse P. Gephart.

VII

Hill Folks

THE MORE remote and landlocked the geographical sector, the more pronounced will be the stamp on men and their folk arts. This truism applies with force to that strip of triangular upland, known as the Ozarks, that straddles parts of Arkansas, Missouri, and Oklahoma west of the Mississippi. On this land of granite ridges and gully-washed farms live an assortment of natives who still cling to old ways, old beliefs, old amusements. Men sleep in cord beds and hunt with muzzle-loading rifles while women operate spinning wheels and homemade looms. To them tall tales of hoop snakes and whip snakes, legends associated with trees, rocks, streams, and Spanish treasure, and stories about the power of witches and the Devil are real.[1] Such beliefs seem to have entered the very fiber of the hill folk.

Although many Ozarkians consider dancing immoral and the fiddle an instrument of the devil, in their play time they manage to amuse themselves hugely in frolics by lamplight (square dances) and, less often, in play-party games, candy pullin's, pie socials, and box suppers. At the same time the provincial minstrels willfully strum the old English ballads as well as the ditties of a later day. Nor are theatricals lacking. While the old showboat melodramas are seldom given, the regular tent or Toby shows are still popular in many parts of Missouri.[2]

Of late years the region has become sharply conscious of its folk treasures. At the annual Ozark Folk

Festival, a crew of entertainers unlock the traditional folk arts. Among these is storytelling, an art developed by constant practice on the Liars' Bench where the local wags and whittlers roll off windies or whoppers or "so-tales" in speech comparable to "smooth corn-likker an' plumb, sweet moosic."[3] Curiously, this speech has hardly changed since Elizabethan times. Through many of the stories runs a droll, theatrical current which speaks for the region. Best known is that piece of folklore supposed to have originated about the year 1840: The Arkansas Traveler. Three generations of backwoodsmen have circulated and embellished this colloquy between the Traveler and the Squatter. The setting is comically theatrical. A contrary, taciturn, fiddle-loving squatter in buckskin breeches and coonskin cap sits placidly on a whisky barrel; his wife, with pipe in mouth, rests in the doorway; near by may be seen a girl, four scrubby urchins, and a boy in an ash barrel. A lost traveler on horseback stops to ask for a night's lodging. Quizzically the native turns aside every question. But once the stranger plays his violin, the whole group leaps into life. Now he must stay; the roads all end, and so he'll have to turn back. The cabin is now at his disposal. This folk jest in folk dialect belongs as much to folk drama as to fiddle music.

To grasp the later and more sophisticated drama of the Ozarks, one must understand the people. Curiously, these hillsmen believe yet doubt. On the one hand they would convince you of their seriousness; on the other, have you disbelieve. They appear to carry their convictions lightly, yet are strongly principled. Though they mock at their own weaknesses, they resent any charge of flippancy. To outsiders, natives in this land of pork, whisky, and corn bread sometimes act as if they were "touched in the haid."

Well-defined native types appear in regional plays by local scribes. As the forces of superstition are bound to clash with enlightened belief, characters rise or fall according to their strength or weakness. In one playlet set in the beginning of the nineteenth century, a half-Indian girl solemnly sees visions and hears the Swamp Spirit. But the doubting youth will brook no such nonsense. Defiantly he takes down an ax and prepares to meet the demon, a tall, ghostly figure in black. Man and ghost grapple for a moment before they disappear. The feeling of horror is credibly sustained throughout.[4] In another quarter, views regarding this "witchin' business" are being exchanged. Natives seriously argue that witches can cast spells on a body, turn milk sour, and perform other feats of magic. "Now, these here witches—thar's ways o' bustin' 'em accordin' to the ol' folks," affirms one cynic.[5] As if to refute this thesis, uttered by a backwoodsman, his child, daughter, wife, and mother one by one fall into convulsions, scream, and faint. Surely they must be bewitched. But the whole affair was planned solely for each to gain personal ends. Against his will the stubborn witch buster is forced to grant to each her wish. The union of femininity with the spirit world proves too much. And the laugh is on the defeated male.

Historic memories of Spanish diggings haunt the cliffs of northwestern Arkansas. It is a fact that the explorer De Soto, led on by tales of gold, found only Indians and mosquitoes. When a modern business man goes digging for gold, he finds nothing but a bare skull. Romance and adventure evaporate in the dull light of today.[6]

The average Ozarkian is a stoic. Fortitude in the

face of hardship and the ability to negate or assert the self are common. The hillwoman of iron rules in a number of dramatic sketches. To indicate but a handful, there is the long-suffering aunt who has been expecting a proposal of marriage, but must lose her man to a golden-haired niece. By this act, however, she manages to regain her self-respect. No longer will she be used as a door mat.[7] An ailing wife decides to remove herself and thus solve the family's hopeless struggle against mortgage, drought, and bad crops. Accordingly, when a heart attack comes on, she does nothing to save herself.[8] Another hillwoman of pioneer stock is torn between duty to her son and duty to her mother. The cause of the dilemma is an heirloom. Shall the spring wheel, a relic one hundred and fifty years old, remain or go? If sold, the son can save himself from arrest; but granny will protest violently. Finally the spring wheel stays, the boy marches off to the penitentiary, and the mother is able to hold her head up after all.[9] A headstrong granmother clashes with the law. She defies the school authorities. No Missouri sheriff can come between her and her grandchildren. But when the island reverts to within the Nebraska line, she gives up her young ones.[10] Equally tenacious but more formidable is the granny who refuses to be moved out of her cabin when the outside world comes into the hollows to blast ground for a dam. Electricity is another word for the devil. "Here I've lived an' here I stay till I'm toted out feet first."[11] But only by her own wish is she carried out of the door in a rocker, feet first. Such is the tough fiber of Ozarkian womanhood as pictured in regional playlets.

The male animal, on the contrary, is exceedingly droll. Side by side with the city slicker, the mountaineer either fades or flourishes. He certainly shows off to advantage in his mastery of a provincial, full-flavored speech. In the spring when the sap's a-running, love can play queer pranks. Two men quarrel over a mountain coquette only to get "the tail-end and drippin's of a raw deal."[12] The maid deserts her two suitors for one of "them damned furreign tour-isters." More canny is the handy genius who invents strange contraptions which he swaps for no-'count things. Slick city agents come to bid for the mining rights on his farm. They despair of ever reaching a settlement until they learn of his regional weakness for swapping. Then follows a series of brazen exchanges in which the local hero wins all his demands point by point.[13] He is brother to two trifling scamps who would rather play checkers than attend to business. In fact, so eager is the storekeeper to be free like the animals to play and to fish that he even arrests himself.[14]

More evenly keyed to our normal level of existence are the rural dwellers of Ain, Grant County, Arkansas —the worried, unhappy farmers who take summer jobs as loggers to eke out a living. They are depicted in *Arkansas Folk Plays* (undated), a trilogy by Clinton Bradford. For pages the conversation unfolds uneventfully until a sudden spark ignites the action. Then a blaze—and the crisis is past! The best of these playlets concerns the inner feelings of a son waiting outside a church while his father is being tried by a congregation for sinning. What had happened was innocent enough. While entertaining friends, the father had grabbed a lady around the waist. He therefore refuses now to repent. Instead he cries out, "They got to point fingers . . . to cast stones." What makes these three pieces significant, slow as the action may be, is the implicit, indigenous notion of sin, church orders, and moral stability.

The folk laureate of the Ozarks is Weldon Stone, a native of Texas and member of the Department of English at the Agricultural and Mechanical College of Texas. Two of his early sketches, *A Darksome Furriner* (1937) [15] and *Courtin' Maisie* (1937), [16] touch on the theme of violation of the stern mountain code. The hill folk eye with distrust "furriners" from the North who dare to invade their mountains. Therefore, when a dark newcomer from New York settles among them, they feel resentful. But presently they are won over by wine and music; and intolerance suffers a defeat. More severe is the punishment administered to those who infringe the moral law. Strait is the gate and narrow is the way. Even appearances are enough to condemn the unwary. A pair of silk stockings and a silk dress carry implications of sin and worldliness even when offered in courtship. But explanations suffice to set things right, and, in racy speech, homely observations on marriage make up for the slight action.

Satire can be a double-edged knife. To laugh at playmakers who sit down to write a folk play is to hit the weaknesses inherent in the type. The result may be contrary to that which was intended. *We Write a Play* (1938) [17] mock-humorously stresses the stock regional elements: mortgage, drouth, storms, hounds, the prodigal son, seduction, theft, murder. Climactic is the revelation that the play cannot be indigenous because it lacks—an idiot! Despite the ridicule, the action at times is too real, too painful to be funny, as in the scene at the lynching where the hounds and the thunderclap are introduced.

Out of the Ozark anthology Weldon Stone has

chosen the most fantastic and original of folk figures, the fine-pretty, irrepressible whittler of Lebanon, Arkansas: Lemuel Skaggs. Five plays[18] about this supreme craftsman deal with his career before and after marriage. Central to the whole is the timeless struggle of the artist to maintain his integrity in a hostile world of crazed, practical moneygrubbers.

Lem, "the greatest whittler of all time," born with an all-fired hankering for something beyond, is a racy, robust folk figure. This genius performs miracles with knife and wood. His skill reaches greatness when he fools the parson and his wife into believing that the rainbow fish he had carved out of cedar wood are real enough to eat. His highest triumph is his carving of a key to the Big Gate of Heaven which, of course, everybody covets.[19]

Lem, the plain mortal, is often driven to make crucial decisions. Temptations and problems beset him. At one time the devil, a sly fellow who makes music on a flute, incites him to carve a statue of Myra before he marries her—although he had promised her to give up whittling. At another time Mammon, a richly dressed stranger in flowing cape who crouches like a buzzard, reproves Lem for wasting "talent in this lonesome Devil-forsaken holler."[20] He holds out alluring promises of riches if he will come away to Hot Springs without Myra. But he rejects the offer and Mammon flies upward out of sight. After Lem has been married a number of years, he has to face another crisis: shall he cut down the biggest tree in Arkansas and make it into furniture and toothpicks? How else can he repay a debt to his father-in-law?

Throughout these plays Myra, his Philistine wife, "a cross atween an angel and a little she-panther"[21] remains a thorn in his flesh. At first she refuses to

marry him unless he quits his "everlastin' whittlin' "
and bends his back to "ploughin' and puttin' seeds in
the ground like ary other man."[22] She cracks the whip,
imposes menial tasks, thwarts him at every turn, and
would even break him. No time for playing or loafing.
She insists that he sell what he makes. Once she goes
so far as to deprive him of his precious knife, without
which he is of no account. When things get too bad,
he repairs to his limestone cave along Little Breakshin
prepared to die. Here he has fashioned for himself a
coffin, sweet-smelling, soft, and cool, to be floated like
a canoe.

For all that, his wife Myra, despite her regular
appearance as counterforce, fails to come alive. She
is streaked with a few primary, dominant traits.

A merry and mischievous fellow, given rather to
mundane pranks than to supernatural doings, is the
devil in *Devil Take a Whittler* (1938). Once he
manifested his power by breathing life into a wooden
image of the Cedar Girl whittled out of a tree. In that
act he seems to reach the height of his magical powers.
He is friendly to the artist but hostile to the wife.
More satanic is the demon Mammon of *Mammon and
the Whittler* (1938) in that he destroys and corrupts
and lays snares fatal to the integrity of the artist.

Despite a veneer of caricature in the portrait of
Lem, he is a pathetic fellow, subject to the needs of the
flesh and the cravings of the spirit. As a free agent he
has to withstand wife, parson, and the public. Like
any other creative worker, he must make continual
adjustments between living and creating; between the
demands of love and the claims of art. In his case the
two are fundamentally at odds. Lem stands as the
self-dedicated artist who must express himself or
perish. Heinrich in *The Sunken Bell* (1896), a play

by Gerhart Hauptmann, is no more distraught a
figure than Lem. The same elements join: pain, frustration, sacrifice, compromise. Though set in the
village of Lebanon, the parable in this saga girdles the
globe.

These "whittler" plays lope along by the power of
conversation, with occasional bursts of action. What
chiefly keeps them agog is the lively and colorful dialect, the playful turns, the pitting of character against
demon on native ground. Quite transparent is the
allegory; while fantasy lights up as an afterglow.

One blemish must be pointed out. Into his most
recent offering, *The Flute and the Vine* (1940), there
are introduced such extraneous figures as Paul Bunyan,
the giant woodsman with his ax, and a troop of dryads
who issue from tree trunks. One of them in dazzling
white, representing Winter, lures the logger and compels him to break his ax. Aside from the incongruity
of the assemblage, this effeminate bit of imagery jangles
like a bell out of tune. The robust Ozarkian imagination has no need of such dainty and artificial props as
seasonal personifications!

Truly the sober fact of the North turns odd under
the Ozarkian sky. When the sturdy and wily mountaineer emerges, he is dabbed with strange tints. But
the face is real, the voice natural, and the feet are
planted squarely on home ground. Not least significant
is the quality of the spoken word—musical, rich, and
nasal. Though possibly a bit lush to "foreign" ears,
it is truly the most unique and refreshing of American
regional dialects.

---

1. Writers' Program, W.P.A., *Missouri; a Guide to the "Show Me"
State* (New York, 1941), pp. 136-37.
2. *Ibid.*, pp. 133 ff., 154.
3. *When the Sap's A-Runnin'*, by Virgil L. Baker, Head of the Division
of Speech and Director of the University Theater at the University of
Arkansas.

4. *The Swamp Spirit,* by Lealon N. Jones of the State Teachers College at Cape Girardeau, Missouri.

5. *Witchin' Racket,* by Virgil L. Baker.

6. *Spanish Diggin's,* by Virgil L. Baker.

7. *Door Mats,* by Stella D. Whipkey.

8. *And Cling to Thee,* by Lealon N. Jones.

9. *Heirloom,* by Lealon N. Jones.

10. *Alsace in Missouri,* by Allean Lemmon.

11. *Feet First,* by Helen S. White.

12. *When the Sap's A-Runnin',* by Virgil L. Baker.

13. *Swappin' Fever,* by Lealon N. Jones.

14. *Triflin',* by Lealon N. Jones.

15. See Mayorga's *Twenty Short Plays on a Royalty Holiday* (New York, 1941).

16. See *Midwest Prize Plays* (Chicago, Ill., 1938).

17. See *One Act Play Magazine,* II (1938).

18. The "Whittler" plays are: *Devil Take a Whittler, Mammon and the Whittler, Cloud Over Breakshin, Rainbows in Heaven,* and *The Flute and the Vine.*

19. From *Rainbows in Heaven.*

20. From *Mammon and the Whittler.*

21. *Ibid.*

22. From *Devil Take a Whittler.*

VIII

Creole and Cajun

THERE IS a hinterland along the Gulf States known to but few. Although actually a part of the South, this ancient *coin de France* sprang from vastly different roots political and cultural. As in the case of Florida, the successive rule by France, Spain, then France again, over a mixture of many strains, produced a fusion of cultures unique in our history. The presence of French and Spanish whites, of Negroes and cross-breeds, contributed to make Louisiana a polyglot organism. Two derivative stocks have retained their native vigor: the Creole and the Cajun.

Once the word "creole" specified the descendants of European Spanish and French colonists from the West Indies. Today in Louisiana, lower Missouri, and in Mississippi the term means a white, French-speaking heir of colonial-French settlers and not, as popularly supposed, a person of mixed white and Negro blood. Likewise, the French patois spoken on the Gulf is called Creole or Gombo.

The French strain is responsible for a colorful street pageant given annually. Exactly when Creole entertainment turned to dramatic expression is not known. Over a century ago young Creoles who studied in Paris, and then returned to live in *La Nouvelle Orléans,* observed the carnival season of Mardi Gras. For those who do not know, it may be well to review this revival of an ancient ceremony as drama. The fun begins with a street parade on the Wednesday before Lent and culminates in a succession of parades, dances, and merrymaking on Shrove Tuesday. Conspicuous is the medieval figure of Rex, the Lord of Misrule, riding high with his retinue. The final parade of brilliantly colored floats illuminated by oil flares carried by hundreds of Negroes belongs to Comus, god of revelry. On the midnight just before Lent the procession ends. Other carnivals are held on All Saints' Day and on other church holidays in southern Louisiana where one-half of the population is Catholic.

Events from the past, no less spectacular, have furnished material for plays. One historic playlet deals with a favorite local hero: that dashing, colorful figure now become legendary, the pirate Jean Lafitte who, with his band, operated off the Baratarian Coast south of New Orleans. It is a historic fact that after Congress passed an act prohibiting the importation of slaves into the United States subsequent to January 1, 1808, Lafitte did engage in smuggling "black ivory" along this stretch of the Gulf coast. It is also a fact that, in 1814, the pirate refused an offer to aid the British in their siege against New Orleans. In *Patriots and Pirates,* by Kathleen R. Coontz, Lafitte swaggers boldly. There has been talk about "pirate folks nosin' up'n de ribber peddlin' black folks and stealin'." The first American governor and his followers discuss the capture of this hunted fellow. Just then the proud Jean enters. He declares his refusal to throw his weight on the side of the British and, instead, he will fight to save the city. They dare not arrest him and thus his offer is gladly accepted. In the old style of romantic bravado and polished speech the pirate is projected ere he makes his grand exit.

Along the parishes of the delta French nobility once held proud sway. Their devotion to things and ways Parisian was deep, and their admiration of French

royalty, intense. Conceivably in such a society claims
to royalty might easily be exploited. *Queens of France*
(1931), by Thornton Wilder, a charming, slight
sketch, holds up to gentle ridicule the victims of a
suave imposter who extracts money from aged do-
wagers by claiming for them high lineage. In and out
of this lawyer's office pass the deluded "queens," all
heirs to the throne of France, deceived and yet ecstati-
cally hopeful.

Tied up with royalty is the spirit of conservatism
which fears any change in the preordained state of
things. Ordinarily a wedding between a middle-aged
Creole of *la haute noblesse* and a youthful consul from
Paris would occasion mild surprise. But when a mob
led by a masked stranger descends upon the royal
mansion, delivers a mock serenade, and then demands
a ransom of three thousand dollars, trouble enters
paradise. In the best French tradition the masked
leader flings jibes at the lady for insisting on a money
marriage for her young daughter. Forced to agree to
conditions laid down by the rabble, the lady and her
groom quarrel. At this point he grows disillusioned
about love and happiness.[1]

The romantic Creoles of New Orleans, as pictured
by George W. Cable in his novels of the eighties,
flickered into life once or twice in our own century.
The stock types, the sudden gusts of passion, the amorous encounters, and the quick defense of honor are
again visible on our stage in one or two plays. Feuds
between highborn Creole gentlemen and visiting Ken-
tuckians over a quadroon, one of the alluring *sirènes*
of the New Orleans of 1835, form the subject matter
of a native opera, *Deep River,* by Laurence Stallings.
Four violent deaths at the end, committed to fine

choral singing, close this piece of prurient theatricalism.

In our own time romance assumes a homelier guise.
Love along the levees can turn bitter as wormwood.
So a few play scribes have discovered. The amorous
flutterings of Creole wenches may not be easily con-
cealed. When occasion warrants they too know how
to dissemble, however. In a deftly handled plot the
wife of a crude owner of a shrimp-canning factory and
of a number of ships near New Orleans awaits her ex-
lover after sixteen years of absence. At length he
enters, now blind and deaf and led by a dog. The two
exchange sweet memories but are chilled by the
presence of the wealthy husband. The Creole wife
finds it hard to recover the old rapture. Soon all is
over. Ironically, the blind man cannot see all the
vulgar splendor designed to impress him. Instead,
he can sniff only the odors from the fertilizer factory.[2]

Equally bitter is the lot of the Creole wife married
to a Yankee but loved by a Creole. Though her un-
demonstrative spouse treats her kindly, she yields
momentarily to a desire to run off with her lover to
New Orleans. Just then her husband, wounded by a
shot, stumbles into the cabin. Her loyalty is instantly
aroused and she refuses to heed the call of her lover.
Soon after, nature rings down the curtain to the noise
of flood waters rushing toward the cabin.[3]

She is typical of the class of "river rats" who squat
in hovels along the levees and bayous on the Gulf
coast as far eastward as the sandy wastelands of northern
Florida. In a group of river plays the monotonous,
ugly, and grim side of their existence is ruefully
exposed. The brunt of misery falls upon the tired
wives, the stoic women with weary eyes and faraway
gaze. They are generally articulate. One of these is

"sick of fish, fish, fish" and yearns for a home on land,[4] while another dreams of raising chickens, pigs, and cows. Throughout her trials her love of finery remains misunderstood and mocked.[5] Calmly and frankly another river wife, a common-law mate, tells her man, "You ain't never meant nothin' to me," and decides to run off with another river rat.[6] The dread of drifting for days on end in shanty boats increases her misery. One disgruntled wife is "tired o' driftin', driftin', driftin' down the river all the time like a piece o' wrecked boat."[7] Usually the hope of relief or escape is blocked by some human or natural agency. It may be the murder of a rival or the elopement of a daughter with the mother's lover. Luckily the girl may escape the drudgery which plagues the mother. Though the river wife will place the blame for her troubles on a dull and brutish husband and remain dejected, in the end she must resume her hateful existence and submit. What makes these plays dramatic is the violent theme: insanity,[8] murder,[9] and despair matched by the mood of the river under the fury of cloudburst and whirlpool, the break of a dam, and the rush of wild waters.

In parishes which make up the plantations and canefields on the delta live the Creole Negroes or colored Creoles. They speak a corrupt French called Gombo, and believe in roots, folk medicine, and conjure. In secret they practice a weird cult of voodooism imported from the island of Haiti. At one time the greatest hoodoo queen, said to have exercised remarkable spells and even to have possessed the power of reviving the dead, the third Marie Laveau, held court in New Orleans. She was attended by a huge rattlesnake as she swayed to the snakelike rhythm of the conjure chant. Her disciples often used their power for such ignoble purposes as revenge in love.

In one playlet the professional snake charmer, a quadroon, rejects her black lover because she loves the
haughty Creole gentleman. But he spurns her. In
retaliation she puts the spell on him and he is brought
in dead.[10]

Equally ceremonial but less weird is the group
picture of the slaves of old New Orleans who used to
gather on Sundays in Congo Square for amusement.
To the music of the *bamboula* ("drum") and the
banza ("bass fiddle"), accompanied by the clapping
of hands and the stomping of feet, men and women
danced with abandon. Their favorite dance was the
calinda. In pantomime with folk music supposedly
enacted during Mardi Gras early in the nineteenth
century, crowds, booth venders, merrymakers, a Negro
couple, a wild dance, a flight, and a murder flash by
in quick succession.[11]

Effective as pageantry, the purely pictorial slowly
fades before the dramatized problems of the colored
folks in a hostile society. The thesis play of mixed
marriage between octoroon and white was fore-
shadowed in 1859 by an old plantation melodrama
which held the stage for years: *The Octoroon; or Life
in Louisiana* by Dion Boucicault, the Irish maker of
plays who dominated the American stage at the time.
It is the story of Zoe, the natural daughter of a planter
who is beloved by her father's nephew, a gentleman
from the North and heir to the plantation. She gently
rebuffs his proposal of marriage. The law forbids it.
In her grief she cries out, "There is a gulf between
us, as wide as your love, as deep as my despair. . . .
That is the ineffaceable curse of Cain. Of the blood
that feeds my heart, one drop in eight is black—bright
red as the rest may be, that one drop poisons all the
flood . . . but the one black drop gives me despair, for

I'm an unclean thing—forbidden by the laws. I'm an Octoroon!"

In these measured cadences intoning the racist theory spoke the tragic figure which was to be drawn less flamboyantly by later scribes. The heroine of a recent play is far less resigned. That she may legally wed her white lover, a Creole quadroon declares herself white in the courts. But her brother, who is a fanatic believer in race purity, will not permit it. Rather than see her marry in violation of his creed he stabs her. Operatically she sings a Creole song as she dies.[12]

Whereas the white Creole is a city aristocrat, the Cajun is a low-class illiterate, a poor white, "the jest of the proud Creole," as George W. Cable described him. The 'Cadian is a descendant of those French Acadians from Nova Scotia who, after being driven out by the British in 1755, found a welcome in Louisiana. The present habitant, who numbers half a million, is a blend of French, Negro, and (as claimed) Indian blood. In damp, lowland marshes along the curving and twisting bayous of Grosse Têche, Lafourche, and Vermilion west of New Orleans, the friendly, easy-going Cajun follows his priests and his impulses, inter marries, farms, fishes, and, on Saturday nights, takes part in all-night country-dances or *fais-dodos* (literally, "go to sleep").[13] Socially he considers himself above the Negro, while he in turn is looked down upon by his white neighbors. He speaks an archaic French patois with borrowings from foreign sources.

Aside from the tent shows which used to operate along the bayous, the drama has been slow to discover these people. A thesis play handles the problem of inbreeding which made mandatory the first-cousin law.

The passage of such a law blasts the hope of marriage between two lovesick cousins. The high-strung lovers wail, the girl cries out in anguish amid much patter of *mon enfant, voilà, hein,* and "No eat, no sleep, no pray for love." To make matters worse, the girl is pregnant. Her only consolation is the church.[14]

Along a bayou in southern Alabama the faint, wailing sound heard from the water has suggested an eerie play. Legendry has it that long ago the resident Indians, driven from the land by the whites, clasped hands and, chanting their tribal songs, walked into the water. Ever since, the spirits of the dead come back to plague certain whites. In this instance a nervous old woman who smokes a clay pipe imagines she hears "sperrits." She swoons when her son enters carrying a dead sea gull—a portent of death—which had beat itself against the door. After Maw is revived, she shrieks and calls out, "Paw." Then she confesses she had pushed her ex-husband into the bayou because he had killed her baby. A moment later, she falls dead.[15]

The tropical passion and sensuousness which invest these few plays from the bayous and backwaters of the Gulf States flow outward to the pictorial and inward to the psychologic. The pageantry with which a George W. Cable once draped the humble habitants of the parishes has been stripped by a generation of skeptics. The former violence of melodrama has been diverted to plausible everyday revenge and murder done to the orchestrated fury of flood and disaster.

Be the actor Creole or quadroon, Cajun or river rat, he is the protagonist expressing himself vehemently and reacting tensely. He or she is but a parcel of explosives smashing against a fixed and irresistible outer wall.

These plays from the Gulf region may measure small in the theater. But in essence they bear the prime quality of the regional play: a dramatic tieup between man and place. In bulk they nurse the seed which awaits only the touch of the master playwright.

1. *Charivari*, by Nan Bagby Stephens.
2. *The Strongest Man*, by Elizabeth H. Sullivan.
3. *Madretta, Addio, The Twilight Saint*, by Stark Young.
4. *The Delta Wife*, by Walter McClellan.
5. *Fixin's*, by Marion K. Coley.
6. *The Delta Wife*, by Walter McClellan.
7. *Drifters*, by Virginia Lee Sneed.
8. *The Fourth Generation*, by Peter G. Meek.
9. *Flotsam*, by Thomas W. Duncan.
10. *Zombi*, by Natalie V. Scott.
11. *Danse Calinda*, by Ridgley Torrence.
12. *Ti Yette*, by John F. Matheus.
13. Writers' Program, W.P.A., *Louisiana; a Guide to the State* (New York, 1941) , pp. 93, 95.
14. *The Cajun*, by Ada Jack Carver.
15. *On Bayou La Batre*, by Bessie C. Moore.

IX

The Northern Border

NOWHERE is the imprint of the aboriginal Indian so evident as along the shores of the Great Lakes. Within this vastness the red man, estimated to have lived here from two to four thousand years ago, raised corn, chanted his prayers, and buried his dead under mounds. Centuries later he engaged in the bloody wars of the frontiers. Today his descendants pursue a quiet existence on reservations and on the tribal lands which dot the lake states of the northern border.

Once upon a time every stream and valley, every river and lake, every rock and hill had its local god in the Indian catalogue. Myths relating to water monsters, raccoons, sturgeons, river beds, bears, and mountains (rescued from oblivion by the late Federal Writers' Project) were passed down the years. Only a small portion of them are known to the white man.

In time, as invariably happens, the cultures of the red man and the white man met and overlapped. Within our own day the best contributions of the two races have found theatrical expression in the easy art of pageantry. Of sixty-odd spectacles in local and state history, notable have been the *Pageant of the Old Northwest,* by Thomas Wood Stevens (1911), *Our Wisconsin, Children of Old Wisconsin, The Gifts They Brought,* and, above all, *The Centennial Cavalcade of Wisconsin* by Ethel Theodora Rockwell, which, in 1936, by the aid of 2,500 actors, traced five hundred years of regional events.

Conscious of this double heritage which has been

responsible for the making of a regional drama, the little theater movement came into being at Madison. The story belongs to theatrical history and deserves to be told straight. In December, 1910, Professor Thomas H. Dickinson, then of the University of Wisconsin, organized and directed an amateur group not connected with any institution: The Wisconsin Dramatic Society. This event, by the way, anticipated both the historic visit of the Irish Players from Dublin and the establishment of little theaters in Boston and in Chicago. The goal was a repertory theater and the object "to encourage the translation, composition, and publication of good plays." The accent was on Midwesternism as an expression of regional life. A separate theatrical branch called the Wisconsin Players, under the direction of Miss Laura Sherry, extended activities to the city of Milwaukee. Since 1914 efforts to establish a free, experimental theater have sent currents of healthful energy flowing throughout the state.

Two volumes of plays and eight issues of *The Play Book* defined Midwesternism flexibly and pointed to the Indian and his clashes with the whites as illustrative material. Several plays of distinction show extreme sympathy for the early dweller on his land. First to be staged was a poetic interpretation by the American poet, William Ellery Leonard. His *Glory of the Morning* (1912) was built around the figure of an actual Winnebago chieftess who lived during the French and Indian War. It unfolds a tale with tender passion. Long ago the French came to the northern border to trade and trap with the Indians. For politic reasons they were not averse to intermarrying. Such a situation forms the basis of the play. A white trader visits his wife for the last time. The white chevalier loves his son, Red Wing, and his daughter, Oak Leaf. He wishes to take his children with him, for his king calls from across the Big Sea Water. His son declines to go along, while his daughter clings to him. The parting words are decisive. "I can no longer do my work in your world; you cannot follow me into mine." After he leaves, the Indian mother stoically resumes her labors.

A second offering by the same author, *Red Bird* (1923), recounts another episode from later frontier history and presents heroic figures in the image of Shakespeare. It is the year 1822. Reds and whites have been at odds. Red Bird, a Winnebago chief, after killing a white man, gives himself up to the whites in the belief that a fellow tribesman, Blue Heron, has been killed. In his cell he learns that he had been deceived and that Blue Heron lives. As a result he dies of mortification. There are fine poetic touches descriptive of woodland and bluff, a sprinkling of songs and legends, and a show of anger at the arrogance of the white man. "The white man's law is the law of Wisconsin. . . . The aborigines must go down before the bringers of civilization." In drawing character the poet neither exalts nor vilifies.

Other hands have worked on the Indian theme. Less psychological and more bustling is a play in libretto form: *Wakuwapi* (no date) by Hartley Alexander. This documentary-poetic reading of an actual event opens in the Bad Lands in 1890, at the mouth of a Cyclopean ruin of the desert under a blue sky, and tells the bloody story of the capture and defeat of two hundred Dakotah Indians. The tale closes with the frantic loss of an Indian infant and the tragic death of both parents. The choral chant rises and falls to the strain of

> Hatred unending
> Of the robber race.

From Minnesota, near by, comes an Indian version of the Romeo and Juliet theme, laid on an island in Lake Minnetonka. It is a nature myth translated into human terms in which the daughter of the Moon secretly meets the son of the traditional enemy, the Sun. By so doing she brings shame upon her tribe. The couple suffer the rebuke of their enraged parents, and, in final despair, meet for the last time and walk into the lake as the maiden sings the Indian love call. Overcome with remorse, the male parents clasp hands in brotherhood. The lyrical lines ripple along in conventional grooves.[1]

The second notable playwright from the Great Lakes region is Zona Gale. To her Midwesternism means simple humanity. *The Neighbors* (1914) does not escape the sentimentalities of her Friendship Village. The whole community flutters in expectation at the arrival of an orphan boy. The prattle of humble folk in cottages is faithfully reported. A later creation, *Uncle Jimmy* (1921), is a likable portrait. For years the old fellow has been splitting kindling and drawling his views on life. "Well, of course, living is always some of a chore." He yearns to go where palm trees grow. Next to a much-traveled aunt he is nothing but a provincial. One day a chance to travel is offered him. He actually sets off, then slinks back to his chopping block in his back yard. After seventy years, habit has chained him. He is human, all too human.

The theater has extended itself throughout the state. Since 1926 when the Wisconsin Dramatic Guild, a state-wide organization, was formed, original play-writing contests and county tournaments of folk dancing, music, and art have promoted rural entertainment. Organized in 1928, the Extension Division of the College of Agriculture, under the supervision of

Ethel Theodora Rockwell, has furthered an interest in community recreation. Thereafter the Bureau of Dramatic Activities carried the message of rural Wisconsin to the folk through hundreds of little theaters. Today, in nearly every one of the seventy-one counties of the state, original plays are produced regularly. A typical example of "a rural pastorale," *Of Folks and Fields,* written jointly by leaders from five counties, presents in song and dance and dialogue the career of the Chester family through four generations. The three acts move from home life to community life, and on to youth facing the future. The scenes are homely and inspiring.

Other local playsmiths have hammered out specific pleas for this and that, for adequate recreation for farm children, for joining farm and 4-H clubs. By strict standards such plays must hold a low place in the scale of drama. Nevertheless, it can be said that the quality of writing is often competent if literal. Plots are simple, the talk is of everyday matters, and the point is driven home straight as a nail. Best of the lot is the sketch which focuses light upon the problem of the lonesome youth who is locked within himself and craves companionship. The proposed remedy is adequate recreation.[2]

The life of the immigrant has suggested themes to a few local play scribes. After 1840, the European tide poured a polyglot stream of German, Norwegian, Swedish, Bohemian, and Polish settlers into Wisconsin. It has been estimated that half of the population was born either in foreign countries or of foreign and mixed parentage in this country. The Germans brought with them a love of the classics. In fact, for eighty-five years, until 1935, they put on old and new plays in German at the Stadt Theatre in Milwaukee.[3]

"Of Folks and Fields," University of Wisconsin

In this way they prepared an audience to receive plays which were to deal with their personal lives on a new soil.

The most obvious theme for the theater would naturally be the clash between foreigner and American. A half dozen such pieces play up the personal problems of Bohemian, German, Swiss, Hungarian, and Norwegian. Memories of the old country stored in heirlooms, in precious shawls,[4] in an old chest,[5] in skill at lacemaking[6] and in Russian cooking[7] lay the basis for plots. Endings generally favor the unhappy wife, the distressed suitor, and the bullied daughter. Sometimes the foreigner has to be chastised and brought to realize that this is America. Sometimes wavering loyalties to the land of birth as against the land of adoption are resolved in favor of this country only after the residents realize that they have at last been transplanted.[8] The jargon is literal transcript while the plots are not complicated. The play that stems from these communities of mixed origins belongs to the folk-nationality class.

As the second generation grows used to American ways, problems of adaptation as thematic material grow less pertinent. Pleas for Americanization give way to broader, dispassionate studies in human relations. A number of playlets accent character in revolt. These conflicts are presented objectively in selective dialogue. The plots are mixed. To illustrate: the overworked farm wife is stirred into self-realization by the arrival of a relative dressed in finery. She disappears for a time and returns from town sporting a new gown bought from her own savings. Still unsatisfied, she expresses a wish to run off with her husband for a vacation.[9] Inner yearnings pass over

into action. Another tired wife, plagued by a drove
of uninvited guests, is driven to extremes. She feigns
a nervous breakdown and insanity. After the relatives
flee, she settles down in peace.[10] Equally desperate is
the newly married wife who craves beauty and music
and sweetness, but is misjudged by her earth-bound
husband and his mother. She is shaken to fury by their
ridicule of her "fine-haired fool ideas." Only when
her mother-in-law leaves the house can the couple sit
down to face their common problems and stay on to
dream together.[11] Finally, two brothers, a college youth
and a farm hand, love the same girl for different
reasons. The first is scorned as a parasite, while the
second is respected as the embodiment of rural virtue.
But the girl will have neither man until she gets some
more schooling.[12] Of such humble stuff is woven the
character plays whose chief value lies in the shrewd
observation and the unaffected mirroring of small-
town manners.

When wit or irony or satire is invoked, the drama
takes wings. That is to say, plays soar beyond the plain
fact of the moment by the power of imagination to
create overtones. It is common to tilt at sanctimonious
funerals in small towns. The theme lends itself to
scourging of hypocrites. In one sketch, while neighbors
and relatives voice their grief in platitudes, the true
friend speaks out against "professional corpse-sniffers."
Under these blasts the respectable mourners wince
but soon fall back upon a defensive sense of duty.[13]

Since 1945 a Wisconsin Idea Theater, under the
direction of Robert E. Gard, has been organized at the
University of Wisconsin and has revived the Wisconsin
idea, as proposed in 1914. The intention is to build a
people's theater.

Mitten-shaped Michigan is planted squarely on all the lakes but one. Three-fourths of her boundary line touches water. This fact accounts for a body of marine lore which lakesmen and schoonermen, who make their homes along the shore, have spread throughout the region. For all that, there are scant traces of water consciousness in the native plays. Thousands of interior lakes likewise have failed to impress the local playsmith. With one exception, the bulk of portraits are those of earth-bound rustics.

The lone play which deals with a lake situation pictures a paralyzed captain compelled to sit and gaze out of a window. Former rough members of his crew invade his privacy and take personal revenge for past cruelties by torturing his beloved grandson. In desperation the captain raises his palsied arm and kills the lakesmen.[14]

Other plays cling to the ground. Such mundane affairs as worrying over one's health until the doctor's verdict tells a farm woman she cannot have a baby,[15] or a mother's anxiety over a tuberculous son because he has been caught selling Bibles to corpses by mail[16] occupy the spotlight of undistinguished plays. Better by far is a study in rural depravity and revenge. Here is an attempt at exploring character. The plot is deftly developed, and the dialogue naturally spoken. Two brothers who have been estranged are united after their father leaves his property to a former wife with whom the old man had not lived for twenty years. Enraged, the two sons vow to burn down the house.[17]

Minnesota, a far northern outpost and fur-trading center, spans the center of the continent. This land of sky-blue waters, rich in resources mineral, animal, and vegetable, shelters numerous nationalities, mainly

Scandinavian, with an infusion of Germans, Finns,
and Poles. Years ago these people cleared the forest,
laid its railroads, built up farming and dairy industries,
organized co-operatives, and in general contributed to
the cultural life of the state. Nor did they forget to
dance the old dances and sing the old songs.

While foreign folk festivals have survived in isolated
areas, these have taken color from their backgrounds.
They could hardly be unaffected by the floating hero
myths and tall tales which circulate along the length of
the northern border. Chief among these is the cycle
of stories relating to the logger, Paul Bunyan. By the
fires of bunkhouses, in logging camps from Maine to
Oregon, the pioneer axman, backwoods giant, and
master logger is a living presence. Who was Paul?
According to legend Bunyan (*Bon Jean* in the French)
is said to have been born of French parents on Prince
Edward Island. He roamed to the border where he
became the boss of a logging camp. Ol' Paul logged in
Wisconsin, Michigan, Minnesota, the Dakotas, and in
the Pacific Northwest, and especially on the Big Onion
River during the winter of the Blue Snow. He rafted
his logs down the lakes. Fantastic stories are told of
Babe the Blue Ox. High and low water levels were
caused whenever he drank. His exact size is not known.
According to one report he stood ninety-three hands
high. According to another, he is supposed to have
measured forty-two ax handles and a plug of tobacco
between the horns.[18]

Since Minnesota is an active logging center, it has
adopted Paul Bunyan as a native son. In proof Brain-
erd, the "capital of the Paul Bunyan playground," has
attracted thousands to the annual Paul Bunyan
Carnivals since 1935, one in summer (fourth week in
June) and one in winter (February). In fact, a statue

of Paul Bunyan eighteen feet high and built of steel and concrete looks down from the shore of Lake Bemidji.[19]

It is interesting to note how each region adds its own touches of coloring to the Bunyan myth. For instance, in Minnesota before 1900, Swedes outnumbered other immigrants in big timber operations and were considered the best loggers. Therefore Bunyan's foremen were of Swedish origin. Other localisms appear in two plays. The first is definitely Scandinavian in tone with fantastic overtones. An old Norwegian lumberjack who ardently believes in his hero incessantly talks about Paul and his exploits, of Babe the Blue Ox, and of the time when Paul cut down trees with one blow. Enter Paul who has returned to earth in human size because he is too big for heaven or hell. He has come "to get good loggers for Sky River Drive" (heaven). Then, together, the two go off. Soon after, blue snow is discovered outside the house, and the swift strokes of an ax are heard. Grandpa is no more.[20]

In the second play, a rambling morality pageant, two folk figures meet: Johnny Appleseed who plants trees, and Paul Bunyan who cuts them down—a happy antithesis. Incongruously the unkempt Johnny is in love with "a dryad in diaphanous green."[21] At once the discord is evident. Robust folk figures and ethereal fairies hardly belong in the same setting. Happily, better plays about the fabulous logger come from regions farther west. These will be considered in their place.

A simple account of ordinary loggers, without Paul, sets the action in a mining camp in the North Woods. The story runs true to expectations. The men are awaiting a woman cook and her daughter. Broadly drawn with a touch of spite are the minor characters of the effeminate minister and the amorous bookkeeper.[22]

Still closer to the soil are three studies of the farmer, son, and wife set within a farming community. Crabbed, twisted lives, bred by misfortunes or warped by old-fashioned notions, fret and stew for different reasons. In one instance a grumbling grain farmer whose foot has been caught in the belt of a thresher nurses his ill will by scoffing at "weather breeders." He enjoys his own perversity and change of heart as a cloudburst passes and sunshine follows.[23] In another play, a father's inherited prejudices against modern scientific agriculture suffer shock when the college-bred youth proves that dry farming can succeed. In the course of the action collateral ideas on the drudgery of farm work and the place of the university in weaning the young away from the one-crop idea sustain the thesis. Scandinavian phrases lend color to the action.[24]

On another farm a self-willed trio chase one another painfully in circles: the pious, bull-headed husband who talks of *my* farm, *my* woman, *my* roof, and *my* food; the worn-out wife in love with the hired man; and the willful daughter expecting a baby. Though the situation is familiar, the handling of emotion is sincere and the action moves rapidly. At one time the farmer pleads, "We're rooted here so deep, it's like we was part of the soil. You can't uproot us without you destroy us."[25]

Despite the hope nursed by the regional colleges that native plays could be artificially created and despite the touring of the Montana Masquers from the Montana State University throughout the mining towns of the North, the drama remains a mud bottom hemmed in by a straggling snake fence.

South of Minnesota and somewhat removed from Lake Michigan lies the Corn Belt. The terrain resembles Minnesota. Here some foreign groups have assimilated, while others, like the Germans, have adhered to Old World ways. Nevertheless, nationalities meet on the common ground of amusement. Pageants like *The Festival of the Corn* have proved popular. Under the joint leadership of the Iowa Farm Bureau Federation and the Agricultural Extension Service at Ames, festivals, operas, and such food skits as *Beans and Bottles* and the *Romance of Bread* have met the simple needs of fun and frolic. In addition hundreds of local unpublished plays have been staged at fairs and cattle congresses, in barns and in neighborhood theaters. Agriculture and culture have tried to meet.[26]

The few printed plays reveal one tendency: bitterness tempered by wry humor. First, the dilatory husband, unmoved by his wife's plea to repair the entrance door, is induced to finish the task only after his wife's death. The neighbors calmly remark that her last wish was to be carried out by the front door.[27] Gently satiric is the intent of the sketch which pictures respectable church-minded folk who expect pious sentiments from the husband who has just been relieved by death of a nagging wife. Instead they hear him say that he is free at last to buy the bicycle he long has craved.[28]

Broadly drawn is the family of German farmers who, having struck oil, align themselves with the oil aristocracy. "We ain't farmers no more," they boast. Only an honorable genealogy will satisfy them now. After the family tree is traced, they learn to their shame that they sprang from low and vulgar forebears. Cabbages, it seems, cannot be changed to roses.[29]

Certain victimized women of this section are drawn

askew in the manner of Benton etchings. Set in the imaginary town of Red Bud, six studies in womanhood by Mark O'Dea touch the extremes of pathos and drollery. First of *Red Bud Women* is the weary, Bible-reading wife neglected by an oaf of a husband who has grown rich. He gives money to the church, talks of buying a tractor, but stubbornly refuses to spend a penny on the kitchen or on house improvements. In vain his wife protests that "the house is always the last thing with men." Before lapsing into insanity she remarks significantly, "shrouds ain't got no pockets." The behavior of the other women borders on the absurd. The portrait of the bride on her wedding night is the one-time feminist's wild dream of the coming woman. The "shivaree" is over and the guests have gone. Alone with her man, the virago thunders against the brute male. She refuses to be a canary, a prize breeder, or an underling. The abashed groom can do nothing but plead dumbly as she rushes out with her bird cage. A sister type is the man-hater. She has rejected the final plea of a former lover who threatens to foreclose. Then she learns that her younger sister wishes to marry the man; in fact, she must have him. Embarrassments on both sides are covered up, and consent is finally wrung. Last are the two village types: the local flirt and the prim school miss. The antics of the flirt compel the wiser woman to counsel the suitor, "Submerge her. Pet her. Stunt her. Dominate her, and she'll love you to her dying day." When the little actress-flirt accepts her man's love as a "lesson" in courtship, the disgusted suitor runs off with the more sensible adviser.

Indiana and Illinois, which press southward, lay claim to our prime historic hero, the young Lincoln. Long a popular epic and folk hero, the Rail Splitter has attracted the attention of writers and artists in every medium. The human face insists on emerging from the cloud of myth. Honest Abe of New Salem, Illinois, about the year 1831, has furnished a core for several plays with varying emphasis on the place and the man.[30] The most earthy play of the set is E. P. Conkle's *Prologue to Glory* (1936), presented in eight scenes. From the lusty wrestling match with the village bully, which Abe enters against his will, to the untimely death of Ann Rutledge, the conflict grows in intensity. The quiet humor, the homely wisdom, the love tempered by reason and melancholy impart nobility to the figure of the future emancipator. Throughout Abe talks a rich, natural speech.

Covering a wider span of years, from 1831 to 1861, is the more popular version based on historical sources, *Abe Lincoln in Illinois* (1940), by Robert E. Sherwood. This skillful chronicle in twelve scenes holds the regional qualities only in the early parts. The twenty-two-year-old drifter into New Salem, a village of fifteen log cabins, takes his place among the great regional characters. In episodes showing the restless spirit, the wildcats of Clary's Grove, "worse'n any old wolves," their remarkable loyalty to Abe, Abe's quiet admiration for Ann Rutledge, his inconsolable grief over her death, his hypochondria and humility, and the beautiful prayer uttered on the prairie for the recovery of the fever-stricken boy—in these respects the playwright has followed the folk pattern of the hero. After Lincoln's departure for Springfield the hero takes on city ways, enters politics, and thus sheds that earthiness which endears him to the folk mind.

Another playlet in miniature presents Abe at the age of eleven. *The Boy Abe* (1941) by Betty Smith, sets him in a country schoolhouse in Buckthorn Valley in

Little Pigeon Creek, southern Indiana. Barefoot and dressed in loose, homespun pants, the boy can answer all questions put to him by his teacher. At this period in his life the motherless lad meets his new mother with her own three children, and shyly acknowledges her tenderness and gifts. The portrait is somewhat idealized as so many historic portraits of the great are likely to be.

A fourth sketch touches on the same event in Lincoln's history when he was twelve. The feud brought on by Abe's love of reading and his father's cussedness is resolved by the arrival of his new mother, Sarah Johnston. When Abe receives some books and a promise of more to come, he is definitely won over. During the marriage ceremony, the father is forced to relent. A pathetic note is struck when the children ask the preacher to preach a funeral sermon for their dead mother. On the whole, the portraits are drawn tenderly though they do not seem too earth-rooted or solidly planted in native ground.[31]

As for the hundreds of minor school plays on Lincoln, worthy as some of them are, the less said the better. The quality that vitiates them is dogmatism.

All in all, these plays from the Great Lakes region find a common denominator in legend, in myth, and in fact colored by the soil. Themes reach back to the historic Indian closely bound in service and in intimacy with the white man. The implicit anger over injustice and the innate pathos voiced in poetic cadences fit mood and theme aptly.

Less classic is the treatment of the master logger whose gigantic tread pounds along the borders of the North. The tone of the local playlets barely suggests the licentious roar, the sly brutishness, and the mountain-shaking laughter of the giant. These come off better in plays set in the Far West.

Far different in key and in temper, the sketches of the darkly brooding Lincoln as a boy come from the pen naturally and emerge under the strokes full length, with a glow on the face.

Finally, in plainer guise and with less artful craftsmanship, trail the dramatic efforts of the obscure recorders whose eye is on the rooted rustic nursing the inner woes peculiar to a hard, physical existence.

1. *Mother Minnetonka,* by Jack Stuart Knapp.
2. *Barred,* by Calista B. Clark.
3. Writers' Program, W.P.A., *Wisconsin; a Guide to the Badger State* (New York, 1941) , pp. 169-70.
4. *The Bohemian Shawl,* by Calista B. Clark.
5. *The Chest,* by Beulah Charmley.
6. *The Maker of Fine Laces,* by Marion M. Grinder.
7. *Russian in Reverse,* by Rose Kapingen.
8. *Transplanted,* by Sari Szekely.
9. *Goose Money,* by Mrs. Carl Felton.
10. *This Way Out,* by Mrs. Carl Felton.
11. *Dreams,* by Calista B. Clark.
12. *Sons of Soil,* by David E. Lindstrom.
13. *No One Can Say,* by Warren Beck.
14. *Mutiny,* by Lee Anderson.
15. *The Provider,* by William A. Compton.
16. *Books for the Dead,* by Hobert Skidmore.
17. *Brothers,* by Lewis Beach.
18. "Paul Bunyan," *Encyclopedia Britannica,* 14th edition, IV, 393.
19. Federal Writers' Project, W.P.A., *Minnesota, a State Guide* (New York, 1938) , p. 361.
20. *Sky River Drive,* by Samuel R. Davenport.
21. *Johnny Appleseed and Paul Bunyan,* by Henry Bailey Stevens.
22. *Lumbering Love,* by Jan Woll.
23. *The Weather Breeder,* by Merrill Denison.
24. *Back to the Farm,* by Merline H. Shumway.
25. *Harvest,* by Oakley Stout.
26. Marjorie Patten, *The Arts Workshop of Rural America; a Study of the Rural Arts Program of the Agricultural Extension Service* (New York, 1937) , Chapter XV.
27. *The Front Door,* by Barbara Busse.
28. *They That Mourn,* by Grant Wood and Jewell B. Tull.
29. *Cabbages,* by Edward Staadt.
30. "Out of the Wilderness: The Salem Years of Abraham Lincoln," a W.P.A. play presented at New Salem State Park, September 26, 27, 28, 1940.
31. *Shirt Tail Boy,* by W. P. Covington, III.

X

Plains and Prairies

FROM THE Great Lakes the transition to mid-America is smooth and gradual. Spaces begin to widen, wheatlands stretch out illimitably, and windswept prairies roll to all horizons. Once claimed by France, ceded to Spain, then given back to France before the United States bought it, this one-time sprawling Louisaina Territory now exhibits traces of multiple culture layers. The population is polyglot and the history as variegated. Group differences express themselves in custom, legend, song, and play. Yet in dramatic expression, unity rules the plains and the prairies.

As among wheat growers in other parts of the world, the primitive instinct of prayer and thanksgiving leads the native to celebrate the seasons. In our day the folk festival has lost its original meaning of fertility and been reduced to one of spectacle mainly. Among the pageants offered in this section of the country may be mentioned *The Dance of the Golden Grain* done in the autumn. After customs and memories tied the settler to the homestead, pride and loyalty flowed over into celebration. Notable among the processionals in the Dakotas, for example, have been *The Pageant of the Dakotaland* at Yankton, South Dakota; the *Covered Wagon Days in the Land of the Dacotahs* at Fargo, North Dakota; and the *Pageant of North Dakota,* also done at Fargo, in which more than "a thousand and more participants, including homesteaders, cowboys, Indians, and persons from city and country,"[1] took part.

Pageantry is merely diffused pictorial drama. Iso-

late a few tableaux and the figures will spring to life in
some playlet. Such a grouping shown over half a
century ago enacted the hard lot of the Easterner eager
to find opportunity for growth in the West. It was a
time of sectionalism when few writers dared tell the
bitter truth about life in shanties on the treeless plains.
Hamlin Garland suffered no illusions about the
romance of farm life in his day. With trenchant
strokes he stripped away the false glamor from the
barren existence in the Boomtown of 1884. *Under the
Wheel* (1890), a play in six scenes, hotly condemned
the tariff, speculation in land by real estate sharpers,
and then made the astounding discovery that in the
eighties there was no such thing as free land! The
message comes by way of a straight plot revolving
about the dashed hopes of a Boston family who go
west. After a succession of miseries including foreclosure, burnt wheat, and crops ruined by storms, the
members of the family are finally squeezed out from
the great free West where men were free to starve!
Warmly the hope is voiced that industrial slavery will
some day be abolished. Again and again blasts against
slums, poverty, rent, wages, the distribution of wealth
and allied problems sustain a central single-tax theory
of society. In this thesis play, probably the first to be
written in this country, the action is loose and episodic
and definitely contrived to prove a set of premises.

For thirty years Fargo has been the dramatic focus
of the Midwest. Outward have traveled the theatrical
currents within the state and beyond. These facts
should be better known. For here on February 10,
1914, at the North Dakota Agricultural College, Alfred
G. Arvold founded the Little Country Theater, a
rural town hall with the best-equipped country-life
laboratory in the nation. Since that time, the drama,

to Arvold, has been "a sociological force in getting people together and acquainted with each other in order that they may find out the hidden life forces in nature itself." As stated by the founder, the purpose of the playhouse was to reveal "the inner life of the country community in all its color and romance" and "to make happy neighbors and contented communities."² Entertainment has included outdoor spectacle, festivals with an agricultural slant, and the acting of such classics as *As You Like It, Faust,* and *Peer Gynt.*

As the benefits of the playhouse have been carried to lonely lives on the prairies, local playsmiths have been tempted to write sketches on the near and the familiar. These have not been too successful by any strict standard of judgment. They try to prove a proposition. They deal with the little red mare, the lazy country boy, the farmer striving to exist, immigrants in a new world, and rural conditions in general. One typical skit reveals farmer folk who have moved to the city. All feel unhappy and out of place, like a bee in a drone's hive. For a time they endure the new life. Only after they are forced to return to the soil does everybody feel happy again. The conflict in *A Bee in a Drone's Hive* (1921) by Cecil Baker, is vague, the talk dull, tone drab, and the point obvious.

While Arvold has done much for the farmer and the neighbors, it remained for a professor to set in motion a movement which was later to bear fruit in another region. In 1905 came Frederick H. Koch to the University of North Dakota at Grand Forks. Five years later he induced his students to organize the Sock and Buskin Society to stage communal projects. Co-operatively they wrote the scenario, words, music, and staged a number of spectacles on a grand scale in open-air theaters. *A Pageant of the North-West,* written in

1914 by eighteen undergraduates, required one thousand homesteaders, cowboys, and Indians to tell the story of the opening of the great Western empire and of the achievements of three heroic Frenchmen: Radisson, La Salle, and La Vérendrye, who had set out to win for France "all the wide wilderness of this unknown region." Scenes of the Lewis and Clark expedition featured a folk figure, the famous Indian, Sacajawea (Bird Woman), who guided the explorers over the dangerous passes of the Rockies. Four other pageant-dramas, based on local history, followed.

After these experiments in the historic pageant-play, the professor concluded that his students were ready to concoct "native prairie plays." They had but to look for their themes on the ranch, the farm, the cowboy trail, and the frontier. In 1917 the Sock and Buskin Society, renamed the Dakota Playmakers, staged series after series of original plays. It was only with the sixth and seventh trial that a handful of embryonic plays began to grasp native themes with surety and to mature out of actual experiences "near to the good, strong, windswept soil." *Barley Beards* (1918) pictured a labor riot in a North Dakota threshing crew. *Me and Bill* (1918) enacted the tragedy of the sad, loony sheepherder pining with grief over his past life and suffering loneliness through the long winter nights in a little sod shanty. *Dakota Dick* presented a comedy of the Bad Lands in frontier days. These early efforts may be considered so many candid-camera shots with dialogue.

From this background of mixed population have sprung a few solid themes handled by university wits. The outline of personalities is sharp and sensitive. The first sketch, in dialect, deals with two generations: a Russian father and an Americanized daughter. The father would marry her off to a stranger. But she refuses. "You have signed me away," she protests. "This is America." Besides, she loves another from the state of Iowa. To her surprise, the suitor turns out to be the very man she loves.[3]

The second, a poignant story by a Carolina Playmaker and by far the most finished product, hinges on the lonely Norwegian farm wife of 1885 from the Red River Valley of the Dakotas. In her isolation, both physical and mental, she has gone insane. Only an interest in flowers and ancestral mementos fills her hours. She fears and suspects strangers and is ever on the defensive. Failure to adapt herself to American ways has turned her inward to daydreaming. When a visitor enters the house, she hides a knife in the folds of her skirt. After an interval she warms into friendliness, chats of her beloved flowers and embroidery, and unrestrainedly showers gifts upon her newly made friend.[4]

A similar housewife who came from the hills suffers homesickness. In fact, she is tortured by memories of hills and flowers. Though she demands a window looking to the south, nobody heeds her wishes. After her mind cracks, hallucinations make real her wish.[5]

Downward from the high plains and buttes of the Bad Lands, across grassy sand hills, Nebraska spreads fanwise toward fertile farm lands on the Missouri River. Here, too, live foreign groups, mainly German, Swedish, Danish, and Czech. The mingling of foreign with native stocks has generated an agglomeration of folk tales, cowboy yarns, and whoppers built around a legendary plainsman, a fabulous Swedish uncle, Febold Feboldson, he who crossed eagles with bees until he had bees as big as eagles.

Nonetheless, such fantastic legends do not go into

Home of The Little Country Theatre at Fargo, North Dakota

the making of plays. Rather do plays prefer to trace the tormented spirits of restless plainsmen past and present. A backward look at the frontier fixes upon unheroic settlers trying to find peace. Back in 1867, the son of a pioneer who felt sick of his barren life on the prairie cried out, "Nothing to look at but grass and snow and a couple of spindling cottonwood trees." As his mother had died of overwork, he declined to follow her example. He would build bridges. But after his father beat him and confessed that he was a builder of fences, the son realized that one could stay at home to build.[6]

On the prairies life runs on unchanged. Tormented spirits may go berserk trying vainly to escape from deadly tedium into brutality or secret joy. Take the case of the selfish farmer who badgers and bullies his help, or the crazed old fellow who beats the drum at picnics. Place into this setting a little orphan cook and a runaway boy drawn together by common suffering and you set the stage for tragedy. When the two youngsters finally decide to run away, the plot takes a violent turn. Caught and brought back to the farm, the boy is beaten to death, and the girl throws herself into the well. Maudlin as the story sounds in the telling, a feeling of inevitability stalks these wild birds. Poetic passages and a tender quality in the writing lift *Wild Birds* (1925), by Dan Totheroh, above much of so-called Western drama.

From the Nebraska sod stem two prominent regional playwrights. The first, Virgil Geddes, has achieved a place in our drama by means at variance with those practiced by most regional scribes. Without benefit of colored lingo or folksy dialect, without cowboy spurs or gaudy costumes, he manages to convey strong regional accents and terse power by a clipped, generalized speech. By the simplest of strokes he paints the melancholy grayness of prairie lives and invests suffering with dignity. Incest without violence, with sex attraction reduced to polar magnetism, is his major theme. In *The Earth Between* (1928) the father, a widower, jealously guards his daughter's virtue. Her will in his hands is as water. By cruel treatment he destroys the hired man who desires the maid. In a burst of suppressed agony the father passionately declares his feelings for his daughter. "You're a woman now. You can take her place." It is then that the daughter senses something between them "like it was the earth itself."

Similar self-torment is expressed in a kind of verbal atonality in the trilogy *Native Ground* (1931). Here the situation is reversed. Now the daughter feels drawn to the farm hand who happens to be her father, though she does not know him as such. They run off and live together without carnal relations. Presently she becomes pregnant by a farm hand and again runs off with her man.

Bit by bit these neurotic women and tight-lipped men unfold in accordance with inner necessity. Either they fly in the face of the law or they bow in submission. They are stripped bare as X-ray plates. Though the plots may sound sordid in the telling, a sense of brooding characterization redeems the drab tones and the sterile hopes.

If Virgil Geddes dips his folks in gray wash, Ellsworth Prouty Conkle soaks his negatives in strong acid. Wherever his eye roves over the Nebraska sand hills, there it lights on rustics, catches their quirks, crotchets, ruling passions, and even traces their very wrinkles. Under his gaze his motley subjects stand naked and a bit helpless, yet they are firmly rooted in the fertile

soil of the region. The village of Peru, in particular,
at different periods from 1849 to 1925 and later,
grounds these provincials.

His period piece, *In The Shadow of a Rock* (1936),
set within the Nebraska Territory of 1849, centers in
the sleepy village of Peru, a slave station on the road to
Canada. But clashes between slave hunters and slave
runners over the issue of slavery brought sharp differences of opinion and action. Through the aid of a
staunch storekeeper, a symbol of hardy womanhood,
two Negro babies delivered by John Brown succeed
in escaping detection. She weathers every crisis, including the death of an absent husband. "Coming to
her is like coming unto the shadow of a rock in a
weary land." Her quiet strength was bound to win for
her eyes were on the future.

Conkle's miniature sketches, published in 1928
under the title of *Crick Bottom Plays,* show up sharply
individualized traits. The lines are fresh and quizzical;
the contrasts human and plausible; the overtones sad
and even sinister. The domineering grandma, sly as
a fox and sharp as a whip, is pitted against the dull farm
hand who comes a-courtin' and unknowingly spits
into a closet which holds her white dress.[7] In another
quarter sit five illiterates talking reverently of the dead
woman lying in the next room. By their own words
they reveal their brutish selves and expose the dead
woman's finer sensibilities. The clod of a husband
coolly announces that the organ she loved will be split
into firewood.[8] In a country churchyard sit two codgers
discoursing on life and death as one of them, the grave-
digger, unwittingly digs his own grave. Their observations suggest the pithy pathos of Gray's *Elegy in a
Country Churchyard* transposed into Nebraska dialect.
"In the eyes a-th' Lord, we is perty small punkin's . . .

The young ones is just out a-pickin' posies, while the
old ones is undoin' their shoe-laces fer th' grave."[9]

Some years later the simple lines of character broke
up into jagged planes. The normal consciousness dis-
integrated into abnormal fragments. As drawn, the
line between the normal and the abnormal is slender.
Twisted selves, dead selves, hard selves, strange selves
stir and droop in *Loolie and Other Short Plays* (1935).
These begin with the erratic pool player whose mind
snaps back to his hen every time his friend asks him
for news,[10] and end with the sketch of the dying grandmother whose simple idea of heaven is a replica of
Peru, Nebraska.[11]

Subsequent characters in the longer pieces go on the
loose. They get tangled up in mischief and must be
untangled by some untoward power. These rustics
from the Nebraska of 1905 do the queerest things for
the queerest reasons. Sometimes a notion sets them
off into wild acts until an accident restores them to
sanity. The total effect is quixotic. *Oxygenerator*
(no date) traces the career of an elderly fellow "allus
settin' a-brewin' somethin'." For two dollars he has
bought a contraption which will cure every ailment.
He decides to sell it. Comical is the scene in which he
stands trial for making improper advances to a neighbor's wife. After his fine is remitted, his salesmanship
reaches a peak. At the schoolhouse he goes so far as to
stage *William Tell* to demonstrate how a boy can be
brought back to life by his cure-all device. But his
exuberance is checked when a little girl discovers that
the machine he is selling holds nothing but sawdust.
Here the pitchman whooping it up, the "brain-worker"
confounding the Philistines ere he himself is con-
founded, is projected with rollicking good humor
couched in fine Biblical image and phrase.

Most grotesque of extravaganzas is *Forty-nine Dogs in a Meat House* (no date). A sex war is on. In self-defense male Nebraskans of 1905 have organized themselves into a society called "The Forty-nine Dogs" because the church women of the town have been conducting a cleanup campaign. Various humorous episodes follow. In this community sex repression in men expresses itself in open ribaldry; in women, in hypocritical crusading. Seriously viewed, the play lightly satirizes the female vice crusader of another day who did not hesitate to pull down the house about her ears.

In an earlier playlet, *Th' Feller from Omaha* (1934), enraged townsmen band together to hound a culprit who has murdered his wife. Wrath mounts to frenzy. One doubting fellow is terrified and hesitates to join the mob of avengers. Personal experience has taught him that the woman may have deserved her death. But the nagging chorus of old hags, hideous and shrill, succeeds in allaying his doubts.

Above all, from the mouths of these grotesques flows a speech at once pungent and characteristic. To an Easterner, the Biblical rhythms may sound over-rich. That is the usual Philistine's charge against poetic rendition of plain speech. It cannot be denied that Conkle re-creates the regional inflection, the tone, and the flavor without loss of earthiness. Like Synge he has put wings on the word.

Squarely across the Midwest stretches Kansas, land of tall cornstalks, of grasshoppers big as mules, of cowboy gallantry, and pungent lingo. The gently rolling plain was once the scene of bloody fighting and border wars. The memory of bleeding Kansas before the Civil War, when Yankee abolitionists and slavers fought to save the state from the curse of slavery, relives in one sketch. John Brown is pictured as a bloodthirsty maniac, a religious fanatic. He kills without hesitation to further the cause of freeing the slaves. Historically this portrait of God's angry man is a vile distortion.[12]

The economic misery suffered by Kansans during the late depression called for theatrical confirmation. Sketches overweighted on the side of fact justifiably plead for the common man in topical and documentary plays. Without doubt the struggle to survive reduces us all to cells and nerves. When frost and heat kill the crops, the old battle of man against the elements breaks forth anew. Besides, an irrational economic system which neglects the tiller of the soil must drive him and his kin to revolt. During and after the depression of the early thirties the plight of a million farm families was desperate. Foreclosure of mortgages by insurance companies, by federal and state credit agencies, and by commercial banks became so common as to be taken for granted. In self-defense farmers united to protect one another by "penny sales." Bids usually ranged from one to four cents. Then the property reverted to the family in want. "Our homes are the only things we have left and we won't consent to have them taken away from us," they insisted.[13]

Especially the farm woman resisted confiscation of property. One wife of a homesteader refused to give up the family organ. A neighbor, against the objections of his selfish wife, offered a bid of five dollars and returned the instrument to the owner. Dazed, she continued to stare blankly before her.[14] On another occasion the united opposition of defiant women halted the sale of a widow's truck farm while the husbands were on the march to Washington. "We the people . . . made the law," they shouted. Armed with pots and pans they bid three cents for a Ford car and equal sums

for farm property until the farm was reclaimed. Tri-
umphantly they shouted, "We did it, together."[15]

When the stomach is full, deeper desires begin to
stir. Music may be more than bread. A mother has
met her daily expenses and managed to save enough
to buy a piano. But her son has stolen the savings. In
spite of what happened, the craving for music continues as strong as before.[16]

A few playlets treat of miscellaneous problems and
situations arising from the life of the farmer. The embittered prairie dweller, despite the terror of dust and
death, clings grimly to his land and habits. Meanwhile, his attitudes are shaped by his occupation. One
such preoccupied owner, while battling to save his
farm from the city sharks, refuses to understand the
longings of his wife or to see the need for beauty.
Only after it is too late does he yield and bring his wife
a red flower in a pot.[17] As for farmers' wives, some
must hide their talents and make sacrifices for the
privilege of rearing a family. An accident may help
them to remain contented to stay on the farm.[18] In
outlying areas parental habits of penny-squeezing may
last longer than needed, even into a time of prosperity.
Children properly resent such habits and demand
certain comforts. By means of three memory pictures
in flash back, the parents see their past unroll from
dust storms and poverty to comparative security. And
they give in.[19]

Something must be said about the plays which deal
with the "river rats" who abide in shacks on river flats
along the Missouri River. Three such playlets aim
to express the bitterness, the drabness, the sodden existence of these degraded whites. The portraits of the
lazy and shiftless men seem to be done with a touch
of caricature. One of these will not abandon his little

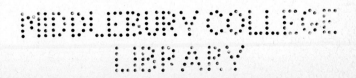

farm though it yields nothing. When he has to choose between the river and his wife, he chooses the river. For consolation he looks forward to some magic island of the future.[20] The other pieces are set in Nebraska and are equally drab. The men are given to thoughtless self-indulgence, while the women show a sturdier sense of duty. They bewail their troubles: a mother over her sick child;[21] a foster-mother over a daughter "always wantin' things." But quickly they relapse into resignation. The external regional details of shack and bare furnishings and little food, as seen by the play reporter, are honestly given. But uncertainties of plot and psychology impair the validity of the portraits. The lazy husband who plans to hold a week-end dance and drinks whisky while his baby is dying arouses hostility. When his excuse of a bad heart actually turns out to be valid, our feelings are thrown into reverse. Is he a ne'er-do-well or a cardiac? What vitiates these two sketches is the intrusion of theater for its own sake. The result is a pair of forced, sudden endings to bring on the final curtain. The dialogue is pallid, and, for the most part, static.[22]

In a land busy with immediate problems of farm and hamlet, little attention can be paid to celebrations of historic events. Before the First World War cities were conscious of their growth and progress. St. Louis, for example, celebrated its one hundred and fiftieth anniversary as a city with an ambitious outdoor, stationary spectacle. In May, 1914, two prominent writers collaborated to put on a chronicle-poem-play, *The Pageant and Masque of St. Louis*. For four days the pageant, written by Thomas Wood Stevens, unrolled the history of the city from the time of the Mound Builders to the Civil War. The clash between Indians and French explorers, the Lewis and Clark expedition, the pioneers of the great West, and scenes from our wars were exhibited before dazzled audiences. St. Louis was represented as a youthful crusader. Separated by an interlude came the second part, the masque, by Percy MacKaye. This part set forth in symbolic language the national and universal meanings underlying the pageant. St. Louis, a symbolic figure, moved among Speaking Persons, Choral Groups, and Presences to develop the theme of the fall and rise of civilization. Other allegoric figures, as well as pioneers, miners, and rangers, came and went as they chanted eloquently. Music played continuously throughout the action. The play enlisted the services of 7,500 citizen-actors who performed on a huge stage erected in Forest Park. For many years this supercolossal performance served as model for community masques given in other cities. In times of peace important cities cheerfully strive to celebrate in grandiose style their origin and development on the dates of anniversaries. In fact, it has become part of our national tradition and public philosophy.

In short, the Midlands, with its wide stretch of territory, has given the nation two major pioneers of the regional theater and their power has been felt throughout the country. Virgil Geddes and E. P. Conkle have written noteworthy and rugged plays. With skill and power they have hewn from the sod regional clods a bit askew, a bit inverted. These folk suffer the bitterness of unfulfillment, the monotony of parched acres, and a touch of sun. What makes their misery all the more unbearable is man's inability to apportion the fruits of the earth justly and equitably.

The Midwestern theater has not been inactive. Numerous centers other than Fargo have accounted for crops of rural plays. Efforts directed toward the

writing of regional plays have been sponsored by such
groups as the Southeast Missouri State Teachers College at Cape Girardeau, Missouri, the Midwestern
Folk Drama Tournament, and the Midwest Intercollegiate Folk Playwriting Contest, spread over nine
states: the last two projects under Lealon N. Jones.
Circulars pleading for a folk drama even suggest scenes
and plots from the life of the folk. The results have
been somewhat better than fair. The successful playlets have been published under such titles as *Country
Life Plays* (Baker), *Midwest Prize Plays* (Dramatic),
Folk Plays for Contests (Denison), *Pleasing Plays of
Country Life* (Bugbee), and *Rural Community Plays*
(Paine).

---

1. Alfred G. Arvold, *The Little Country Theater* (New York, 1922),
p. 56.

2. Marjorie Patten, *The Arts Workshop of Rural America; a Study of
the Rural Arts Program of the Agricultural Extension Service* (New York,
1937), p. 43.

3. *Lita's Man*, by Charles Burke.

4. *Sigrid*, by Margaret Radcliffe.

5. *A Window to the South*, by Mary K. Reely.

6. *Last Flight Over*, by Allean Lemmon.

7. *Sparkin'*.

8. *Minnie Field*.

9. *Things Is That-A-Way*.

10. *Loolie*.

11. *Little Granny Graver*.

12. *John Brown of Pattawatomie*, by John F. Alexander.

13. *Our Lean Years*, by Fred Eastman.

14. *The Organ*, by G. Edward Pendray and Kenyon Nicholson.

15. *Woman's Might*, by Jude Storm.

16. *Bread*, by Fred Eastman.

17. *Black Harvest*, by William B. Sears.

18. *Compensation*, by Anne Ferring.

19. *The Lean Years*, by Mary K. Reely.

20. *The River Rat*, by Mary Paxton Keeley.

21. *The Dance*, by Anna Best Joder.

22. *Dola's Learnin'*, by Anna Best Joder.

XI

Indian-Spanish America

IF YOU draw lines on a map of the United States south of the thirty-ninth parallel and west of the Mississippi, bounding the states of New Mexico, Arizona, Oklahoma, and Texas you isolate a geographic unit known as the Southwest. This actual blend of South and West, this arid land of adobe houses and pueblos, of desert, mesa, and mountain, has been ruled successively by the Indian, the Spaniard, and the American. Different origins and histories of these ethnic groups have helped build a drama of variegated yet blended strains.

Dramatically speaking, the land of little rain is primordial ground. The basic pattern is Indian. Athwart the two states of New Mexico and Arizona extend the largest tribal lands in this country bearing the largest single Indian aggregate of 89,586 persons (1940 figures) in an area equal to that of Massachusetts, New Hampshire, and Vermont. On this terrain dwell the pastoral horse-riding Navahos, in hexagonal hogans; the agricultural Hopis or Pueblo Indians who, since 1848, have remained in peace and in isolation in six Arizona villages; the ceremonious Zunis and Apaches who still practice the cult of the masked gods; and the Walapai and the Papago.

Essential to the faith of these tribes is the deeply inrooted feeling of oneness with the tribe. The link which binds the individual with the group is the traditional tribal prayer dance or sacred ritual untouched by foreign influences. In a land where water is life, the dance for rain becomes one long prayer. The primitive belief that by imitating an action one can get what that action suggests is translated into the up-and-down movement that brings rain. After the rain has brought the desired corn and other earth products there comes united cause for thanksgiving through prayer. From January to December, therefore, in pueblos and at sings, the Indians perform their dances in the following order: buffalo, eagle, turtle, spring, corn, summer-corn, harvest, sunset, harvest-corn, and the Navaho fire chant.

Best known to outsiders is the nine-day snake dance ritual of the Hopis, a colorful spectacle of monotonous dance movements addressed to nature. Second to the snake dance is the annual fiesta and summer-corn dance of the Domingo Indians, given at the pueblo of Santo Domingo thirty miles south of Santa Fe. As Mother Corn is the source of life to the Indian, the dancers wear cornhusks about their loins and in their hair as they move intently from street to street. Equally important are the harvest, rainbow, hunting, and basket dances of the Zunis, done by masked dancers with remarkable powers of mimicry.

The dance easily steps over into drama. Again and again mimic representations in solemn or light mood not only enforce tribal unity but provide entertainment. Most striking is a comic pantomime, the mountain chant of the Navahos, in which clowning characters, seminude, daubed with white clay, and wearing the spectacles and whiskers of the white man, draw howls from the crowd.[1]

Dance sequences which act out myths of creation have long interested the white man. Investigators have lived with the Indians in the hope of penetrating the meaning of such dances and have subsequently

published their findings in journals of folklore. Here
and there an inquisitive playmaker has watched their
ceremonies, listened to their tales, and taken pains to
translate into dramatic form the mood and the event.
First to immerse herself in Indian culture was Mary
Austin, who pleaded for an understanding of the
aborigines and set about creating a folk drama. In
fact, she hoped to start a school of regional writing
which would interpret the one race to the other. With
the ardor of one who opens new casements upon
strange vistas, she penned a number of highly poetic
Indian dramas. One of these roots in the Southwest.
Against a primeval, timeless background she blends
myth, psychology, and mysticism. The myth of the
power of deathless life over time comes to full expression in the dance drama of *Sekala Ka'ajma* (1929).
Among rocks and mountains in the desert of the Gila
River, and in the pre-Columbian past, men in costumes and women dancers welcome the handsome
Sekala, the Deathless One. He seeks the wind's trail
for Hot Wind has ravished his wife. Then follow
mystic chants that intone the birth of our hero begotten
by the coupling of the Fairest Maiden with the Sun, a
drum dance, and mystic explanations about "the dance
of substance at the will of spirit" together with prayers
to the "father of life unending." After this prelude
the plot begins to move. Climactic is the confrontation
scene in which two contestants throw a medicine stick
back and forth until Sekala pierces the snake ring. The
two play trick for trick, shield against shield, and dance
against each other. The end is decisive. Hot Wind
vanishes, sunlight floods the scene, and a Song of
Victory bursts forth:

To thee our thanks we cry.

This clash of primitive passions couched in frank, sex symbols denotes fertility winning over aridity. As the struggle unfolds in poetic terms, as image and phrase succeed each other, the high solemn note rises from the quaint speech of *thee* and *thou*. Mystic rhythms tend to hypnotize eye and ear and overpower the will to believe. The play reads like a literary translation from Indian myth into white man's verse.

The Mary Austin style has not been altogether salutary as an influence. Succeeding scribes have handled aboriginal material in that curiously mannered and Indianized style which has become traditional. Later plays by other pens exhibit less of the mystic strain and also less embroidery. Two playlets will illustrate the point. A Zuni folk tale explains the lack of rain by the fact that a giant has swallowed the clouds. Moreover, he rolls young men over the cliff. In turn they vow to destroy him. Together with the Spider-Woman they sew up the giant's eyelids into cobwebs, then roll the blinded giant over and ask him for rain.[2] In the story of the Zuni Indian turkey girl we find a parallel to the Cinderella tale. Though she can dance and be gracious, she is scorned by the handsome Indian youths. By the secret advice of the turkeys she is enabled to turn beautiful and win the love of one youth. But once she returns to rags, she is despised as before. In the end she leaves sadly by the trail.[3]

Partly Indian is the plot dealing with the white ethnologist who has lost his memory and taken to himself an Indian maid from among the Hopis. One day he is discovered in a pueblo by his long-searching wife. For the moment he recovers; but when his mate offers him a drink, life again becomes a mirage. In sharp contrast the ceremonial language of the natives stands out against the blunt talk of the whites, the simple child of nature against the cultured white lady. Indian chants punctuate the dialogue.[4]

Once a part of New Spain and rich with memories of Spanish history stands New Mexico. Centuries ago these rock shelters and high plateaus cut by canyons witnessed explorations, conquests, and massacres. It was here that Francisco Vásquez Coronado, in 1540, entered to seek the Seven Cities of Cibola and the land of the Quivira. In place of gold he found mud walls and reeds. Four hundred years later, in 1940, the Southwest commemorated the event by more than two hundred festivals which included Spanish fiestas and Indian dances. *The Coronado Pageant,* written by Thomas Wood Stevens, and the folk festivals, under the supervision of Sarah Gertrude Knott,[5] aimed to create an epic mood by the use of Indian and Spanish themes through song, dance, and scene.

Though Coronado's expedition failed, it opened the way to further Spanish occupation and left behind a trail of legends and tales. Conquistadores spread an interest in dramatics wherever they went. They used them as a weapon of conquest and conversion. Such plays as they put on were straight propaganda pieces, borrowed or written by missionaries in the New World to be performed by Spanish soldiers on horseback. An old script, probably retouched, furnished the central idea: the defeat of the Moorish army and the acceptance of the Christian faith. *Los Moros y Los Cristianos* (The Moors and the Christians), through pantomime and mimicry, served as a parable to Christianize the heathen Indian. Since 1598, the year of the first equestrian play to be shown on American soil,[6] the descendants of the Spanish colonists in the district

of Rio Arriba have periodically edified their com-
patriots by a revival of the play.

Religious drama is still common in the Spanish
settlements of New Mexico, though less so than thirty
years ago. In fact, every town has its own patron saint
whose feast day it commemorates in its own way. Plays
known locally as *pastorales* may be performed any time
during the Spanish Christmas season, which extends
from December 16 through January 6. These variable
folk plays, in the medieval sense, are done on improvised stages by religious casts. Scripts are often con-
solidated, portions omitted, and improvisations allowed. Reverently they present the sacred story in
simple, homely terms. The religious *auto sacramental*
or religious play, which was popular in Europe during
the sixteenth century, drew its material from the Old
and New Testaments: from the one, *Adam and Eve*
and *Cain and Abel;* from the other, the *nacimientos*
or stories of the birth of Christ. Beginning with the
theme of the marriage of Joseph and Mary, the cycle of
pastorales ran through the familiar incidents of the
shepherds watching their flocks by night, the Three
Kings, and the account of Christ's meeting the doctors
of Jewish law in the Temple.

First of these popular nativity plays, in the order
of production, is *Las Posadas* (The Shelter). Nine
nights before Christmas young people march behind
the images of Mary and Joseph from house to house
singing religious songs. They ask shelter for Mary but
are refused admittance because Satan presumably hides
behind every door. On the ninth night, the Blessed
Pair are recognized, doors are thrown open, and they
are admitted. Merrymaking follows.

On Christmas Eve little bonfires for the Christ
child, *El Santo Nino* (the Holy Child), are lighted be-

The Eagle Dance, New Mexico

fore house doors and in the streets. Night processions with cedar torches move through the pueblo of Taos.

Most popular is *Los Pastores* (The Shepherds), the tale of the shepherds who, while watching their flocks, hear the angel's song at the Nativity and decide to go to Bethlehem. A bit of rough play is interpolated when the Archangel Michael and Lucifer wrestle and the Evil One is thrown to the ground. But the fall is only momentary! Lucifer summons his legions of hell and devils rush in from everywhere. Promptly they are stopped by Michael who points to the Christmas star and the illuminated manger. Then travelers approach; some buy the Child *tamales*. Finally the shepherds return to their camp, singing as they pass into the night. The original text has been corrupted by the introduction of new scenes, new lines, and new phrases, such as the long speech of the Devil to St. Michael, and odd bits of humor. Strangely, the play preserves the form and versification of the classic drama of the sixteenth century.

Another version, acted out in San Antonio, Texas, every winter introduces some mock-serious moments when six devils wearing masks, tusk horns, and long black mantles covered with spangles, emerge from and retreat into Hell-Mouth. Together with Satan they hear the news of the birth of the Child which had been previously announced by the shepherds. The familiar duel between Lucifer and Michael offers a bit of comic byplay.

On the sixth of January, the Spanish Christmas, the Magi on camels ride past the balconies. Then the holiday is fittingly observed by a short play, *Los Reyes Magos* (The Magi Kings). The piece opens in customary medieval fashion with the lines:

Atención, noble auditorió
A nuestra composición.

The Three Kings seek the manger. On the way they stop at the court of King Herod but change their routes when Herod orders the Innocents to be slaughtered. In the end, Herod is deceived by a band of rustics.

Other sacred plays like *La Virgen de Guadalupe* (The Virgin of Guadalupe), based upon the legend of the miraculous apparition are performed from memory year after year. Many of these sacred plays have been borrowed by and molded to their present uses by the Indian. For example, The Passion Play has been re-enacted during Holy Week by the pious Yaquis in the little village of Pascua. Also, near the Mexican border, an annual three-day Feast of San Francis Xavier has been celebrated annually in December for 250 years at San Xavier del Bac Mission by the peaceful Papago Indians. *Los Matachines* (The Clowns), a bit of Spanish foolery, more dance than play, has been done by the Pueblo Indians. In the most recent *Los Comanches* (The Comanches), Indians clash with Spaniards but are eventually converted. Three different versions show the savages in attitude of submission, once to the Holy Child and twice before the Spaniards.

All three strains—Indian, Spanish, and American—mingle in an annual fiesta held since 1927 at Santa Fe. Indian dances precede a Memorial Procession of our Lady of Victory, which, in turn, is followed by the De Vargas Pageant, a panorama of historic events extending from the entry of Diego de Vargas, who recaptured the province from the Pueblo Indians in 1692, up to present-day events.[7]

Contemporary American plays on Spanish religious themes are few. One authentic modern morality in English draws its conflict from the last surviving sect of the Flagellants, founded three hundred years ago in Spain, *Los Penitentes*. At one time almost every male Catholic in New Mexico belonged to this group. Yearly they revive the Passion Play without the whippings or scourgings which once were not suppressed. Anyone chosen to play the Christ generally enjoys prestige and even worldly success. In *El Cristo* (1926), by Margaret Larkin, one such candidate refuses to suffer on the cross for so gross a purpose as to elect his father sheriff. He spurns this degraded use of a holy privilege. Rebuked, he gives up his chance to another less scrupulous than he. Then he flings himself before the altar and prays.

On the historic theme of resistance by Mexican feudal lords to westward expansion by the United States, one play has been written by Maxwell Anderson: *Night Over Taos*. Here a Mexican chieftain, with his two sons and faithful followers, represents the last flicker of Spanish rule north of the Rio Grande. This imposing leader realizes that he cannot hold out against superior forces. What is worse, a sentiment of democracy is growing up in one of his sons. In accordance with his code of honor, he exacts the supreme penalty from his son. Skillfully joined scene by scene, the events roll on swiftly to an appointed end while the speech ripples along in semipoetic stage verse. Yet the stage properties turn into cardboard and ghosts, and the pageant fades into insubstantial air.

Native as the Indian dance dramas and Spanish *pastorales* may be, the two are at variance with American myth. The frontiersman and pioneer had to believe in a power greater than himself and thus create demigods incarnating his fierce love of freedom and scorn of law. He found them in the bandit, the rover, and the cowboy. From West to East ran the bandit theme in story and song as exemplified in the saga of Billy the Kid, of Jesse James, and such. Eventually, the exploits of these heroes passed from legendry to fiction, and then into the drama.

The setting of several plays is the old West where primitive passion often raged unchecked. Billy the Kid, he who is supposed to have sent twenty-one souls into eternity, stamps the boards in an old revenge melodrama: *Billy the Kid* (1906), by Walter Woods. Within the old frame moves the idealized bandit. Throughout, a reverence for the prowess of the eighteen-year-old wonder boy is manifest. The action is cluttered with such jumbled episodes as threats of reprisal, reluctance to kill, outbursts in saloons, and the reunion of young lovers. Other pieces show Billy in the role of benefactor. He comes upon the scene to do a good turn. After some sparring, this hero of the plains, this "quickest drawin', straightest shootin' guntoter in the territory," consents to be merciful when a Sister of Charity pleads with him to save a life. When someone intervenes, he is silenced by a shot; and another notch is added to Billy's gun.[8] The story is colored by an infusion of Westernisms. Still benevolent, Billy, in another play, unconsciously persuaded two lonely sheepherders on a mountain slope in New Mexico, when they vow to turn *bandidos,* to go straight. So scared are they by the hero's toughness that they decide rather "to work hard and sleep good," and yes, even "to eat good."[9]

Equally notorious is the career of Jesse James from

Missouri. A swiftly told plot aims to humanize the man and to reveal likable qualities. Events move on a plane of credibility instead of adolescent hero-worship. In the end the bandit comes to grief through treachery.[10] "But the dirty little caoward who shot Mr. Haoward, He laid po' Jesse in his grave."

While the early wild version of Billy the Kid was drawing cheers from audiences, a finely wrought study of West and East was making dramatic history. In *The Great Divide* (1906), by William Vaughn Moody, the Arizona frontier was painted in fresh, poetic colors. The admirable scenes of a cabin on the desert, followed by those of the adobe cabin in the Cordilleras, set the stage for a battle of codes: that of the effeminate Puritanic East against the freer, less inhibited one of the West. The regional coloring conveyed by language somewhat polished, though refreshingly original for the time, is broadly Western but not too recognizably regional nor folkish. The didactic turn of events toward the end shunts toward ethical debate and gives the victory to the belief that self-respect can be regained through suffering and discipline.

Later playwrights did not trouble themselves about so complex a character as Stephen Ghent. Instead, they flash, in short sketches of incident, such wild characters as the gunman, the outlaw, the kidnaper, the vagabond and other species of the "bad" man. They act like tabloid newspaper villains, dogged by an evil star. Sometimes the gunmen are captured by the Americans they try to terrorize,[11] or the notorious prowling outlaw is unsuspectingly captured by a tenderfoot unaware of his bravery.[12] Or again, when kidnapers rush into a lonely cabin to demand the use of a horse, they are trapped by Benito, the hired boy, who telephones a fake warning that the dam at the

head of the canyon has burst.[13] Finally, the accidental
shot into the night by a rover kills the innocent maid
who promised to meet him before he left by the trail.[14]
Sufficient unto the story is the plot. The dialogue is
generally sprinkled with such Spanish phrases, oaths,
and mixed lingo as *bueno, hombre, savvy, Madre de
Dios.*

More inwardly turned is the desperado, now a
family hero, who returns to his home hopefully with his
moll, a burlesque queen. He hopes to be safe in the
hideouts of Oklahoma. But he can find no peace. "No,
things ain't the same," he complains. The old fears
and jumpiness will not desert him. Torn within himself, he makes off again—this time to certain death.[15]

Along with these native types appear a host of
Southwestern figures caught in the web of circumstances for the moment: the sheriffs, the bartenders, the
tenderfeet, the sheepmen, cattlemen, town miners and
such. These will appear more distinctively in plays of
near-by regions.

Oklahoma, land of mesquite and sagebrush, of
cypress and pine, is rife with Indian lore. For here,
finally settled the Five Civilized Tribes: Cherokee,
Choctaw, Chickasaw, Creek, and Seminole. In addition, thirty smaller bands of Indians on twenty-seven
reservations are scattered throughout the territory on
land granted to them for "as long as grass grows and
water runs." In fact, the largest Indian population
of any one state is concentrated in Oklahoma: 63,125
(1940 census) .

Of Indian legends which have reached the white
man, two have been turned into play form. No hidden
meanings tantalize the mind in these simple tales
which assume stage presentation. The first, taken

from the Choctaws, symbolizes the growth of corn.
Answering the call of hunger, the daughter of the
Great Spirit comes to earth as corn. After a period of
four moons she turns out to be the Green Corn Goddess herself.[16] Set to music and told in running verse
is the tale of White Hawk, the Shawnee Indian hunter
noted for his aim and swiftness. Pursued by maidens,
he rushes into the magic circle, woos the returning
maid, and loves her. But presently the hunting fever
and the desire for companions prove too strong and he
leaves. On his return he learns that his beloved has
vanished. After a period of mourning he meets her
again. Then both are claimed by the Great Spirit.[17]

Other playlets hark back to the early history of
Oklahoma and Indian Territory and present a dismal
record of battles, lawlessness, and massacre endured by
the hardy frontiersmen. In a land of red clay, dirty
rivers, and parched prairies the struggle to maintain
family life must have been disheartening. Wives were
the worst sufferers. Yet so strong was her faith in
Oklahoma that one wife passionately decided to stay
on and build the red land even after her husband had
been shot for refusing to give up his mining claim.[18]
Later settlers, equally hopeful, looked forward to
something brighter and better beyond. A bit reluctantly, two settlers sink roots and hope for the best.[19]
To be sure, the next year's crops will be good enough
to pay off the mortgage.[20] In this way the good settlers
lived from year to year.

In our own day the bitter plight of the Okies admits
of no such optimism. The gruesome struggle of a
tenant farmer against dust, a tuberculous daughter,
and the land agent who will not renew his lease is
painted in dark colors. His case is typical. Rail as he
will at "big machines that grind out profits" or plead

for co-operatives, he and his neighbors seem powerless
to stop the ruthless tractor that rips down the frail
house.[21]

Noteworthy among Oklahoma playwrights is the son
of a cattleman of Cherokee blood, born and bred in the
old Indian Territory: Lynn Riggs. Since 1921 he has
written more than eighteen plays, of which eleven
have been published or produced. His characters stem
straight from the native trunk. In a semifantasy,
Cherokee Night (1936), the author pleads the cause
of the Cherokees. Hunted down and chained to the
wall the Amerindian, by necessity, turns inward to
dreams of action. Ill at ease in a Christianized world,
the part-Cherokee nurses his vision of forebears only
to be awakened into an alien world. In a series of
flashes, the racial self of the Indian unfolds against
odds in a world where God is a white man.

This author's other creations live feverishly and
force the issue. They crave space in which to expand.
In the Indian Territory of 1905 the wild spirit smashed
at barriers and exploded into lawlessness. Hell-bent
for mischief, the self-assertive roarer in *Roadside* (or
Borned in Texas) (1930) rushes pell-mell into and
out of trouble. He just can't be arrested, this wildcat
"crazy as a suck-egg mule." In the end he carries off
his wild mate. The road wins against the plow.

The same wild energy that knows no check possesses
the brutal father who, by dint of hard work, has acquired 160 acres of land. In *A Lantern to See By*
(1928), whose plot, by the way, bears some resemblance to O'Neill's *Desire Under the Elms* (1924),
this self-willed farmer tyrannizes over his sensitive
son and his pregnant wife, and seduces the maid who
succeeds her. In opposition stands the son, a muddled

weakling who also has some claims on the maid. Only when he kills his father does his brain fog lift.

Of the same stuff is the neglected daughter turned prostitute in *Sump'n Like Wings* (1928). She wills to live her own life in town with a boy whom she loves. Though trapped by circumstances, she resolves to fight it out until she wins.

This same spirit of dogged resistance, of exaggerated will, animates the young maid who insists on marrying the Syrian peddler. Luckily, events turn in her favor when a number of unconscious remarks, mistaken for artful threats, impel her widow-mother to consent. Continuity and colorful speech make a tightly knit playlet of *Knives from Syria* (1928).

The fret and fever in the veins of two high-school students come to a sad end in *Big Lake* (1927). By chance the two find themselves in a murderer's cabin, and by mischance they are killed. Across this tragedy slashes like a knife the stupidly prim and complacent precepts of the school teacher.

In one supreme effort Riggs joined the threads he had previously spun. Wistfully he returned to the Indian Territory of his father. The iron will and the adolescent crudity give way to mature love and ecstasy tempered by affliction in *Green Grow the Lilacs* (1931). Sinister shadows of human hate mar the hasty romance which ties the singing cowboy to the scared maid. Effective as theater are the magnificent scenes of the bawdy "shivaree" in the hayfield, the abortive fire, the scuffle, and the accidental death. Throughout the action the tang and agony that once marked the bold free life of the West come to fullness. Notwithstanding, the blare of local allegiance is too loud, while the folk material of song and folk say is too thinly painted over and a bit too consciously spread.

Cut from the same granite block is the headstrong niece bent on exposing the sham of conformity. She is the logical end result of overweening self-confidence touched with abortive satire. The heroine of *Russet Mantle* (1935) moves among stage types. Some cryptic criticisms of our civilization and our accepted values ring true. "But the rigor and terror of man against man never ceased." Indignation flames to white heat. "Machine guns mowing down men in Wisconsin. Men and women hounded and flogged and tortured in San Francisco. Riot squads, strikebreakers, nausea gas, bayonets and starvation! And voices crying out, for what? A little bread, a little sun, a little peace and delight." Unfortunately, such fine utterances do not flow from situation. The ending collapses, and the figures vanish into air.

The accumulated angers and darts end in neurosis. The sick will, blocked and deflected, seeks fulfillment in incest. Hate begets hate until evil destroys itself. A neurotic Hedda Gabler of the plains madly loves her absent brother, clashes with every member of her family, and causes the death of another and of herself. How she acquired her unhealthy passion is never explained in dramatic terms. The incest theme in *Cream in the Well* (1941) moves ahead by jerks and shocks. The talk of mules, horses, cows, and working on the land sounds extraneous.

All in all the plays of Lynn Riggs—to quote his own expression—"have a slight edge beyond realism."[22] He achieves his effects by the use of violence, fury, incest, murder. In the very creation of these hell roarers and furies who crave the right to fight and build and dream, the individualists of an early day go to seed. The line begins and ends in the self. When these selves rise above the normal, they turn grotesque;

and lawlessness winds up in neurosis. As one who
views the Western scene, Riggs falls into the error
shared by his own tough people. He makes a virtue
of bafflement and inversion. With one of them, he
seems to whimper, "We don't know where we are."
Actually, were the settlers of 1905 and later so faint-
hearted? It is hardly likely that the struggles "between a man and his inner glowing core" were resolved
by futile sobbings or angry denunciations. As were
once the pioneers, so are their present descendants
men of decision and action who have learned to temper
their egos. It is presumed that they have at last found
a lantern to see by. Valid as the playwright's claim
may be to turn psychanalytic, it is certain that moods
and inversions and talk do not make the whole personality come through. Be that as it may, the background
of belief and folkways remains authentic, and the
mastery of flexible speech rhythms and poetic idiom in
the mouths of unique individuals is unmistakably impressive and indigenous.

Today oil is king in Oklahoma. The invasion of
industry attendant upon the discovery of oil has
brought new subjects to folklore and to the drama.
Among the oil drillers, a series of legends has clustered
about the phenomenal figure of Kemp Morgan, tank
builder, driller, and operator extraordinary, as well
as about a great gray wolf who is blood cousin to Babe
the Blue Ox.

Thus far plays have fought shy of these two figures.
Instead, a few have dramatized the humble toilers in
the oil field. The common theme voices a common
hope: namely, that the miracle of oil will pull these
hard-pressed natives out of their poverty. Also, youths
back from college hope to discover signs of oil. But
dramatic surprise insists that a lucky accident, like

dropping a stick of dynamite into a well, will bring the golden gush. When it comes true, Oklahoma suddenly becomes the promised land.[23] However, a bidder for oil land must take his chances. Expectations rise and fall when offers to buy land with sandburs, cockleburs, wire grass, and all seem futile. But the repudiated sale turns out happily for the owner of the property when oil is actually discovered.[24]

The hope of an oil boom and its actual arrival according to schedule can play tricks with character, and even undermine it. A self-assured and positive female who reigns over her less-assured neighbors in near-by Texas wilts into insignificance when their lands are leased for oil as hers were. Deflated, her only comfort is to leave the village to go around the world with her husband.[25] The portrait of regional pride in this instance takes on universal meaning.

In the wake of oil drillers have come fatalities. Machinery in the fields has claimed its victims. And the repercussions on family life can be painful indeed. Mother love bears the full strain on the death of a husband, a son, and now a second son. At this critical moment, sister love feels obliged to follow human impulse on her marriage day. The currents merge in a poignant sketch.[26]

Finally, when oil gushers are found on farm land, the farmer must choose between oil or wheat. Habit will keep the bullheaded farmer rooted to the ground and scornful of any offer. "A man don't let outsiders take over a place he's seen his kith and kin fight for that way." The same stubbornness dictates his views on newcomers, schooling, new devices, and roustabouts. True to his principles he resists the entreaties of his son, his daughter, and his wife. He will not sell.[27]

Midway between the two oceans unrolls the widest
stretch of the Southwest: Texas. Woodland, plain,
and desert give diversity to breadth. Within this vast
area move lumbermen and planters, sheepherders and
cowpunchers, wheat growers and dry farmers.

Texans have always been intensely proud of their
history. In many communities processions, pageants,
and plays of notables, set within a frame from the past,
have been exhibited. Some of this material bears a
strictly local interest. Now and then a wide panorama
of incidents, written in the customary florid style of
pageantry and lavishly mounted, boastfully projects
the spirit of Texas for the admiration of the country.
The entire history of the state from 1685 to 1846
passes in review in *Westward the Course of Empire*.[28]
Another comprehensive pageant with words divides
the last century of Texas history into periods of
progress by ten decades. Lovely sisters wearing Grecian
robes enter one by one to declaim the glories of the
state from the time of the early settlers to the present-
day "vast and thriving country." The procession ends
in a riot of wild flowers and stage business carried on
by allegoric figures of Mother Earth, Father Sun,
Flora, and others.[29]

Over a century ago the clash of armies battling for
supremacy shook Texas. In the war for independence
from Mexican rule in 1836 occurred the bloody siege
of the Alamo. For thirteen days a handful of men
held off a superior force under Santa Anna. Finally
the Americans were brutally slaughtered in the chapel.
This disastrous siege burnt deep into the hearts and
minds of Texans. "Remember the Alamo" rang
down the century until playwrights, heeding the cry,
revived the dire and tragic episode.

To date, the most ambitious piece on the Alamo

traces with deliberate oratorical effect a timely analogy
between the early incident and the present world
crisis. The scene is the courtyard of the mission-fort-
ress of San Antonio de Valero. Here stand the small
band of Americans ready to defend Texas against the
superior Mexican army. They reject the proffered
terms of surrender. Loyal sentiments measure the
morale of the fighters. "We live for Texas—we are
ready, if necessary, to die for Texas." The Mexican
tyrant is branded as "this field who thrives on lies."
At one time the forlorn and discouraged *Americanos*
debate their cause. Shall they give up? No! "No
nation today lives to itself alone. If liberty dies in
Texas, its promise for mankind everywhere passes into
jeopardy." Next morning the massacre climaxes the
plot. With his last breath a doctor warns, "No just
peace is possible with the dictator."[30] Definitely this
topical treatment of a heroic incident is a trumpet call
for united effort in a time of crisis. Texas digs into its
own past to warn the world.

A more recent playlet shows the same fighters at the
Alamo bitterly arguing about their peril in strong,
soldier language. The way to retreat has been left
open, but nobody wishes to take advantage. When a
diminutive Mexican from a near-by hamlet enters with
twenty men, the bewildered Americans are no longer
afraid, and they accept his services to cross the line.[31]

One month after his bloody defense, the Americans,
under Sam Houston, at San Jacinto defeated and captured the Mexican general. This campaign is regularly
celebrated at San Antonio by a fiesta. Of the plays
which have staged this battle, one version in five parts
and with choral music shows events leading up to the
success of the commander in chief of the Texas army.
Laments, cries, and curses in the manner of a Greek

play proclaim somewhat artificially the fall of the last
of the missions, the flight of the *Americanos,* and the
final stand.[32]

For the moment the scene narrows to a peaceful
log cabin where, in 1831, homesick colonists are be-
wailing their lot. Then there enters on her first trip
westward the sprightly and adventurous Mrs. Mary
Austin Holley, the first historian of Texas. After she
speaks to the settlers, she arouses their faith, idealism,
and enthusiasm. And they resume the task of building
a fine, new world.[33]

Thirty years later the residents of St. Cooper were
disturbed by a strange event. It was the time of border
clashes between white settlers and Comanche raiders.
A white girl had been kidnapped as a child by Comanche Indians, had married an Indian chief, and
borne him children. Having been captured, this squaw
and her papoose were brought to a white settlement
where she was recognized as white by her blue eyes.
The natives tried to befriend her and to find her kin.
But, unable to speak English, all she could mumble
was her name.[34]

Central to Texas lore is the cowboy. At one time
Texas, as the land of boots and saddles, of roundups,
rodeos, and barbecues, was the capital of the romantic
Wild West. In the long hours of night-herding and
range-riding, while the cowpuncher rode his herds
northward to Montana, he manufactured and regaled
himself with endless stanzas about love and danger, of
monotony and pleasure. When he met his fellows, he
invented folk heroes who were but glorified cowboys.
One of these, the principal of an unpublished play,
was Pecos Bill, "the great granddaddy of all cowboys,
who once mounted an Oklahoma cyclone and traveled
across three states."[35] In *Bill and the Widow-Maker,*

by E. P. Conkle, done at the University of Texas, the
hero is conceived in jesting mood and reduced to near-
human proportions. His career is traced from the
day he fell off his parent's wagon as an infant to the
time of his death in scenes which shift from the open
prairie on the Pecos River, to Nebraska, and back to
Texas. In the beginning the child talks wisely to Don
Coyote, a local folk figure who hates "inhumans as
cruel as thorns and cactus." He joins the coyotes. Before long he meets cowboys, grabs a lasso, and catches a
cow. Up to this point the story sounds like a mild fairy
tale. One day he sees the purple stallion, Widow-
Maker, and falls in love with it. So smitten is he by
this "conquering splendid purple stallion" that he
renounces his animal kingdom. After this event the
narrative takes on regional strength. Borrowed from
native legendry is the episode of Nellie who mounts
the horse and is thrown over the moon and back to
earth where she jounces on her bustle and keeps on
jouncing. The last act, complete in itself, stiffens into
satire. Bill, just out of jail, finds himself in an alien
world. He doesn't like fences and farmhouses. He
craves space and freedom, bewails the fact that only
gentlemen are left, and begins tearing down fences.
Bill's final fall is traced to love, to rustlers, and to fences.
Unhappily, this chronicle play fails to bring Bill into
full focus.

The impulse to wrest gold from the earth has moved
men at all times, including the playwright. Strange
tales of secret Spanish mines and buried bullion, and
fantastic legends of icicles of silver and pebbles of
gold are still exchanged in the Big Bend country of
Texas, land of mountain, canyon, and mesa. Gold is
where you find it, say the prospectors. Negating this

"Precious Land," by Robert Whitehand, University of Oklahoma

proverb E. P. Conkle sets against the mountainous terrain of the Panhandle a grizzled explorer who, with his burro, has spent forty years seeking gold. One day he actually finds the precious ore. Instantly he dreams of luxury. But cold reason reminds him of the discomforts of wealth. He must die in bed and go home to his Arminty. All this time the burro speaks to him reproachfully. The prospector then makes his decision. "Fine t' be goin' on searchin' . . . prospectin' . . . right now. . . . No fambly chitter-chatter, no civilized grub t' have t' eat, no Legislatoor, no clean shirts t' wear all around . . . no . . . no. . . ." And he merrily continues his journey. Behind the paradox of *Gold is Where You Don't Find It* lies an intensely human and universal figure: the simple, happy, and carefree rover.

As the laughter of a Conkle dies beyond the crags, the plains come into view again. Here the cry of distress from unhappy victims rises from several plays. Characters must make painful decisions to escape dilemmas. The rustler, the sharecropper, the dust victim all move in a maze of happenings and vainly seek a way out. A desperate border thief of cattle blurts out angrily, "Just a slave to a piece of grazin' land. Just a chunk of gumbo . . . mud." His fate is sealed in theatrical fashion when his wife decides to shoot him when he hides from the law.[36] Equally pathetic is the case of the baffled sharecroppers who feel the injustice of "farms on the halves" and rail at the miserable returns they receive—compared with the easy money in town. In fact, one hard-pressed youngster sees no solution to the problem except just dying.[37]

Vividly pictured is the plight of dust victims on the roads of Texas. One family trundling a push-wagon westward to California cannot shake off memories of "a mailbox a few hundred yards off down the public road." The parents bitterly complain that "you can't fight dust cause it ain't nobody." On the way their little girl coughs her lungs out, dies of pneumonia, and is buried. The final love scenes of stranger and daughter, and the mother's funeral, are sentimentalized.[38] Finally, during the black blizzard of April, 1935, black clouds of dust filled eyes, ears, and mouth and water in the pail proved undrinkable. In such a windstorm hunger drives parents, against the tearful plea of their child, to kill the last rabbit left alive. As a result the child carries out his threat to kill himself by running out into the storm.[39]

Between the rhapsodic declamations of Grecian maidens in pageants and the heartsick wail of a child in a dust storm runs the gamut of Texas themes in plays. The variety of events thus treated is practically as wide as the region itself. Conspicuous has been the trend toward worship of the past. With it has traveled a lusty optimism and bravado inseparable from pioneering. In the process the drama has singled out a local demigod as typical: namely, Pecos Bill. But it has been left to a region farther north to do justice to the cowboy.

In short, the drama of the Southwest has aimed to follow the triple lines of culture laid down by the Indian, the Spaniard, and the American. Though the lines run parallel they generate currents that often move as one. The Indian theme enters the drama of this region on timid feet and lingers awhile. The rich heritage of Old Spain and Mexico of three-and-a-half centuries has left permanent markings on the folk arts and the folk drama. Only within the past century, after the *Americano* overran the region, have his own ups and downs led him to create local demigods wherein he found dramatic release in rough historic figures.

Theatrical activity in such centers as Dallas, Waco, and Austin has been lively. Among the plays produced have been the regional works of such superior craftsmen as Mary Austin, E. P. Conkle, and Lynn Riggs.

1. *Indians at Work* (Washington, D.C., Office of Indian Affairs, October 1, 1937) , p. 30.
2. *The Giant Who Swallowed the Clouds,* by Susanna Myers.
3. *The Turkey Girl,* by Sarah M. Williams.
4. *Mirage,* by George M. P. Baird.
5. Director of the National Folk Festival held annually.
6. For some of these facts I am indebted to Arthur L. Campa's *Spanish Religious Folktheatre in the Spanish Southwest,* first and second cycles (Albuquerque, 1934) .
7. Hartley Alexander, "The Fiesta Theatre at Santa Fe," *Theatre Arts Monthly,* XI (January, 1927) , 27-34.
8. *Chico,* by Harry C. Gibbs.
9. *Manana Bandits,* by Betty Smith and Chase Webb.
10. *Missouri Legend,* by Elizabeth B. Ginty.
11. *Public Citizen Number First,* by John E. Walsh.
12. *Stick 'Em Up,* by Gordon Clouser.
13. *Flood Control,* by Milward W. Martin.
14. *Frontier Night,* by Chase Webb.
15. *Last Refuge,* by Noel Houston.
16. *Chisbaohoyo,* by John W. Dunn.
17. *White Hawk,* by Teresa Strickland.
18. *The Red Land,* by Robert Sturgis.
19. *Banners of the Soil,* by Ernest Chamberlain.
20. *Storm Clouds and Wheat,* by Harold K. Crockett.
21. *Tenant Farmers,* by Elliot Field.
22. "When People Say Folk Drama," *Carolina Play-Book,* June, 1931, p. 40.
23. *The Promised Land,* by Horace W. Robinson.
24. *Very Crude Oil,* by Stella D. Whipkey.
25. *The Reign of the Minnie Belle,* by Virginia B. Weaver.
26. *Derricks on the Hill,* by Robert Whitehand.
27. *Precious Land,* by Robert Whitehand.
28. By Alice Mary Matlock Griffith.
29. *Dramas of Daring Deeds,* by Bessie Lee Dickey Roselle.
30. *We Are Besieged,* by Sam Acheson.
31. *God and Texas,* by Robert Ardrey.
32. Samuel Asbury, "A Provincial Drama Ritual," *Southwest Review,* Winter, 1930.
33. *Westward People,* by John W. Rogers, Jr.
34. *The Rescue of Cynthia Ann,* by John W. Rogers, Jr.
35. Writers' Program, W.P.A., *Texas; a Guide to the Lone Star State* (New York, 1940) , p. 93.
36. *Across the Border,* by Colin Clements.
37. *Sharecroppers,* by Arthur McC. Samplay.
38. *West from the Panhandle,* by Clemon White and Betty Smith.
39. *Dust,* by Edna Muldrow.

XII

Peaks and Prospectors

WESTWARD toward the continental divide the land takes on glory and grandeur. Natural formations of rock and peak, of canyon and glacier, make up a scenic wonderland surpassing all loveliness. Against this range of the Rockies once moved Indians, foreign explorers, native scouts, trappers, and later the pick-and-shovel crew who were to scar and deface acres of good earth in search of the elusive gold and other precious metals.

Where nature is so overwhelming, man and his works must appear trivial. The far-flung panorama is in itself so mighty a pageant as to need no verbal text. But man in his littleness aspires to match or approach this grandeur symbolically through the dance, music, and words. Man-made pageantry in graphic terms tries to equate the beauty of national parks and the joy of having subdued a wild land to human habitation. Wyoming, therefore, points with pride to the vastness of God's country, the Far West, and in particular to its own past hardihood. Of nine recorded pageants which glorify the state, *Veedauwoo* (Earth-Born) (1925), by Mabelle L. De Kay, in five episodes based on fiction and history, conveys a pretty allegory. Before a miniature geyser in Yellowstone Park an assembly of pixies, elves, and spirits dance at the creation of Wyoming. The state is personated by a comely maiden loved by the Earth Spirit. Indians, trappers, traders, Kit Carson, cowboys, sheepmen, and cattlemen pass by. In the end the State and Earth-Born marry to signify the awakening of the soul to the beauty of Wyoming. As if to surpass the glorious abstractions, the text rings with highly ornate passages.

Regional history has furnished incidents for several sketches: mere plot pieces with a dash of local background. During 1849 and afterward, it was customary for pioneer parties to be led by frontier guides into the great Rocky Mountain basin. Clashes between tough guides and "them there dudes" must have been common. A roughneck and a dude quarrel over a refined girl. Pistols flash, a shot rings out, and the dude's body rolls beneath the boot of the heartless guide. Horrified, the playful girl accuses herself of murder.[1]

To the pioneers of 1862 the Pony Express brought news, adventure, and fatalities. It took ten days for two hundred riders and five hundred horses to carry assorted mail to California. To send one package of three ounces cost thirty dollars in postage. In one particular play the question is: "Will Pa's letter containing five hundred dollars, addressed to Sacramento, get through?" Meanwhile, the daughter has taken a fancy to one of the pony riders. Then one day another express rider, wounded by rifle shots, walks in. As the girl dresses his wound, he casually blurts out the news that her lover has been cut down by a band of Indians. But he hastens to assure her that the overland mail has, nevertheless, gone through.[2]

The hammering of the golden spike which tied together the railroads of the East and West near Ogden, Utah, in 1869, motivates one play. Paw and Maw, wearing store clothes, are not happy. They fear the railroad as "tools of the devil," and detest "the big injine." Amid "thars" and "I swars" they denounce the firebox along with other contraptions like the

threshing machine. Just then a shrill whistle of the
train blasts their ears as it thunders by. They suffer
the terrors of the damned. Nevertheless, they have
been guilty of buying a sewing machine. The tone of
the play is mildly jocular, and the surface tints are
those of a bright chromo.[3]

In the Rockies folk tales and legends of buried
treasure have been current for more than a century.
Even before gold was discovered farther west, numerous stories of lost mines like the Great Mother Lode
and the Madre de Oro, of Spanish wealth, lost canyons,
and mocking mirages in the desert, circulated up and
down the Rockies. Naturally, when the pioneer pressed
forward to stake his claims, these tales colored his
hopes and excited his imagination. As gold mining in
the mountains became a reality, the store of fables and
tall tales, called "whizzers," grew. But so did the
prosaic day-to-day gamble. Fortunes won, fortunes
lost, was the refrain of the adventurer in frontier
mining towns.

A sheaf of plays objectively sketch the background
of mining field and frontier. One dynamic chronicle
play, *Bonanza,* by Janet D. Shafroth, covers a span of
years from 1859 to 1896 and moves between Washington, D.C., and Denver, Colorado. It catches the stir
of pioneer effort, the easy optimism, the lawless will
operating in a man's world. In the progress of the
central character from hotelkeeper to millionaire to
outcast, the play traces the continental changes from
wagon to railroad, from poverty to wealth. Quick
fortunes made by speculation and lost as quickly bred
the flashy type represented by the aggressive gambler,
the illiterate sensualist, and the charming patron. He
rushes from venture to venture, snatches at romance,
climbs to slippery heights, and drops into the abyss.

Undaunted at the end, the bankrupt still hopes to strike a new mine. Although the miner's lingo of grubstake, rathole, salt the mines, pay dirt, jumping claims, and so on sounds authentic, the central character is an aggregate of traits instead of a rounded personality.

As if to distrust the golden dream, contemporary one-act plays stress the forlorn hope nursed by miners and their wives in a mine that has petered out. Diehards are subject to last-minute seizures and insist that they will open a new vein in the rock. But such expectations are never realized. When the impatient wife will no longer cope with loneliness and failure, a train of domestic miseries follows.[4] Sometimes, too, the miner will be torn by conflicting duties. He yearns to stay on to find a new vein while his mate, a former trollop, longs to be married and move away. Complications involving a father-in-law who is a lazy dotard fond of hunting lead to her dismissal.[5] Her only course now is to take up with the ranger. Another forlorn wife must act quickly in an emergency. Trapped by circumstances when her husband, a disappointed miner, is murdered by his own brother, whom he had never met, the wife feels obliged to play the game of make believe to deceive the inquiring sheriff.[6] Slightly different is the problem of the Slavic youth, a coal miner, who must choose between love and learning. He hopes to escape drudgery by accepting a scholarship. "No more coal mines; no more dirty work," he vows. When the long-expected prize arrives, he must give it up because his ladylove weeps and protests.[7]

To the mountaineer not engaged in mining, the temptation to violate the hunting laws must be strong. A play or two deals with such a situation. Lucky the hunter who escapes the penalty for poaching. He may do so by his wits, however. It is common for hunter and game warden to face each other for a showdown. On a game preserve in the West Elk Mountains such a scene is enacted. Unannounced, the game warden enters a cabin in search of deer killers. He sits down unbidden to eat venison. In the meantime the hunter sneaks out to hide the carcass of the poached animal. Presently the tables are turned, and the warden is ordered out of the house.[8]

As in the case of the fast-dwindling Shakers of the East, the three-fifths of the population of Utah who call themselves Latter-day Saints make up a people with a faith, a revelation, and a tradition of their own. Essentially a religious folk, they have not made of religion a shackle. That is why they have never banned hymn-singing, proper dancing, and play acting. In fact, a tradition of play acting and playwriting goes back as early as 1830. From the start the elders put high value on the spiritual worth of recreation. Their first leader, Joseph Smith, "prophet, seer, revelator," organized a dramatic company and himself acted in a play at Nauvoo, Illinois. After the same pattern, his successor, Brigham Young, played the part of the High Priest in *Pizarro* and helped build the Salt Lake Theater in 1861. Other local wards, in the fifties and sixties, organized dramatic societies modeled on those of Salt Lake City. Rehearsals were opened with prayer, and smoking and drinking were forbidden. Like the Spanish missionaries long before them, they chose drama as the medium of instruction.

At first plays were pragmatic; that is, angled to provide spiritual yet wholesome release for the faithful. Few of these scripts have been preserved. If they have, only the faithful few knew them. Like other re-

ligious sects, the Mormons have found pageantry and
outdoor spectacle effective in presenting to their followers their concepts of the sacred and the pictorial.
Among these have been three pageant-dramas by J.
Karl Wood which dealt with the story of the prophets
Mormon, Elijah, and Lehi; while a fourth, *The Message of the Ages,* shown in the Tabernacle in 1930,
depicted the visit of the first Mormon missionaries to
the American Indians in the winter of 1830. This
centennial celebration was played for thirty nights by
fifteen hundred men, women, and children. In 1937
another huge pageant, shown also in the Tabernacle,
commemorated one hundred years of Mormonism in
Great Britain. More exalted is the Passion Play
modeled after that of Oberammergau: *The Zion
Canyon Easter Pageant.* An impressive centennial
pageant was presented at Salt Lake City as part of
the state centennial celebration in 1947.

It is interesting to note that, in the 1850's, anti-
Mormon prejudice was rife among the Gentile playmakers. Anything Mormon was sure to be bitterly re-
viled. Several specimens of melodrama show the intolerance of outsiders toward Mormon leaders and the
much-advertised cult of polygamy. Malicious jibes
at the Saints, aimed to amuse rough audiences hidden
in clouds of cigar smoke, showed by indirection the
tenacity of the sect to push forward its holy mission.
There was *The Mormons; or, Life at Salt Lake City,*
a stage piece written in 1858 by Thomas Dunn English,
in which the Mormons are slandered as hypocrites,
sensualists, polygamists, and even murderers. Those
who join the church do so from petty and venal
motives. Further, the Saints supposedly hate the
United States Army for killing their Prophet. Brigham
Young is pictured as a monster of duty, a despot who

glories in his power and misuses the gift of visions to command marriages. The plot which ties these diatribes together turns on the problem of rescuing from the iniquities of the Saints a newly married young sectarian, his wife, and their friend. A second play, *Deseret Deserted; or, The Last Days of Brigham Young,* written by (Club, goes farther in its venomous attack and shows up Brigham Young as a bloodthirsty drunkard who dreams of Mahomet's harem and emulates the splendor of his paradise. In the spirit of farce, the play is peppered with gags, puns, and witticisms.

Recent plays written by the faithful, to be presented before Mormon audiences, bear unmistakable qualities both spiritual and dramatic. These are given not only at the annual April conference but throughout the year in every ward of the church.[9] Often plays are written purposely to dramatize the M.I.A. (Mutual Improvement Association) theme for the year. As one sectarian put it, "At the beginning of each Mutual year, we have a passage of scripture which we carry through the months as a spiritual influence on our thinking." Among player groups The Deseret Theatre officially sponsors plays in Salt Lake City, while the Murray Players at Granger, Utah, directed by Nathan and Ruth Hale, put on plays written by this pair.

Plays accentuate positive themes and deal with Utah, the Mormons, and the pioneers. Many of them are moralities designed to impress and convert. As such they must conform to church policy as laid down by the Drama Committee of the General Boards of the Mutual Improvement Associations at Salt Lake City. Their Mutual officers, as a matter of fact, have controlled the stage since 1910. Briefly, plots must be moral and entertaining at the same time. This means a strict adherence to six commandments: No Deity on the stage; no blasphemy; no vulgar language; no use of tobacco, tea, or coffee; no killing for the sake of killing; and no condoning of divorce or infidelity.[10] Since 1929, the chosen pieces have been published from time to time as the *M.I.A. Book of Plays* and these have served as the source of plays for the ward or stake leaders throughout the church. A few years ago there were 531 wards in Utah.[11]

Through these plays there runs a quiet faith in the law as set down by the Prophets and in the rightness of divine guidance. Along the way they catch up so many pebbles of Mormon doctrine. Texts are sprinkled with allusions to implicit faith in prayer as an inner need. Nature often responds miraculously because the missionary spirit operates in trusting minds and hearts. Respect for elders is a recognized practice. The world, in short, is a theater where good works operate under the benevolent inspiration of Joseph Smith and Brigham Young.

While the background of most plays is a generalized area for a discourse on Mormonism, doctrinal points are touched upon lightly as in passing. References to disapproval of tobacco or snuff or alcohol, to hatred of light conduct, divorce, and the flouting of the teachings of Elders and the Prophets are casual. The plea and the message generally rise above the plot. The tone may be said to be more ethical than theological. At the same time a sureness of aim gives a confident flow to the stream of events as if the controlling purpose made all sequences feasible.

Strong indeed must be the historic sense of a people who have suffered and sacrificed for the faith. As in the plays of Joseph J. Cannon, stage settings picture the ports of Liverpool and Copenhagen where immigrants yearn "to get to Zion, to gather in the valleys of the mountains." They stand ready to face trials and death, spurred on by a faith "in the Gospel . . . the Lord."[12] Invariably they are driven by some domestic need. Always they plead, "Our children must be in Zion." And so, "Our faces are turned toward Zion," the supreme goal of their hopes and their dreams.[13]

Other plays, notably those by Nathan and Ruth Hale, dramatize the hard lot of the early Mormons as they battled their enemies in 1830 and later. Plural settings jump from settlement to settlement, from New York State to Salt Lake City. The stop at Nauvoo, Illinois, gave the wanderers a breathing spell for several years. Actual events are followed closely. Forced to leave the state of New York, they suffered martyrdom at the hands of mobs in Missouri who burnt down their houses, drove them naked on the march, massacred many of them, and vowed to exterminate the sect. When they finally reached Nauvoo, their prophet, Joseph Smith, was arrested and shot. But nothing stopped these hardy adventurers from pushing on and spreading their message.[14] Once settled in Utah, the pioneers continued to struggle against barren soil and drought and Indians.

In *It Shall Keep Thee* three generations of Mormons are projected against a background of southern Utah. The tone is light. The authors seek to prove that church members need not necessarily be long-faced. The love story which holds the plot together is subordinated to the major problems of the settlers.

A pioneer fable of faith and struggle is *Handcart Trails* (1940), by Ruth Hudson Hale. It rumbles along from Iowa City in the midsummer of 1856 to South Pass, Wyoming, late in October. The cast of twenty actors includes five members of the church, eight converts, and seven outsiders. The love story affords a pretext for showing opposite points of view. The maiden has given up everything for her religion while the rejected suitor stays outside the faith. Meanwhile, a band of English and Scottish converts join the party. They mean to carry all their possessions in two-wheel carts and they hope to reach Zion before the snow falls. Their faith stiffens or slackens with circumstance. Misery follows them to the mountains where snow and wind, hunger and sickness, cold and death tax their courage to the utmost. But they hold out. At last the rescue wagons come, and the Lord's promise will now be fulfilled. By his time the doubting lover is so impressed that he joins the Saints.

From the historic outline emerges the exhortation to courage and belief. But didacticism here flows over into melodrama. At one time the heroine firmly but solemnly declares, "I can never give them up! . . . I cast my lot with these people in Iowa and I go with them to the valley."

The familiar frame holds three successive generations. The types have been established. There are the blunt, knowing grandparents who look with sad eye upon the blunders and peccadillos of youth. They counteract the doubts and flippancies and challenges of the young. For in time the children will grow up and learn to see the truth. Meanwhile the parents carry on the business of everyday living, suffer the slings and arrows of adversity, the intolerance of neighbors, and the prejudices of the Gentiles. Meekly they offer prayers, serve one another unselfishly, and wait for deliverance from evil. True to instinct the children follow an unorthodox line while they question. They even go so far as to fling blasphemies in the face of hunger and danger and sometimes yearn to run off to more friendly surroundings.

Transparent devices are used in other plays to drive home a point. One author is too anxious to persuade, and overloads the moral. The contrast of those who stay at home and fail to achieve worldly acclaim as against those who climb the worldly ladder only to be kicked down to the bottom is naïve.[15] Another play-maker resorts to allegories of Time selling experience to Youth and Youth hesitating to pay the price but willingly going through the gate that leads to the M.I.A.[16] Still another scribe overworks coincidence in the casual finding of a twenty-dollar gold-piece at the bottom of a jam jar—which saves an indigent family from starvation. Indeed, the money has arrived promptly in answer to a child's prayer.[17] Finally, when action gives way to exhortation to demonstrate in the last act how strong can be the lure of the Mormon creed,[18] violence is done to dramatic credibility.

Despite the frequency of the pioneer theme, it is strange to note that so few plays are rooted in the soil. One, *The Rescue,* by Annie D. Palmer, reads like an indigenous transcript since it follows the line of Mormon legendry. The plot is well constructed and mounts to a plausible conclusion. The indecisions and conflicts are handled capably, while the talk of rattle-snakes, drought, crickets and gulls conveys a feeling for the dry and unfriendly soil. Between dejection and hope moves the tide of emotion. Despite the invasion of crickets, the harried settlers vow to stay on because "our prophet leader recognized this place as soon as he saw it as the one he had seen in visions, and with firm decision and prophetic voice he designated the spot where our temple shall be built." Finally comes the miracle from Heaven: a flock of gulls sweep in to devour the pests. Here pioneer life in a folk setting is honestly and earthily set down.

In most of these theatrical pieces a belief in the justice of divine intervention insures the inevitably happy ending. Now a neighbor with a jug of water arrives in time to minister to a sick family just as a flock of quail fly in. Now a sister declares herself ready to stay up all night to nurse a child with a fever. Wondrous, indeed, is the strange healing of a blood clot regarded as fatal, not to overlook the resuscitation of a frozen child. With a jolt such plots come to rest on a prayer, a reformation, a conversion, or a rescue.

One impressive dramatization, *Corianton* (1933), based upon the Book of Mormon and taken from the works of B. K. Roberts by Orestes Utah Bean, combines the pictorial with the doctrinal set against a foreign setting. Through a plot peopled with Aztecs from South America in the year 75 B.C. runs an alegory of good and evil. The Nephrites try to win back to their fold the dissenting Zoramites. Corianton, the missionary son of the High Priest, personifies Mormon tenacity. Tense scenes dealing with greed, defiance, denunciation, and love keep the action taut.

Above a score of plays not available to outsiders have been penned around the lives of the two Mormon leaders. Minor plays strike minor chords. But always the didactic finger pinches the tail of the plot.

In short, Mormon drama, as far as the collectible data show, is conspicuously employed to keep alive the faith of a people in their scriptures: *The Doctrine and Covenants of the Church of the Latter-day Saints.* While Utah has bred no Eugene O'Neill or Lynn Riggs, it has begot a group of ardent scribes whose earnest message means more to them than individual names. At the same time it must not be forgotten that art and propaganda are not necessarily incompatible.

It is possible for artistic merit and religious precept to be wedded.

From pageantry to didacticism runs the Rocky Mountain train of regional plays. Outdoor spectacle to match the mountains utters the grandiose in high stage terms. The picturesque works to the disadvantage of profundity. Though regional sketches on dudes and pioneers must needs be fleeting and rootless, nevertheless the Pony Express and the railway did serve to bring to the fore simple pioneer portraits of early Americans. As for the miner and his kin, the dramatic struggle seems to revolve about members of the family as they try their luck. For the miner it was generally a clear question of survive or perish. Patiently he waited for a "last-stand" strike, for that one more round to blast in opposition to the piteous whimper of wife or mistress. Finally, this most unique of regional blends ends in a collection of plays dealing with Mormon life and faith. It is natural for a people who cannot easily forget the pangs of ancestors to harp on the theme historic. The result for our theater has been a shelf of stage pieces ardent and competent. It is clear that these Mormon scribes have tried to be humane and didactic. It is regrettable that the pieces they have contrived are more conscious of the preachment than of the presence of desert and hill, of wind and rain.

1. *The Boomer*, By E. Stoker.
2. *Two Hundred Riders*, by Guernsey Le Pelley.
3. *The Machine Age*, by Estella Kelley.
4. *Shooting Star*, by Jack W. Lewis.
5. *Last Day of Grouse*, by Orin Mack.
6. *A Lady and the Law*, by George W. Cronyn.
7. *Trains*, by Evelyn Emig Mellon
8. *Sit Down to Supper*, by Glen Haley.

9. During the year 1941 there were some five thousand performances.

10. See the pamphlet on *Theatre Arts* by Dr. T. Earle Pardoe of Salt Lake City, published by the General Boards of the Mutual Improvement Associations (Salt Lake City, Utah, 1942), pp. 19-20.

11. Writers' Program, W.P.A., Utah; *a Guide to the State* (New York, 1941), p. 94.

12. *Love One Another,* by Joseph J. Cannon.

13. *The Emigrants,* by Joseph J. Cannon.

14. *Light for Tomorrow,* by Nathan and Ruth Hale.

15. *Success,* by Elsie C. Carroll.

16. *Through the Gate,* by Sybil Spande Bowen.

17. *Things Not Seen,* by Della Morrell.

18. *Conversion,* by Elsie T. Brandley.

XIII

Trail to Oregon

THE LAND is still young in the Pacific Northwest. It was only a century ago that hardy travelers drove their oxen and mules across the arid sands, forests, streams, and passes, and cut deep ruts into the Oregon Trail. In their wake they dropped the seeds which were to spring up into ballads, legends, songs, and tales. Today ancestral memories of trials and adventures, of friendly greetings and sudden death still haunt the countryside of Montana, northern Idaho, Washington, and Oregon.

In this segment of fertile territory people regard their flora tenderly. Seasonal pageants glorifying the fruits and flowers of the earth are notable. In Idaho the Cherry Festival in June, a pageant-parade with displays of luscious fruits, and the annual Flower Show in August testify to the gratitude of the inhabitants for the natural abundance of the earth. Portland, Oregon, goes so far as to stage masques, May revels, and, on the occasion of the rose celebration, the brilliant spectacle of *Rosario, the Pageant of the Rose* (1925),[1] which allegorically demonstrated the influence of the rose upon progress and civilization.

The Northwest is strongly region-conscious. Of pictorial-scenic celebrations with strong local flavor, four can be singled out as noteworthy. *The Spirit of Idaho* (1925), in eight episodes, presents the development of the state from the covered-wagon days to 1925. Two other pageants by Talbot Jennings draw on events from pioneer history. The first, *The Light on*

the Mountains (1923), is performed every ten years
by the student body of the University of Idaho at
Moscow with the aid of Indians who dance the old war
dances; the second, *Footprints West* (1926), is a
"marching pageant picturing the development of the
state from the days of the fur-traders to the era of
machinery." It should be pointed out that in one
scene of the latter the regional heroine, Sacajawea,
the Bird Woman, appears.

Missionaries, Indians, and whites gathered to take
part in the greatest of religious festivals ever staged on
the Pacific coast: *The Flotilla of Faith,* which was
done by the late Federal Theatre in Portland and Vancouver in June, 1939, as part of a three-day Catholic
centenary in the Northwest. The spectacle re-enacted
the arrival of an "appointed missionary for that part
of the diocese of Quebec which is situated between the
Pacific Ocean and the Rocky Mountains." After
months of travel the explorer-missionaries were supposed to have reached Vancouver where they were
welcomed by settlers, workers of the Hudson's Bay
Company, and the native Indian tribes. "Again Vancouver became a trading-post with Indians and trappers mingling at the stockade with bugle and drum
announcing the approach of the Blackrobes."[2]

The trail of the Indian in the Northwest is everywhere. Indian totem poles and place names testify
to his former possession of the region. Numerous
reservations house different tribes. The Indian's sense
of tribal unity finds easy outlet in the dance, the costume, and the scene. Some years ago a gigantic processional in which two thousand aborigines took part
as paid performers unrolled a wide panorama of events.
Westward Ho has been described as "a dramatized

version of what the Indian thinks the white man wants
to see."[3]

A closer view of the Indian as a human being shows
him grappling with an inherited ritual. If he conforms,
he may cause disaster; if he rebels, he may free himself.
Two playlets play up both sides. The first, set in a
grove of the Blackfoot country in northern Montana,
where once roved the Cheyennes, tells a bloody story.
Tenderly drawn are the portraits of the faggot woman,
an adopted captive of the tribe, and her son, Young
Hawk. One day he captures a Cheyenne warrior who
turns out to be his father. Soon after, the father, to the
horror of his ex-wife, unwittingly scalps his own son.
As in other Indian plays, the speech is clipped and
stylized.[4] The second offering narrows to a patch of
soil on the higher coast country of the Chinooks, a
people who dwell in settlements of permanent wooden
houses. In one hut live two brothers. They idolize a
wooden carved figure of wife to one, lover to the other.
In fact, they have made a ritual of their devotion. But
when two lost girls who have run away from undesirable suitors enter, the mourning husband undergoes
a change of heart, while the younger and more devoted
worshipper continues to pray before the image.
Throughout are heard the drumbeats and love songs
typical of the tribe.[5]

The story of the white man's possession of the region
has been told again and again in history and in fiction.
But the drama, always a laggard, has dealt scantily with
the westward marchers. In the last century melodrama
blustered through with a few lurid pieces about
the pioneers.[6] Within recent years one serious study
tells the familiar tale of emigrants who allowed nothing
to stop their journey to Oregon. Around the everyday struggles crowd the elemental fears, dangers,

hungers, and loves known in the 1840's. *Distant
Drums* (1932), by Dan Totheroh, restores a foothill
meadow in the Snake Indian country of 1848, some-
where between Fort Hall and Fort Boise, where "an
emigrant train of covered wagons has come to rest in
an improvised stockade drawn up in a circle and
chained together for protection." Indians surround
the place and demand the white squaw. What should
the pioneers do? The squaw is the wife of the leader
and is beloved by another. She decides to answer the
summons. When the desperate lover rushes after his
lady, he is killed. The train can now go through to
Oregon! Pale as the bare recital may be, the background of fact and character is established authenti-
cally. There is an attempt at showing human strengths
and failings. The horrors suffered during the march
are probably understated. Dramatically, however,
the action is thin and external.

More lurid and rousing was life in Montana after
the gold rush. The mining towns were roving ground
for prospectors, desperadoes, and vigilantes who moved
restlessly across the Far Western scene. Two lusty
plots by Betty Smith and Robert Finch unfold against
a wild and wintry landscape in a supply station in the
Montana Territory of 1864 and 1870 respectively. In
both plays a blizzard is blowing. Nervous bandits commit murder for gold dust and the map of a claim.
Then they hurriedly bury the body in the snow. But
before the curtain drops the two villains take the
wrong path to look for the claim. The mood of
Montana Night (1938) is one of tense expectancy,
and the characters are broadly sketched. The second
piece bears traces of fantasy. There is the prospector
who has exchanged some gold dust for supplies and is
waiting to return to his claim. An Easterner, who has

come overland to try his luck, talks of Indians and road agents. The station proprietor is worried over his partner's riding with gold across the divide. A dream motivates the rest of the action. The line in *Murder in the Snow* (1938) wavers a bit unsteadily and at times sinks to the level of old Western melodrama.

As Montana is primarily a cattle country, the cowboy rides through several plays. Of these, two, written by the writing pair just mentioned, are acted out in a bunkhouse on a Montana ranch starkly limned against a distant snow-capped peak. Cowpunchers sit around talking, joking, and singing. The light falls upon an injured cowboy who lies dying of a broken leg. He dreams of returning to his folks in Ioway. Suddenly a strange cowboy in black shirt, black tie and black sombrero quietly enters and sits near the dying cowpuncher. Not long afterward the Black Rider carries off the dead man on his white horse. Quietly from the narrative of *Western Night* (1938) issues a sense of something better to come in an imaginary world "beyond the valley."

Long winters make the cowpuncher gloomy and restive. When, in addition, the food is bad, the boss mean, the weather cold, and the bunkhouse draughty, it is hard to control him. The only effectual way to hold him is to entertain him or stir his fancy. Such a situation is brought to focus in *Summer Comes to the Diamond O* (1940). Bored cowboys listen with fascination to the spun yarns of a stranger in white. He tells romantic tales of his wanderings and of his big ranch, and invites all present to Mexico where it is always warm and where lovely senoritas are plentiful. But the dreams he arouses are blasted when a sheriff enters to arrest the fine talker who has never been out of the state. Not only is he touched in the head but he must answer charges for stealing a horse. The men will not be beaten. They need his yarns to keep up their spirits. Accordingly, they agree to bail him out.

Granted that these four pieces make much of the external clash of events and of background color to meet the demands of good theater, the linking of details about the Far West succeeds bit by bit in establishing mood and place. The last two plays stir the deeper sympathy by virtue of a play of fantasy.

Logging in the Northwest has long been a major occupation. *Timberline Tintypes* (1938), by Yasha Frank, a series of sketches revolving about logger life in Oregon, was put on by the Federal Theatre. Loggers are by nature an imaginative lot. Their folk yarns of animals and bull teams, their tall tales of the master logger, Paul Bunyan, form the subject of pageant and play as they do in regions elsewhere along the Canadian border. Two theatrical pieces in semi-satiric vein deride the weaknesses that go with giant-hood. In the first play the giant towers above the peaks of the Rockies. When at work he creates uncouth lumberjacks who in their lusty way roar:

> We is th' lumberjacks
> Ear-chawin' reptyles.

Paul's prime fear is that his men will fall for women. He does everything he can to avoid this calamity. Accordingly, he hopes to stupefy his workers by gluttonous feeding. Comical is the scene which describes doughnuts large as rubber tires rolling off the machines in mass production. But feeding does not satisfy his men. During Paul's absence, women are admitted, and his men pair off. Then religion and finance combine to render the giant powerless. He shrinks to human size, learns the tricks of business and politics, and turns bank president in a poor community. Guilty of the human weakness of larceny, he is expelled by the enraged women. At this point the plot takes an unexpected turn. Paul's strength now returns and his men go back with joy to lumbering while the women demand alimony. This light burlesque delivered in rapid-running lines of verse points to the obvious conclusion that gianthood is too weak to withstand the onslaughts of femininity, theology, and finance.[7]

Paul and the Blue Ox, an ambitious spectacle play in eight scenes, by E. P. Conkle, done at the University of Iowa, presents Babe the Blue Ox resting above the rim of pines and hill. Paul is pictured as fearful of discontent which might lead to revolution. Paul would go logging in the Big Auger and even harness the Aurora Borealis. An equally powerful giant, Pat the King of Europe, is introduced. Four of his followers scheme to sow discontent among Paul's men. The loyal followers, who have been warned again and again never to think, eventually discover their rights. The rest is obvious. After the loggers have left in a body, Paul swears a mighty oath to get even with the traitor. He overcomes his rival, Shot Gunderson, the Iron Man of the Mountain. But his men are lost to him forever. Judged by the script, this play shows a lack of balance in the scenes. The action straggles and aims to convey a sense of bigness by hell-roaring. Besides, there is a touch of comic sophistication in viewing gianthood as dull-witted and in sustaining the point that brute strength without brains cannot hold out against the superior wiles of sex.

Level with the earth stand the afflicted folk from

"No More Frontier," by Talbot Jennings, Drake University Theatre, Des Moines, Iowa

ranch and forest in the Cascades who must struggle against malign circumstances to keep alive. These gaunt, careworn victims are sometimes articulate, sometimes reticent—and sometimes resigned. Life to them is bitter as gall. Representative plays strike the sad chord. There is the trackwalker's wife who has become embittered toward life following an accident involving her husband. She conceives an insane hatred of God. In retaliation against what she calls Fate, she refuses to swing the lamp that will halt a train approaching a landslide. And the train crashes.[8] As the motivation is merely announced, the ending seems theatrical. Another wife, whose husband has hardly spoken to her for some time, and who has taken to drink, feels she cannot go on. But she never probes the cause of her husband's misery. Had she questioned a lonesome sheepherder, she might have learned that the man had been slowly going blind since their marriage.[9]

Elsewhere, on a ranch, a tuberculous son dies in poverty, his condition made worse by snow and rain, and by the greed of a rich neighbor. The disgruntled father can only whimper, "We slave . . . and all we get is just a living."[10] In the forest dwells an embittered grandfather who is constantly badgered by his son and by his son's wife about his pension. He feels he is too old to live. Before signing off, the old man saves his beloved grandson from arrest. As he dies of poison, he mutters something about big pines cracked by the wind, "broken . . . on . . . the mountain."[11]

More theatrical, and reminiscent of *Trifles*, by Susan Glaspell, is a minor tragedy from the Coast Range. A husband, the sheriff, and relatives are searching for the missing woman. By a slow gathering of feminine clues the wife's cousin concludes that the woman had been murdered by her husband. Follows the confession. He did it because his wife's nagging became intolerable. What brought on the crisis was an inhuman act. When he fed his dog in the cabin "she fetched a tea kettle of hot water an' throwed it on the dog." This was too much for him, and he killed her.[12]

On such elemental themes rest these latter playlets. The core problems of land dwellers seem imbedded in the hard rock of their habitat. Unable to mold their own lives, they are forced to submit to forces which bear down upon them. Nature overwhelms them literally. The mood is thus grim and gray.

The lovely panorama harbors more gloom than sunlight; happiness seems curiously absent from the affairs of the men. When reality can no longer be borne, fantasy enters to befriend the victim or to spin the yarns which will cause momentary forgetfulness. Luckily, the pioneer, the miner, the cowboy, the logger, and the rancher are never idealized.

Limited as the dramatic repertory of the Northwest may be, the cycle is practically complete from seasonal celebration to the drama of folk close to the soil. If play after play were placed in a pattern as in a mosaic, one would discover an index to the spirit of the region. Unfortunately, no one play thus far has blended sky, earth, and Westerner into one potent whole vibrant with Western stir and color and speech.

And how painfully restricted has been the choice of stage types. Had our playmakers possessed the same ardor for exploration as had the Forty-niners, they long ago would have drawn characters from a humanity which includes sheepmen, cattlemen, farmers, dairymen, hunters, and ne'er-do-wells. They also would have discovered themes and plots in the lives of the Chinese, the Japanese, the Basques, and the Finns, not to overlook the old settlers scattered over timberland, grassland, and mountain pass.

It is unfortunate that the dramatic output of the Northwest does not keep pace with the theatrical activity of the region. Such excellent playhouses as the Civic Theater of Portland, together with three others in Seattle, namely, The Repertory Playhouse, the Showboat Theater, and the much-advertised Penthouse Theater of the University of Washington contain all the equipment needed to create an experimental drama built from good, native material. Instead, repertoire has followed the safe, conservative lines of the classics and of Broadway hits. Play lists show no instances of regional or indigenous pieces. Far more courageous was the policy of the Federal Theatre when it offered *Timberline Tintypes, Prologue to Glory, See How They Run,* and similar offerings. Happily, experimental pieces and original one-acters have been put on by the Montana Masquers from the state university in Missoula and, since 1943, by the Tryout Theater in Seattle for the encouragement of new plays by new writers. Yet the results, worthy as they are, have not justified the hopes of the promoters of the regional drama.

1. By Doris Smith.
2. Flanagan, Hallie, *Arena* (New York, 1940), pp. 311 ff.
3. Writers' Program, W.P.A., *Oregon; End of the Trail* (Portland, Ore., 1940), p. 39.
4. *Kills-with-Her-Man,* by Hartley Alexander.
5. *The Wooden Wife,* by Alice Henson Ernst.
6. See the next chapter.
7. *Paul Bunyan,* by R. L. Stokes.
8. *The End of the Trail,* by Ernest H. Culbertson.
9. *In the Darkness,* by Dan Totheroh.
10. *Cloudburst,* by J. Carl Weaver.
11. *Broken Pines,* by Charles Hilton.
12. *It Took a Woman,* by Laura Miller.

XIV

Pacific Panorama

THAT THE Golden State, teeming with natural abundance from olives to oranges, from roses to redwoods, in a valley lying between high ranges, should likewise supply the world with a crop of sunkist drama seems a foregone conclusion. Nothing is impossible in California. Regionally there are two Californias: the North of the gold rush, the mining camps, the Sierras of fiction, and San Francisco, town, port, and grove; and the sunny South with its more placid valleys and deserts, the land of Ramona, of Spanish friars and missions, Los Angeles, and San Diego. In fact, southern California may be considered a projection of New Mexico; a garden in a reclaimed desert.

The mixed history of the region has been one succession of upheavals: Indian clashes, Spanish rule, and Anglo invasions from the East. So rapidly did one civilization impinge upon the other that the traditions and cultures did not blend but rather remained separate. Consequently, the aggregate of myth and legend still presents a puzzle to the historian and a hunting ground to the literary explorer. Baffled like other observers, the play scribbler hardly knows how to utilize the wealth before his eyes. No Bret Harte of the drama has appeared to point the way.

It was not until the Anglos and the Spaniards learned to live amicably that the play spirit began to function freely. Spanish pageantry, with its color and gravity, began to reappear in natural amphitheaters in grove and woodland. These fiestas suggested to the newcomers similar but colossal dramatizations of nature myths, Indian legends, allegories, and even such topical subjects as *Wally for Queen,* the story of Edward VIII. The result has been a line of rich and varied spectacles mounted on more than thirty stages in amphitheaters on hillside and mountain slope, oak grove and redwood forest.

Most famous of outdoor spectacles is the grove play. This fusion of masque, opera, and drama is mounted lavishly against a backdrop of redwoods. From the foot of a wooded hillside, framed by trunks of enormous trees to form a natural proscenium, rise natural platforms in receding order. In such a setting the annual play is given by the Bohemian Club in its private redwood grove in Sonoma County, seventy miles north of San Francisco. The history of this institution is worth a note. In 1879 a group of writers, musicians, printers, and actors met to put on an annual "midsummer high jinx," both literary and musical. After 1902 the open-air picnic became the formalized grove play. The first to be shown was fittingly called *The Man in the Forest,* by Charles K. Field. It dramatized a legend of Indian tribes. Since then other librettos have been written by distinguished writers. For the most part the productions have stressed outdoor pictorial effects, grandiose dialogue, and primordial scenery. Only five scripts to date have touched directly on native character and on regional themes. Other grove plays include the Mount Tamalpais Play and the annual Semper Virens Club Forest Play in Santa Cruz County.

It is but natural that primordial scenery should unfold the aboriginal Indian. Indian myths lend themselves to outdoor presentation. In time a white man was bound to discover the real Indian as fit subject for reflective drama. The first craftsman to recognize the dramatic value of the life and lore of the Indian as material "sprung from our own soil ready to hand" was Mary Austin. By way of example in 1911 she wrote a long play in free verse set in the foothills of the Sierras: *The Arrow Maker*. Here she tells the story of the Medicine Woman of the Paiutes crossed in love. "Her heart is full of bitterness and there is no room in it for the gods." The Chisera, "the mateless woman denied love and children," stands as the embodiment of feminine will. Her constant lament rises like a personal plea. The play exploits a layer of Indian beliefs and customs; but of Indian psychology, only one acquainted intimately with the inner life of the Pacific Indian can presume to say how much.

In *Fire* (1914), a drama in three acts written "in broken verse and with a folk rhythm,"[1] glimmer mystic intimations of man and creation. The dramatized tale is one of many legendary animal creations of the coyote current in the valleys of central California. Briefly outlined, Coyote carries in its mouth a flame which must be passed on. An unhappy Indian husband who absents himself from public worship secretly, yet joyfully, seeks the company of the outlawed Beast Brother. At the same time the angry elders of the tribe pronounce their red brother delinquent, accuse the Beast of profaning the fire, and bring charges against the heretic. He will not renounce the Beast Brother. Unrepentant and still holding high the flaming brand, he and his squaw march off. As in *The Arrow Maker* the same insistence on personal volition, the same defiance of whatever restrains the good impulse, rings boldly from the pages of this beast fable.

Based on an Indian theme *The Acorn-Planter* (1916), a grove play by Jack London, focuses upon the first man of men, Red Cloud, who would make life more abundant. As he lies dying he marks the passing of time. In the white man he recognizes a brother acorn planter and the possessor of a superior life formula. Amid the sober Indian talk, stylized and interspersed with lyrics, occur such passages as "I am the Fire-Bringer; I stole the fire from the ground squirrel and hid it in the heart of the wood." The play ends on a chord of hope.

> Lo, the New Day dawns,
> The day of brotherhood.
> The day when all men
> Shall be kind to all men,
> And all men shall be the sowers of life.

More operatic than real, this forest play does not presume to explore Indian mores or psychology. Instead, native braves, heroically projected, incarnate earth poetry, semimystic and semioracular. The Indian is but a peg for high-keyed oratory.

Another dramatized creation myth of the California Indians embodies their race concept of the First Man. Indians constantly revert to the beginning of things. When the world was young and before men were yet created, no hope lived in the heart of the Eagle Mother. To her was given the task of guarding an eagle's egg which would breed a son. When six enemies crept in to steal the egg and maliciously danced around the mother, she chased them off. On the seventh day a red cloud floated across the scene to herald the arrival of the Eagle Child and with him the hope of the race of immortal men to come.[2]

An Indian myth which aims to explain queer noises heard in a canyon is embodied in the pageant-drama called *Tahquitz,* which is presented periodically in the Tahquitz Bowl. An evil spirit haunts Mount San

Jacinto. At the same time a Cahuilla Indian who had
been killed for abducting Amutat, the most beautiful
girl of the tribe, returns to seek her or some equally
beautiful maiden.

Whereas the Indian pageant and the play on Indian
themes have been formal products manufactured by
English-writing scribes in recent times, the Spanish
fiesta was a matter of slow growth from dance and song
during the period of colonization by Spanish pioneers.
Within this outpost of empire, Spaniards and Mexi-
cans of New Spain enjoyed outdoor entertainment.
Their missions permitted the fandango with choral
accompaniment. In this century a picture of the missions has been drawn broadly in *The Mission Play,* a
festival of song, dance, and episode. For ten weeks
each year, between 1912 and 1932, at San Gabriel
Mission near Los Angeles, this three-act performance
re-created the story of the founding of Christian influence in the West. Scenes showed the first settlement
at San Diego in 1769, under the firm leadership of the
Franciscan, Fra Junipero Serra; the missions at their
peak in 1784; and the decline of the missions after
secularization.

Since 1920, except during the war years, another
production, *The Pilgrimage Play,* has been presented
annually in summer in the Pilgrimage Theater, set
in El Camino Real Canyon in Hollywood. The story
of Christ reverberates from the hills in twelve scenes,
with a prologue and epilogue.

The land of Ramona insists on repeating the stirring
plea in behalf of the Indian year after year amid the
settings of the story. Since 1923, in the Ramona Bowl
at Hemet, the open-air *Ramona Pageant,* originated
by the late Garnet Holme and based upon the novel

by Helen Hunt Jackson, impresses natives and tourists by its solemn ceremonial. The annual presentation has been resumed since the termination of the war.

Contemporary playlets which glimpse life under Spanish occupation re-create the atmosphere of pastoral frontier and romantic love. One such piece introduces the foreign *renegado,* guilty of love and treachery, escaping in an American vessel and being subsequently captured and tried in court. The long speeches in genteel verse, interpolated with lyrics, ring with Shakespearean cadences.[3] Equally exciting must have been the game of smuggling furs across the frontier. Trappers like Kit Carson had to use their wits to get out of tight places when "gringos" and "greasers" clashed. To escape paying the mandatory license fees for furs, Kit and his fellows seek sanctuary in a church.[4] There Kit meets the lovely Josefa, who promises to see him again that night. But his major concern is to get a rope and two horses with which to flee. Fidelity in love, when suspected, may turn tragic. In another play,[5] the mistress, the maid, and the *amante* form the usual classic trio. The weak caballero, upbraided for faithlessness, is stabbed by the maid after her mistress exposes his treachery. Notwithstanding, she regrets her act. Culturally the Spanish period links California with New Mexico and Florida.

Then came the Anglos. When gold was discovered by a workman near Coloma, throngs of *Americanos* descended like locusts upon California. By 1850 gamblers, fortune hunters, and actors had swarmed into the state hungry for wealth and excitement. After grubbing in the hills, miners stood ready to scatter gold dust in gambling saloons and in cheap fandango houses. The rough spectators also applauded

Richard III, their favorite play, in "makeshift theaters of the mines as well as in the 'histrionic temples' "[6] of San Francisco. Here their insatiable appetite doted on all varieties of farce, comedy, melodrama, and travesty. Wildly they cheered the extravaganzas and wagon shows from across the mountains and the farces of topical allusion like *The First Night; or, The Virgin of California* (1856).[7]

Local extemporizations on the Don Juan legend like *The Lady-Killer of San Francisco* (1855), or a loose putting together of local materials on gulling an Englishman in *The Duke of Sacramento* (1856), or *A Live Woman in the Mines; or, Pike County Ahead!* (1857)—these reveal the raw beginnings of a local drama of authentic character and picturesque lingo.[8]

At the same time short farcical afterpieces on the gold rush began to take shape. With them arrived a set of robust stage types who shot their way through the melodramas of the period. They exhibited the usual primitive traits and strong passions, yet betrayed human longings and weaknesses. Their speech was free and racy as was natural to men who passed their days amid rowdy camps in the absence of women. Types crystallized. The tough miner is shown up in plays as externally rough but tender within. He was the "bad man" who used oaths liberally but worshipped babes and women from afar. While he might hearken to the voice of morality, he lived the life of the sinner between spasms of remorse. Whenever a good woman arrived, the gold hunter idolized her. For it was she who generally befriended the rough miners, spread cheer and fellowship in the saloon, but remained apart like a chaste goddess. Sometimes, indeed, she succumbed to love and then had to leave her world of men for her special choice of mate.

In the absence of love, friendship became the ruling passion and bond between men. The true and stead-fast partner who sacrificed his own life for his friend became a familiar type in oral tradition as in fiction and in plays. In the standard repertory of the seventies and later, the miner, the gambler, and the widow hardened into stereotypes. Beneath the clash of in-cident and coincidence, improbable as they sound to modern ears, runs a commentary on the manners of the Gold Coast which did not preclude current undis-guised prejudices against an alien race.

One strikingly regional figure of the day who darted across the stage at intervals was the Oriental or "heathen Chinee." His presence must be explained by the fact that, after the discovery of gold, thousands of Chinese immigrants came to the West Coast to serve as miners, laundrymen, farm hands, and do-mestics. By 1852 there were twenty thousand of them, respectable and faithful workers. Two years later their coming was resented by unemployed native miners and their presence denounced as contract "coolie" labor. They were ridiculed as the "pigtail," "John Chinaman," and "the almond-eyed Celestial." Riots broke out. So intense had the feeling grown by 1871 that the residents of Los Angeles perpetrated a Chinese massacre in which nineteen Chinese were hanged by a gang of mobsters on the charge that one of them had shot an American.[9] Even after this event riots did not cease. With shadings that vary but little, the defer-ential "Chinee," a target of white prejudice, material-ized in several plays of the time. His was, of course, a minor role.

Prior place must be given to indigenous characters created by early recognized dramatists. The first full length play on California life is generally attributed to Augustin Daly. *Horizon* (1871), a melodrama, presents the improbable story of the disappearance of a worthless father with his daughter from Washington Square to the wild settlements of the Far West. Here, amid the rough Westerners, the father is killed but the charming daughter is protected by the "bad man." Along the way one detects rude portraits almost real. The speech is natural and the plot well contrived. Beneath the negligible story runs a cynical view of the "dirty" Indian and the "crafty Chinee."

Bret Harte followed with another improbable story of a repentant father in search of the son whom he had driven from his home: *Two Men of Sandy Bar* (1876), taken from his story, "Mr. Thompson's Prodigal." From a regional point of view the center of interest falls on the laundryman, a heathen Chinee as unreal as an apparition. The language of Hop Sing sounds like bad pidgin English. "Me plentee washee shirtee... always litee litee on shirtee alle time . . . me no likee tomollow."

An intermediate piece which enjoyed a vogue in this country and abroad was *My Partner* (1879), by Bartley Campbell. The absurdity of the plot is beyond telling. Here the bond of partners is sundered by love for the same woman. Sharply contrasted are such regional figures as the rough-natured miner and the libertine. Throughout the story abuse is heaped upon the head of the Chinese whose conversation is comically stagy. "Me too muchee chin chin, alle samee Melican man."

Two plays which reflect the riotous living along the Sierra frontier and show the influence of Bret Harte came from the pen of Joaquin Miller. High lights and shadows fall across the once-popular *Danites in the Sierras* (1877). Here again appears the widow before whom the rough miners grovel in awe. They are piqued because she befriends a young boy who is, in reality, a girl in disguise. She is one of many who are being hunted by the Danites, a secret society of Mormons ostensibly resolved to murder the enemies of the Prophet. (The Mormons denied the existence of any such secret society of fanatics.) Again "a helpless little Heathen" named Washee Washee is the butt of the white man's dislike of Orientals.

The second play, *Forty-Nine: an Idyl Drama of the Sierras* (1882), unfolds a wild, preposterous plot. Pathetically drawn is the patient Argonaut who struggles to see his wife, his babe, and his dog once more. Amid gambling scenes stalk such regional puppets as the pioneer who sticks to his tunnel even after hope is gone, the overworked maid, the saloon-keeper's daughter, and the old Negro servant. A moral exhortation on success closes this museum piece. Openly expressed once more is the author's prejudice against Mormons and Chinese.

Wrought in the same style and also set in the Sierra is *The Girl of the Golden West* (1905), a glittering melodrama by David Belasco, which closes the cycle of gold-rush dramas. It is the old story of the girl and the bandit. Again the female keeper of the saloon, chaste and self-reliant, evokes the homage of the miners. But she falls in love with an outlaw. Although condemned to be hanged, he is freed by the gang, and the couple leave for the East. Love has reclaimed villainy. Forgotten at last are those "undesirable" outsiders, the Mormons, Indians, Chinese, and others.

Of late, shadows have begun to fall across the terrestrial paradise, to darken the sky and landscape of hawks, buzzards, and coyotes. In a number of recent sketches the unpleasant facts about men who still

seek gold, who struggle with the earth and wrestle
with personal problems, the fruit pickers, farmers,
ranchers, have reached the stage. In short, the "lonely
lives blown across the trail,"[10] in the words of Mary
Austin, have finally blown into the theater. Against
the desert move eccentric mortals. There is the whimsical hermit, Death Valley Scotty, who, as legend has
it, lived alone in the early years of this century in a
tin shack near his gold mine and not far from his
friends, the Hopi Indians. One day, led on by revenge,
two brothers enter this secret zone. When they meet
Scotty, they learn the facts about their uncle, an ex-
partner of Scotty. He had been shot when he grew
wild with the heat. Just as the two strangers raise
pistols to shoot the veteran miner, they are shot by
Hopi Indians.[11] The story mounts steadily to the
climax.

Allegorically presented in a minor sketch is Youth
driven on by restless desires to take the trail across the
Mojave Desert with Hope and Memory as guides.
The figures and background are real.[12]

In more realistic vein is the couple on the
desert discouraged by poor soil and plagued by wind.
For ten years the wife has seen the wind kill everything, including her children. Further, she has felt
the power of the desert that "keeps wrapping itself
about you until you become part of it." She decides
to run off. At the last moment she sees through the
villainy of her lover and decides to stay on. Curiously,
the experience has purged her.[13]

More acute are the problems of ranch wives and
daughters in a fertile country. Sometimes they are
the victims of their own habits; sometimes they are
marked for death. Three instances will suffice. In a
remote ranch house an unhappy mountain woman,

married for thirty years, has always been hopeful of flight at a given moment. The time is now ripe. As she was brought up from the valley into the mountains by a peddler's wagon, so she has sworn to return by the same route and the same conveyance. According to a standing agreement she asks the peddler to take her down. But when the husband in the fields whistles three times, she sinks into a chair and moans, "I'm not coming. . . . I'm not coming." Habit has chained her.[14]

In the prune country a farmer's wife, against the orders of her husband, is feeding a tramp. Suddenly he notices a cracked teapot on the upper shelf. Experience has taught him that stolen money is hoarded there. He upbraids the wife for stealing but carries off the money. Then the wife vows that "it ain't goin' to be no more."[15]

Pathetic is the incident of the daughter of a wealthy grape dealer in the vine country. She primps before the mirror on the day she is to parade as queen of the grape festival. As her parents dote on her fair looks, a shot, meant for her father, is fired through the window by a rival racketeer.[16] And death has smitten the vineyards of sunny California.

To sum up: the three cultural streams, Indian, Spanish, and American, have flowed down the years along parallel lines. This fact may explain why no distinguished cargo has been delivered. It is not difficult to separate the three resulting types of plays. First, the grove play which furnishes natural scenery as background to grandiloquent words and music is California's attempt to match art with nature. The impetus to dramatize the life of the aborigine honestly and movingly started with the earnest pleading of Mary Austin, observer and student of Indian life. Secondly, the Spanish mission period in Western history added a dash of color and gravity to native theme and costume. Finally, conceived in hatred as a target of the white man's prejudice, is the quaint Oriental who lived his hour as a regional puppet.

Among the creators of a wild, frontier melodrama number Augustin Daly, Bret Harte, Joaquin Miller, and David Belasco. Their footprints still shine in the sawdust trail of the gaslit era. What stultified their inventions of yesteryear was rant, reverence, and revenge. Notwithstanding the silly and boisterous plots, there is ample evidence of faithful and vigorous reporting of the mood and manners of the time and the locale.

Far different in approach and effect is the theater of two humanitarian forerunners: Mary Austin and Jack London. They did not hesitate to draw upon modern lore and psychology to create character somewhat after their own egos.

In line with other theaters of the country, the non-commercial play directors at Pasadena, Santa Barbara, and Carmel, as well as established university groups in the state, have recognized the need of writing one-act plays "in modern colloquial idiom expressive of the contemporary American scene."[17] Laudable as this aim must sound, there has been little effort to exploit local and regional material in spite of numerous annual theater tournaments.

To say that the drama, far less than fiction, has hardly caught the sweep and meaning of the California landscape is to state a fact. Perhaps, when the Pacific playwrights cast the sun out of their eyes and merge fertility, beauty, and design into a happy synthesis, the Golden State may deliver a crate of plays native as the coyote and the burro and indigenous as the scrubby mesquite in the desert.

1. Mary Austin, *Earth Horizon* (Boston, Mass., 1932), pp. 320-21.

2. *The Golden Eagle Child,* by Joyce E. Lobner.

3. *The Renegade,* by Isaac Flagg.

4. *Bride Out of Beaver,* by Grace Williams.

5. *Miguel,* by Glenn Hughes.

6. George R. MacMinn, *The Theater of the Golden Era in California* (Caldwell, Idaho, 1941), p. 84.

7. Constance Rourke, *Troupers of the Gold Coast, or the Rise of Lotta Crabtree* (New York, 1928), p. 116.

8. MacMinn, *op. cit.,* pp. 236-37, 239-40, 246-51.

9. Writers' Program, W.P.A., *Los Angeles; a Guide to the City and its Environs* (New York, 1941), p. 41.

10. In *Earth Horizon* (Boston, 1932), Austin, *op. cit.,* p. 296.

11. *Death Valley Scotty,* by James Milton Wood.

12. *Desert Smoke,* by Dwight L. Clarke.

13. *The Wind,* by Agnes Emelie Peterson.

14. *Day's End,* by Alice Pieratt.

15. *The Cracked Teapot,* by Charles C. Dobie.

16. *Good Vintage,* by Dan Totheroh.

17. From a circular issued by the Berkeley Playmakers, 1940.

XV

A Note on Rural Plays

THE NEED for grouping plays, as herein followed, should not be permitted to shut out a pack of dramatic pieces because they fail to indicate locality. Such waifs and strays move within or near a regional boundary notwithstanding. The fact that the setting may not be registered is no sign that the play is not rooted. Let there be no mistake about that. The broadest designation of a setting, contained in such prefatory phrases as "west of the Mississippi," "on a mountain slope," "latitude so and so," may be misleading or spurious. Unless the text confirms these designated tags by native customs, lore, and speech, the regionality may be in question: a mere label with no actual tie-up. More restricted, and therefore more recognizable, will be the area indicated by such common designations as "a colonial farmhouse," "any farm district," "a chicken farm," "berry fields," and others.

Across this continent there are thousands of parcels of land and properties which answer to such descriptions. What makes them truly regional for stage identification is the set of concurrent clues within the text. Allusions to snow-capped mountains, a hamlet near by, a town or wood or road, together with passing references to sagebrush, cactus, dust storms, or to intense cold, will help point to some patch of ground or neck of woods within a definite region.

In the absence of other evidence to yield a native clue, one way of identification is by localisms or provincialisms taken in bulk. The experienced eye and ear can hardly fail to recognize the familiar "paw and maw," "air ye," "purty," and "as well as common" as coming from the southern Appalachians; the broad "a," "git" for get, "ben" for been, "jest" for just, from the Middle West; the foreign locutions like *bueno, bonita, poco, hombre,* and *savvy,* which clearly point to the Southwest.

As a matter of fact, an unrooted play is an anomaly. If the action runs its course in a boardinghouse or country home, or some indeterminate spot between town and village, with characters assembled from scattered points, the play is neither here nor there. But where, as in the case of *Let Freedom Ring,* the people are forced to uproot themselves at the risk of losing their earthy freshness, the struggle to keep their rural selves intact does not negate regional qualities. Finally, when characters exhibit ingrained habits and traits associated with a supposed region, unnamed, and seem almost outgrowths of earth which may be identified as New England or the Midwest or the Pacific coast—in short, when their folkways are unmistakably authentic, we have the elements of a rooted or regional play.

It must be stressed that the rural or rustic drama has begotten a bastard species which flourishes in the hinterland. Thousands of such plays are listed in publishers' catalogues under the heading of "rube" plays. Generally the plot unfolds a battle of wits between city slicker and country rube with the odds in favor of the country cousin. The stock situation is reversed with glee. Characters rush in and out, blurt forth blatantly the most glib nonsense, romp and frolic to slapstick until the curtain drops on a mad finale.

Most prolific dispenser of rustic antics is Walter

Ben Hare. He has penned about 250 comedies for a far-flung country and small-town audience. Two of his successes will define the type: *Deacon Dubbs* from Sorghum Center, West Virginny, written in 1916, and the ever-popular *Aaron Slick from Punkin Crick,* copyrighted in 1919 and signed by the pen name of Lieutenant Beale Cormack. *Deacon Dubbs* uses such stock situations as giving the deacon an oversupply of punch supposed to be water, holding down an auction bidder in an old well, the sudden appearance of an estranged husband to interrupt a wedding, the hired girl running after the farm hand to pop the question— all sentimental sauce for good, red hokum. The actors recall in caricature early American and British stock types like the big, jovial warmhearted farmer (Joshua Whitcomb), the wolf in sheep's clothing (villain), the brave little schoolmarm, the village cutup, the richest girl in town, other sensual females, and the hired girl in love with the hired man. The story of extortion and arrest, punctuated by moments of hilarity, ends in the death of the villain, the promise of a double wedding, and noisy country dancing.

Most popular of "rube" comedies, said to have been staged above fifty thousand times, is *Aaron Slick of Punkin Crick,* "an old tale of rural virtue triumphant, of city vice thwarted."[1] Amid sport and bustle on the Oklahoma farm, the crooked speculator falls into his own net, outwitted by old Aaron, "slicker'n a corn-stalk fiddle." Hilarity runs unchecked over such bromides as screaming at sight of a mouse, falling into a pan of dough, and hiding in a clothesbasket. In and out dash the stereotypes: the charming widow waiting for a proposal, the regular tomboy, the crooked speculator, the wily rube, and the hesitant wooer. The humor is gauche. "Gee whiz, I'm so glad, I could kiss a Dutchman." The sentimental smear over Punkin Crick where "everybody knows everybody else and likes everybody and is just as happy as the day is long" is downright ludicrous, even in a farce. A sudden proposal, together with plans for "going back to Oklyhomy," brings on the final curtain.

Another practitioner, Henry Rowland, has penned a number of rustic comedies with glib, singing titles. Some of his pieces are included among the following jingling hilarities. Taken at random from publishers' catalogues they read: *Silas Green from New Orleans, Silas Smidge from Turnip Ridge, Mrs. Tubbs from Shantytown, The Cousin from Coon Ridge, Aunt Minnie from Minnesota, Amy from Arizona, Sophie from Sandysville, Sunbonnet Jane of Sycamore Lane, Aunt Billie from Texas, Redheaded Royalty from Arkansas, Ma Simpkins of Simpkinsville*, and lots more.

Suggested by these yokel titles have come a number of better written and more probable plays on the country slicker. The victory is still with the country oaf in a plot supposedly funny. Character is still subordinated to run of events, while the sense of place is hardly developed. Two examples will suffice. A farmer near Chicago has claimed the balance due on twenty acres of land. His claims are ignored. To his annoyance a highway has been built across his land and the land resold to the state. In anger the owner shuts off the highway, fences off his section, and builds a tollgate across it. His sons collect quarters from passing cars. The farmer now has the baffled state officials at his mercy. In the end he has collected an exorbitant sum of money.[2] In the second instance, rural folk outwit the city sharper. By circulating rumors of rich oil deposits, they sell a ranch at a high price. In the end the rumors prove to be unfounded.[3]

Rafts of cheap rural plays, designed to tickle the yokels until they howl themselves hoarse, are being dispensed across the country. That they enjoy wide popularity is no cause for tears; they are in a sense a measure of the dramatic taste of the provinces. Producers and directors, when pressed for a choice, select the ready-made piece which brings the loud laugh and drops cash into the box office. Especially in a time of war do these sure-fire numbers, these rube pieces entitled *Uncle Josh Perkins, Simple Simon Simple, The Late Mr. Early, Aunt Abby Answers an Ad,* and *The Wacky Widow,* draw crowds to the footlights.

The prospect is not too gloomy. Here and there in some unexpected quarter, some college laboratory, community playhouse, clubhouse, and trade union hall, efforts are being made to reject the yokel standard for an honest projection of the farmer, the mountaineer, the cowboy, the riverman, the sharecropper, the miner, and the like. In fact, a new brood of native folks, rooted in the ground and stretching from ocean to ocean, is sprouting in our drama. What is needed is more intensive cultivation and wider dispersion. One condition is paramount. The rural audience must be taught, if it does not already know, to distinguish the true from the false, the genuine from the shoddy; and to accept the emergent regional species as a truthful mirror of men and manners in our country and in our own time.

1. "Aaron Slick of Punkin Crick," *Life* (March 14, 1938), pp. 24-27.
2. *Country Slicker,* by Howard Buermann.
3. *Fingerprints,* by Myrtle Giard Elsey.

XVI

Up From Roots

IT WAS NOT so long ago that American scholars looked dubiously at the American drama. They raised quizzical eyebrows as they asked whether any such thing actually existed. Today, no doubt, many are asking if there is a regional drama in the United States. It is hoped that the preceding chapters have answered this query. Any attempt to explore the drama of the backwoods, the small towns, the hamlets, prairies, mountains, and deserts, will uncover a heap of material neglected if not ignored by the ordinary investigator. For the seeds of a local and native drama have been generating in our soil since 1866. It may be stated as a definite fact that, since 1909, the regional drama has taken on a sizable dimension and a corresponding importance.

What of the harvest that has sprung up from these roots? Can we draw any generalizations from the present crop of pageants and playlets and long plays slowly piling up on the shelf? While, for the moment, the making of regional pieces has been arrested by the post-war need for frivolity, it is true that a quantity of substantial and beautiful work has appeared. One conclusion is clear: a uniquely indigenous species, a genuine homespun variety of play worthy of being called our own, has arrived to challenge attention.

We are hardly yet accustomed to the idea of a *regional* literature. Somehow, the last sector to be discovered or developed is the near-at-hand. Curiously, the word "regional" has acquired motley associations of limitation and narrowness and poor writing that usually go with such words as "provincial," "yokel," and "outlandish."

The concept of regionalism should once and for all be freed from the bonds which unfriendly critics have fastened upon it. The commonplace observation that the regional can be universal must be trotted out. One may belong to a patch of ground like Pancake Hollow and still be a citizen of the world. Thus a play may be rooted in Balsam Gap and still represent, in miniature, the passions and impulses felt outside that area. Your true regional scribe aims with Blake "to see a world in a grain of sand." Euripides never shrank from being called an Attic dramatist. Nor was Thomas Hardy averse to being referred to as the novelist and historian of a region called Wessex.

In any survey, every mound and hill must be counted before we can linger in the mountains. Of the hundreds of plays and playlets discussed in this book, many are demonstration pieces, conscious dramatizations, experimental essays toward native expression of native problems on native soil. There must be hundreds of other playlets, no less important, which have entertained as many audiences but have not been set down in print. As such they may be considered preparatory offerings, initial drawings or models on which will be built the full-rounded and matured plays like *Porgy* and *Ethan Frome* and *Desire Under the Elms*. To dismiss the minor attempts as negligible would be the height of critical arrogance. Rough and crude as some of them may be, they bear a likeness to this thing called man. Ultimately the product will represent a perfect fusion of scene and culture, of man and poetry.

The regional play is recognized by its casual, unstudied plot line. It comes close to our everyday humanity, though it is sunk inward as is the play of idea and crisis. Action does not erupt violently nor cry out for soft music. The tempo is the tempo of living common to men in the cabin, the gulch, the prairie, the mine, and the cottage, in tune with the rhythm of nature itself. As such this does not rule out the skillful use of art in dramatic devices which make for unity and compactness.

Contrariwise, too many of our contemporary hits have been dominated by the story. Technique is still the god of the Broadway stage. Action must be plotted in neat, mathematical lines; surface emotion must be high-pitched to make an impression. That is why the humble theme is so often scorned, and language degraded to mere mumble and ejaculation.

Admittedly, dramatic themes bear a resemblance the world over. Human passions fall into patterns more or less alike. Nobody denies that the farmer, the lumberjack, the cowboy hate and quarrel and love. But each is still subject to impression and modification as a human organism, especially when hemmed in by mountains or haunted by wide horizons or conditioned by wind and rain and snow; the way of the boss and his neighbors, the customs of his fathers, and those intangibles which every region breeds. As such the direction of thinking and acting will necessarily be determined by the outer, physical world. If to these circumstances are added the facts of ill-health, poverty, and hard work, the aggregate of human protoplasm will be shaped to what it is. And to the degree that the human creature will resist or surrender to his little world will the action be dramatic.

The true regional play stresses the setting, the mores, the folk beliefs and folk wisdom uttered by the characters. These are more than stage trimmings. They are the essential lines which form the composition; the motifs which govern conduct and give identity and value and meaning to the whole, not only as document but also as writing. Often indeed, the language in which the native, his mate, and his brood articulate their fears and desires comes close to good, Biblical speech. Many an earth-born creature utters wisdom old as the hills yet fresh as the morning breeze. While speech alone does not make the play, any more than plot does, it rounds out and colors and illumines the whole. Many a dramatic classic reduced to diagram without the redeeming touch of poetry would read like stark melodrama or fairy tale. When the regional play catches the homely accents, the folk idiom of a Lynn Riggs, an E. P. Conkle, or a Weldon Stone, the drama may be said to approach the condition of poetry.

As to tone or mood, generally the regional play takes on a somber gray even in comedy. That may be so because life in our provinces is far from gay. Sobs are more common than belly laughs. With hard conditions of living still facing certain groups in our country, with man to man still inhuman (see the lynching plays), with superstition and witchcraft and narrow codes of conduct still operating in the backwoods, moments of conflict must end in bitterness and defeat. It is to be expected, then, that the struggle will be recorded by the playwright on dark plates.

A final checkup of native playwrights who have contributed over 670 items to the regional drama of this country shows that at least twenty have caught the true lineaments of earthlings at war with their environment in plays which have taken their place in our modern repertory. These plays have lasted for more than two and sometimes three decades. Not only have more than a dozen of these plays actually been produced on Broadway stages but they have been read and studied and mounted in hundreds of communal theaters across the United States. If any sign of the universal is to be seen, it lives in these plays rather than in the flashy and fleeting offerings given in many an urban theater.

To call the regional drama "tributary" to Broadway is a gross impertinence. Tributary to what? No drama is centralized in any one capital. The drama is larger than any one district or theater or period of time. It is unfortunate that the theater west of the Hudson has too long aped and envied the successes of the big metropolis. Hollywood and Manhattan may be the center of theatricals, but they cannot supply the genuine wares spun on the ground from homely materials; the real stuff out of which hundreds of scribes in every corner of the country for some time have been carving their theatrical images.

A brief word about the theater, which must remain subordinate in this study of the drama. If the American drama of the future is to expand and flourish, the 200,000 noncommercial groups scattered across the states must be supplied with fresh, living matter. Broadway hits and artificial medleys of jokes and stereotypes which whip the jaded taste must be resisted. The better regional plays on hand must offer their rich content for presentation and at the same time encourage the making of new plays in kind. The easy formula of slick penmen cannot possibly encompass the variegated lives which make up the life in every region of our vast country.

Before the regional play can become a national institution, we may have to train audiences to perceive the beauties inherent in the homespun personalities on the farm, the ranch, in the miner's shack and logger's hut. By making our choice of plays from the provinces habitual, playgoers will eventually discover that North Creek and South Bend hold suspense and surprise, passion and wisdom. Already in some college laboratories or in communal playhouses, from unsuspected nooks, eager minds are committing themselves to creating a people's theater. The experience of the late Federal Theatre showed that the people are ready to receive honestly wrought plays by native craftsmen on native subjects set against native scenes. When audiences learn to enjoy the interplay of human experiences drawn from Polecat Ridge or Lake Minnetonka, the dramatic awakening will have come.

The time for a people's theater is overdue. It may be that the separate states will have to endow their theaters as Virginia now does, and for managers and directors to exercise more care and discrimination in their choice of vehicles. Certainly the Federal Theatre showed courage and independence in this respect. Studio or campus or resident theaters, indigenous and permanent, must serve as a reservoir of new talent. The fact is that more than a hundred well-equipped theaters across this country stand ready to serve as centers for bringing to the people genuine American dramas. Besides, a national group, founded in 1925 under the presidency of George Pierce Baker, can well direct and guide a national people's theater. It is the National Theater Conference, a nonprofit, co-operative organization of directors of community and university theaters, organized collectively to serve the noncommercial theater. The central office is at the Western Reserve University of Cleveland, Ohio.

Once we fill the nation with active theaters run by progressive leaders anxious to exploit our native, dramatic resources, we shall be well on our way toward dramatic and theatric maturity. Then, should we piece together the regional exhibits across the country, we shall discover a pattern that spells the United States of America.

Bibliography

Bibliography

I. COLLECTIONS OF PLAYS
CONTAINING REGIONAL MATERIAL

All University One-Act Plays. Franklin, Ohio: Eldridge Entertainment House, 1931. 11 plays.

American Folk Plays, edited by Frederick H. Koch. New York: D. Appleton-Century Co., 1939. 20 regional plays.

American Plays, edited by Allan G. Halline. New York: American Book Co., 1935. 18 plays.

American Scene, The, edited by Barrett H. Clark and Kenyon Nicholson. New York: D. Appleton & Co., 1930. 34 plays.

American Scenes, edited by William Kozlenko. New York: The John Day Co., 1941. 12 plays.

Appleton Book of Short Plays, The edited by Kenyon Nicholson. First and second series. New York: D. Appleton & Co. 1926-27. 12 plays in each.

Banner Anthology of One-Act Plays, The, edited by Leslie H. Carter. San Francisco, Calif.: Banner Play Bureau, 1929. 15 plays.

Best One-Act Plays of 1937, 1938, 1939, 1940, 1941, 1942, 1943, 1944, edited by Margaret G. Mayorga. New York: Dodd, Mead & Co., 1938-45. 12 plays in each.

"Blackfriar Series of Original Plays," edited by Lester Raines. University, Ala.: University of Alabama, 1940-41. Over 40 plays. Mimeographed pamphlets.

Carolina Folk Comedies, edited by Frederick H. Koch. *(Carolina Folk-Plays,* fourth series) New York: Samuel French, 1931. 5 regional plays.

Carolina Folk-Plays, edited, with an introduction on folk-play making, by Frederick H. Koch. (First series.) New York: Henry Holt & Co., 1922. 5 regional plays.

———. Second series, *ibid.,* 1924. 5 regional plays.

———. Third series, *ibid.,* 1928. 6 regional plays.

Christian College Prize Plays, edited by Mary Paxton Keeley. Columbia, Mo.: Christian College, 1934. 6 plays.

Contemporary One-Act Plays, edited by William Kozlenko. New York: Charles Scribner's Sons, 1938. 10 plays.

Contemporary One-Act Plays of 1921 (American), edited by Frank Shay. Cincinnati, Ohio: Stewart Kidd Co., 1922. 20 plays.

Cornell University Plays, edited by A. M. Drummond. New York: Samuel French, 1932. 10 plays.

Country Life Plays. Boston, Mass.: Walter H. Baker Co., 1936. 8 plays.

"Dairymen's League Health Pamphlets." Issued by the Home Department, Dairymen's League Co-operative Association, Inc., 11 W. Forty-second Street, New York City.

Dakota Playmaker Plays. First series. Boston, Mass.: Walter H. Baker Co., 1923. 4 plays on colonial themes.

Fifty Contemporary One-Act Plays, edited by Frank Shay and Pierre Loving. Cincinnati, Ohio.: Stewart Kidd Co., 1920.

Fifty More Contemporary One-Act Plays, edited by Frank Shay. New York: D. Appleton & Co., 1928.

Folk-Plays for Contests. Chicago, Ill.: T. S. Denison & Co., 1940. 7 plays.

Grove Plays of the Bohemian Club, edited by Garnett Porter. Vols I, II, and III. San Francisco, Calif.: Press of the H. S. Crocker Co., 1918.

Harvard University: Plays of the 47 Workshop, edited by George P. Baker. New York: Brentano's, 1918. 4 plays.

———. Second series, *ibid.*, 1920. 4 plays.

———. Third series, *ibid.*, 1922. 4 plays.

———. Fourth series, *ibid.*, 1925. 4 plays.

International Plays. Chicago, Ill.: The Dramatic Publishing Co., 1936. 6 Wisconsin plays.

Lake Guns of Seneca and Cayuga and Eight Other Plays of Upstate New York, edited by A. M. Drummond and Robert E. Gard, Ithaca, N. Y.: Cornell University Press, 1942. 9 plays.

Midwest Prize Plays: Prize-Winning Plays from the Midwestern Folk Drama Tournament, with preface by Lealon N. Jones. Chicago, Ill.: The Dramatic Publishing Co., 1938. 7 plays.

Negro History in Thirteen Plays, edited by Willis Richardson and May Miller. Washington, D.C.: The Association Publishers, 1935. 13 plays.

New York Rural Plays. Chicago, Ill.: The Dramatic Publishing Co. 1935. 6 plays.

"New York State Rural Life Plays." New York: Samuel French, 1928. 8 separate pamphlet plays.

One-Act Plays, edited by Barrett H. Clark and Thomas R. Cook. New York: D. C. Heath & Co., 1929. 12 plays.

One-Act Plays for Everyone, by Dan Totheroh. New York: Samuel French, 1931. 11 plays.

One-Act Plays for Stage and Study. First to ninth series. New York: Samuel French, 1924-38. 21 plays in each volume.

Out of the South, by Paul Green. New York: Harper & Bros. 1939. 15 plays.

Pageants of Our Nation, edited by Anne P. Sanford and Robert Haven Schauffler. New York: Dodd, Mead & Co., 1929. Vol I, Eastern States, 7 pageants; Vol. II, Midwestern States, 9 pageants.

Plays and Pageants from the Life of the Negro, edited by Willis Richardson. Washington, D.C.: The Association Publishers, 1930. 8 plays and 4 pageants.

Plays of American Life, by Fred Eastman. New York: Samuel French, 1934. 9 plays.

Plays of American Life and Fantasy, edited by Edith J. R. Isaacs. New York: Coward-McCann, 1929. 18 plays.

Plays of Negro Life, edited by Alain Le Roy Locke and Montgomery Gregory. New York: Harper & Bros., 1927. 20 plays.

Plays of the American West, by Robert Finch. New York: Greenberg, 1947. 15 plays.

Plays of the Harvard Club. Vol. III, second series. New York: Brentano's, 1919. 4 plays.

Plays of the Harvard Dramatic Club. Vol. II, first series. New York: Brentano's, 1918. 4 plays.

Pleasing Plays of Country Life, edited by Blanche H. Pickering and W. L. Miles. Syracuse, N.Y.: The Willis N. Bugbee Co., 1930. 17 plays for young folks.

Prize-Winning One-Act Plays, edited by Billie Oneal. Dallas, Tex.: Southwest Press, 1930. 5 plays.

Representative American Plays, edited by Arthur Hobson

Quinn. Fifth edition, revised and enlarged; New York: D. Appleton & Co., 1930. 28 plays with bibliographies.

Representative One-Act Plays by American Authors, edited by Margaret G. Mayorga. Revised edition; Boston, Mass.: Little, Brown & Co., 1937. 25 plays.

Rural Community Plays, edited by Mary Thomson Johnson. Dayton, Ohio: Paine Publishing Co., 1925. 10 plays.

Short Plays for Modern Players, edited by Glenn Hughes. New York: D. Appleton & Co., 1931. 12 plays.

Six Plays for a Negro Theatre, by Randolph Edmonds. Boston, Mass.: Walter H. Baker Co., 1934.

Stage Magazine, comp. *Forty-Minute Prize Plays,* edited by Grant Wood and Jewell B. Tull. New York: Dodd, Mead & Co., 1936. 6 plays.

Tested One-Act Plays, edited by Oscar E. Sams, Jr. New York: Noble and Noble, 1939. 13 plays.

25 Non-Royalty One-Act American Comedies, compiled by William Kozlenko. New York: Greenberg, 1943.

25 Non-Royalty One-Act Plays for All-Girl Casts, edited by Betty Smith. New York: Greenberg, 1942.

20 Prize-Winning Non-Royalty One-Act Plays, edited by Betty Smith. New York: Greenberg, 1943.

Twenty Short Plays on a Royalty Holiday (1937-40), edited by Margaret G. Mayorga. New York: Samuel French, 1941.

Twenty Short Plays on a Royalty Holiday II (1940-43), *ibid.,* 1944.

Types of Modern Dramatic Composition, with an introduction by George Pierce Baker; edited by Leroy Phillips and Theodore Johnson. Boston, Mass.: Ginn & Co., 1927. 20 plays.

University of Chicago Plays, Skits & Lyrics, edited by Frank H. O'Hara. Chicago, Ill.: University of Chicago Press, 1936. 6 plays.

University of Michigan Plays, edited by Kenneth T. Rowe. Ann Arbor, Michigan: George Wahr, 1929. 5 plays.

———. Book two, *ibid.,* 1930. 6 plays.

———. Book three, *ibid.,* 1932. 10 plays.

University of Utah Plays, edited by Roland B. Lewis. Boston, Mass.: Walter H. Baker Co., 1928. 7 plays.

Wisconsin Community Plays. Chicago, Ill.: The Dramatic
Publishing Co., 1935. 6 plays.
Wisconsin Plays, edited by Thomas H. Dickinson. First series.
New York: B. W. Huebsch, 1914. 3 plays.
———. Second series, *ibid.,* 1918. 4 plays.
Wisconsin Rural Plays. Chicago, Ill.: The Dramatic Pub-
lishing Company, 1931. 5 plays.
Yale One-Act Plays, Vol. I, edited by George P. Baker. New
York: Samuel French, 1930. 6 plays.
———. Vol. II, edited by Walter P. Eaton. New York:
Samuel French, 1937. 9 plays.
Yearbook of Short Plays, The, edited by Claude M. Wise and
Lee O. Snook. First to sixth series. Evanston, Ill.: Row,
Peterson & Co., 1931-1940. 25 plays each, except fifth
series which contains 15, and sixth which contains 23.

II. BOOKS AND PAMPHLETS
CONTAINING REGIONAL REFERENCES

ALBRIGHT, H. DARKES "A Survey of Small-Community Drama
in New York State (1936-39)." New York: Rockefeller
Foundation, August, 1939. Mimeographed report.
ALLSOPP, FRED W. *Folklore of Romantic Arkansas.* Vols. I
and II. New York: The Grolier Society, 1931.
ARVOLD, A. G. *The Little Country Theater.* Special circular
(May, 1938), issued by the North Dakota Agricultural
College, Extension Service. Fargo, N.D.: North Dakota
Agricultural College, 1938.
BAVELY, ERNEST, ed. *Yearbook of Drama Festivals and Con-
tests.* Cincinnati, Ohio: The Educational Theatre Press,
1939.
BECKWITH, MARTHA W. *Folklore in America; Its Scope and
Method. (Folklore Foundation Publication No. 11)*
Poughkeepsie, N.Y.: Vassar College, 1931.
BEEGLE, MAY PORTER, and JACK RANDALL CRAWFORD. *Com-
munity Drama and Pageantry.* New Haven, Conn.: Yale
University Press, 1916.
BLAKE, BEN. *The Awakening of the American Theatre.* New
York: Tomorrow Publishers, 1935.
BOND, FREDERICK W. *The Negro and the Drama.* Washington,
D.C.: The Associated Publishers, 1940.

BOYER, MARY, ed. *Arizona in Literature.* Glendale, Calif.: The Arthur H. Clark Co., 1934.

BROWN, STERLING A. *Negro Poetry and Drama.* Washington, D.C.: The Associates in Negro Folk Education, 1937.

CAMPA, ARTHUR L. *Spanish Religious Folktheatre in the Spanish Southwest* (first cycle). *(University of New Mexico Bulletin, Language Series,* Vol. V, No. 1; Whole No. 238) Albuquerque, N.M.: University of New Mexico, 1934.

————. *Spanish Religious Folktheatre in the Spanish Southwest* (second cycle). *(University of New Mexico Bulletin, Language Series,* Vol. V. No. 2; Whole No. 245) Albuquerque, N.M.: University of New Mexico, 1934.

CARMER, CARL. *The Hurricane's Children.* New York: Farrar & Rinehart, 1937.

CARTER, JEAN and JESSE OGDEN. *Everyman's Drama; a Study of the Noncommercial Theatre in the United States. (Studies in the Social Significance of Adult Education in the U.S., No. 12)* New York: American Association for Adult Education, 1938.

CLARK, BARRETT H. *An Hour of American Drama.* Philadelphia, Pa.: J. B. Lippincott Co., 1930.

COWAN, ROBERT ERNEST, and ROBERT GRANNISS COWAN. *A Bibliography of the History of California, 1510-1930* San Francisco, Calif.: John Henry Nash, 1933.

DAVIDSON, DONALD. *The Attack on Leviathan; Regionalism and Nationalism in the United States.* Chapel Hill, N.C.: University of North Carolina Press, 1938.

DAVIDSON, LEVETTE JAY, and PRUDENCE BOSTWICK. *The Literature of the Rocky Mountain West, 1803-1903.* Caldwell, Idaho: The Caxton Printers, Ltd., 1939.

DICKINSON, THOMAS H. *The Case of the American Drama.* Boston, Mass.: Houghton Mifflin Co., 1915.

Dramatic Index, The, edited by F. W. Faxon. (An annual, 1909-1940.) Boston, Mass.: Boston Book Co., 1909-40. Volumes for 1936, 1937, and 1938 edited by Mary E. Bates.

DRUMMOND, A. M. *Plays for the Country Theatre. (Cornell Extension Bulletin, No. 53)* Ithaca, N.Y.: New York State College of Agriculture, June, 1922.

FINCH, ROBERT. "Folk Playmaking in North Carolina." Chapel Hill, N.C.: University of North Carolina. Typescript in office, Drama Department.

FLANAGAN, HALLIE. *Arena* (photographs by Federal Theatre photographers). New York: Duell, Sloan and Pearce, 1940. Lists of Federal Theatre productions.

———. *What Was Federal Theatre.* Washington, D.C.: American Council on Public Affairs, 1939.

GARD, ROBERT, and OTHERS. *How to Choose a Play and How to Write One. (Cornell Extension Bulletin, No. 449)* Ithaca, N.Y.: New York State College of Agriculture, November, 1940.

GREEN, PAUL. "Folk Drama." *The National Encyclopedia* (New York: P. F. Collier & Son, 1935), XI: 355.

———. *The Hawthorn Tree; Some Papers and Letters on Life and the Theatre.* Chapel Hill, N.C.: The University of North Carolina Press, 1943.

HAZARD, LUCY LOCKWOOD. *The Frontier in American Literature.* New York: Thomas Y. Crowell Co., 1927.

———. *In Search of America.* New York: Thomas Y. Crowell Company, 1930.

HENRY, CATHERINE. "Bibliography of Pageants in the United States." 46 parts in 4 volumes. New York: New York Public Library. Typewritten copy.

HINKEL, E. J., and W. E. McCANN, eds. "Bibliography of California Fiction, Poetry, Drama." Vols. I, II, and III. Oakland, Calif.: Alameda County Library, 1938. Mimeographed.

HOUGHTON, NORRIS. *Advance from Broadway; 19,000 Miles of American Theatre.* New York: Harcourt, Brace & Co., 1941.

Iowa State College, Extension Service. "Home Project Playlet Series." Ames, Iowa. Iowa State College, n.d. 6 playlets.

JOHNSON, JAMES WELDON. *Black Manhattan.* New York: Alfred A. Knopf, 1930.

KEISER, ALBERT. *The Indian in American Literature.* New York: Oxford University Press, 1933.

KELLY, MARY EVA. *Village Theatre* (England). London: Thomas Nelson and Sons, Ltd., 1939.

LA FARGE, OLIVER. *As Long as the Grass Shall Grow.* New York: Alliance Book Corporation, 1940. Photographs and text.

LAWSON, HILDA J. "The Negro in American Drama." Unpublished thesis, University of Illinois, Urbana, Ill., 1939.

LEWIS, BENJAMIN ROLAND. *Pageantry and the Pilgrim Tercentenary Celebration, 1620-1920 (University of Utah, Extension Division Service, Bulletin, Vol. X, No. 4)* Salt Lake City, Utah: University of Utah, 1920.

LINDSAY, JOHN S. *The Mormons and the Theatre.* Salt Lake City, Utah: Century Printing Co., 1905.

LINDSTROM, D. E. *Dramatics for Farm Folks. (University of Illinois, College of Agriculture and Agricultural Experiment Station, Circular 372,* October, 1936) Urbana, Ill.: University of Illinois, 1936.

LINDSTROM, D. E., and SARAH JANE SHANK. *A List of One-Act Plays.* (University of Illinois, College of Agriculture, Extension Service in Agriculture and Home Economics) Urbana, Ill.: University of Illinois, 1937.

LOCKE, ALAIN. "The Negro and the American Theatre." In *Theatre: Essays on the Arts of the Theatre,* edited by Edith J. R. Isaacs. Boston, Mass.: Little, Brown & Co., 1927.

LOGASA, HANNAH, ed. *Regional United States.* Boston, Mass.: The F. W. Faxon Co., 1942.

LOGASA, HANNAH, and WINIFRED VER NOOY. *An Index to One-Act Plays.* Vols. I, II, and III (1900-1940). Boston, Mass.: The F. W. Faxon Co., 1924-41.

McCLEERY, ALBERT, and CARL GLICK. *Curtains Going Up* (index of community theaters). New York: Pitman Publishing Corporation, 1939.

MACGOWAN, KENNETH. *Footlights Across America: Towards a National Theater.* New York: Harcourt, Brace & Co., 1929.

MacMINN, GEORGE R. *The Theater of the Golden Era in California.* Caldwell, Idaho: The Caxton Printers, Ltd., 1941.

McWILLIAMS, CAREY. *The New Regionalism in American Literature.* Seattle, Wash.: University of Washington, 1930.

MAJOR, MABEL, and REBECCA W. SMITH, eds. *The Southwest in Literature.* New York: The Macmillan Co., 1929.

MANTLE, BURNS. *American Playwrights of Today.* New York: Dodd, Mead & Co., 1938.

MARABLE, MARY HAYS, and ELAINE BOYLAND. *A Handbook*

of Oklahoma Writers. Norman, Okla.: University of Oklahoma Press, 1939.

MAYORGA, MARGARET G. *A Short History of the American Drama.* New York: Dodd, Mead & Co., 1932.

MOORE, ARTHUR ULRIC. "Art, Community and Theatre." Unpublished thesis, Cornell University, Ithaca, N.Y., June, 1936.

MOSES, MONTROSE J. *The American Dramatist.* Revised edition; Boston, Mass.: Little, Brown & Co., 1925.

———. "Plea for Folk Basis in American Drama." In *American Theatre as Seen by Its Critics, 1752-1934;* edited by Montrose J. Moses and J. M. Brown. New York: W. W. Norton & Co., 1934.

ODUM, HOWARD W., and HARRY E. MOORE. *American Regionalism; a Cultural-Historical Approach to National Integration.* New York: Henry Holt & Co., 1938.

PATTEN, MARJORIE. *The Arts Workshop of Rural America: a Study of the Rural Arts Program of the Agricultural Extension Service.* New York: Columbia University Press, 1937.

PAYNE, LEONIDAS W. *A Survey of Texas Literature.* New York: Rand McNally & Co., 1928.

PERRY, CLARENCE ARTHUR. *The Work of the Little Theatres; the Groups They Include, the Plays They Produce, Their Tournaments, and the Handbooks They Use.* New York: Russell Sage Foundation, 1933.

Play Actin': Midwestern Folk Drama Tournament. Cape Girardeau, Mo.: State Teachers' College, 1938-39.

QUINN, ARTHUR HOBSON. *A History of the American Drama from the Beginning to the Civil War.* Second edition; New York: F. S. Crofts & Co., 1943. Valuable, extensive bibliographies.

———. *A History of the American Drama from the Civil War to the Present Day.* Revised edition; New York: F. S. Crofts & Co., 1936. Extensive play lists.

REED, P. ISAAC. *The Realistic Presentation of American Characters in Native American Plays Prior to 1870.* Columbus, Ohio: Ohio State University, 1918.

ROCKWELL, ETHEL T. *American Life as Represented in Native One-Act Plays.* Madison, Wis.: University of Wisconsin, 1931.

——. *Historical Pageantry; a Treatise and a Bibliography.* *(State Historical Society of Wisconsin, Bulletin of Information No. 84,* July, 1916.) Madison, Wis.: State Historical Society of Wisconsin, 1916.

——. *A Study Course in American One-Act Plays.* *(University of Wisconsin Bulletin,* IX, No. 3) Madison, Wis.: University of Wisconsin, 1927.

ROGERS, JOHN WILLIAM. *Finding Literature on the Texas Plains;* with a representative bibliography of books on the Southwest by J. Frank Dobie. Dallas, Tex.: Southwest Press, 1931.

ROLLAND, ROMAIN. *The People's Theatre;* translated from the French by Barrett H. Clark. New York: Henry Holt & Co., 1918.

ROURKE, CONSTANCE. *Troupers of the Gold Coast, or the Rise of Lotta Crabtree.* New York: Harcourt, Brace & Co., 1928.

"Rural and Folk Theatres," *Encyclopedia Americana,* XXIII, 778. With bibliography.

Rural Cultural Arts in Wisconsin. *(University of Wisconsin, College of Agriculture, Special Circular,* June, 1940) Madison, Wis.: University of Wisconsin, 1940.

SANWICK, HELEN M. "The Development of the Negro Character in the American Drama from 1767 to 1934." Unpublished thesis, University of Washington, Seattle, 1934.

SAVAGE, GEORGE MILTON, JR. "Regionalism in the Drama." Doctor's thesis, University of Washington, Seattle, 1935.

SOBEL, BERNARD, ed. *The Theatre Handbook and Digest of Plays.* New York: Crown Publishers, 1940.

SPICER, DOROTHY GLADYS. *Folk Festivals and the Foreign Community.* New York: The Woman's Press, 1923.

TAYLOR, C. W. *Life of the Mormons at Salt Lake City.* 1858.

TURNER, FREDERICK JACKSON. *The Frontier in American History.* New York: Henry Holt & Co., 1928.

——. *The Significance of Sections in American History.* New York: Henry Holt & Co., 1932.

United States. Copyright office. *Dramatic Compositions Copyrighted in the United States, 1870-1916.* Vols. I and II. Washington, D.C.: Superintendent of Documents, 1918. Since 1917 two supplementary volumes have been issued. These list all plays and films copyrighted in the United States.

WHITMAN, WILLSON. *Bread and Circuses: a Study of Federal Theatre.* New York: Oxford University Press, 1937.

Wisconsin State Historical Society, Collections, Vol. V, Nos. 77-86, 1915-17.

WITTKE, CARL. *Tambo and Bones, A History of the American Minstrel Stage.* Durham, N.C.: Duke University Press, 1930.

Works Progress Administration. Federal Theatre Project. "San Francisco Theatre Research Monographs." First series, Vols. I to VIII. 1938.

———. "Play Lists, Nos. 15 and 17 (Rural II and Rural III)." Washington, D.C.: Library of Congress, 1937.

———. "Negro Plays." (No. 24) Washington, D.C.: Library of Congress, 1938.

Writers' Program, W.P.A. *American Guide Series* volumes for every state and the principal cities, prepared by the Federal Writers' Project and issued by various publishers, 1938-45.

III. PERIODICAL REFERENCES
TO DRAMA, THEATER, REGIONALISM, FOLKLORE

ALEXANDER, HARTLEY. "The Fiesta Theater at Santa Fe," *Theatre Arts Monthly,* January, 1927.

ALLISON, TEMPE ELIZABETH. "Folk Version of the 'Processus Belial' in America," *Publications of the Modern Language Association,* 53:622-24, June, 1938.

"America in Drama and Song," *London Times Literary Supplement,* September 9, 1939.

"American Play Stuff," *Theatre Arts Monthly,* March, 1931.

ARMES, ETHEL. "Community Drama Activities," *Theatre,* July, 1921.

———. "Dramatic Activities Fostered by Community Service," *Theatre,* December, 1920.

ASBURY, SAMUEL. "A Provincial Drama Ritual," *Southwest Review,* Winter, 1930.

ASHBURN, BERNICE. "The Florida Play Contest," *Quarterly Journal of Speech,* November, 1931.

ATKINSON, J. BROOKS. "South of Times Square," *The Carolina Play-Book*, September, 1928.

AUSTIN, MARY. "American Folk," *Folk-Say*, 1930.

——. "A New Medium for Poetic Drama," *Theatre Arts Monthly*, November, 1916.

——. "Drama Played on Horseback," *Mentor*, September, 1928.

——. "Folk Plays of the Southwest," *Theatre Arts Monthly*, August, 1933.

——. "Indian Detour," *The Bookman*, February, 1929.

——. "Regionalism in American Fiction," *English Journal*, February, 1932.

BAILEY, J. O. "Negro Players in Southern Theatres," *New Theatre*, July, 1935.

BAYLEY, C. JR. "Plays for California," *Theatre Arts Monthly*, July, 1934.

"Beginnings of Negro Drama," *Literary Digest*, May 9, 1914.

BOTKIN, B. A. "The Folk in Literature: an Introduction to the New Regionalism," *Folk-Say*, No. 1, 1929.

——. "Folk-Say and Space," *Southwest Review*, July, 1935.

——. "We Talk about Regionalism," *Frontier*, May, 1933.

CALKINS, MARION CLINCH. "The Folk Theatre," *The Survey*, November 10, 1921.

CAMPBELL, MARIE. "Survivals of Old Folk Drama in the Kentucky Mountains," *Journal of American Folklore*, January, 1938.

CANDLER, MARTHA. "American Community Drama," *Drama*, November, 1919.

CARMER, CARL. "The Making of an American Dramatist," *Theatre Arts Monthly*, December, 1932.

——. "Alabama—Material for a Dramatist's Note-Book," *Theatre Arts Monthly*, December, 1930.

CAROLINE, FREDERICK. "Folk and Passion Plays," *Theatre Arts Monthly*, June, 1931.

CASON, C. E. "Regionalism," *Sewanee Review*, October-December, 1931.

CHURCH, JULIA MORROW. "Dixie Plays on Broadway," *Holland's*, May, 1929.

CLARK, BARRETT H. "Our New American Folk Drama," *English Journal*, December, 1927.

——. "Paul Green," *Theatre Arts Monthly*, October, 1928.

CLARK, JUNE. "Twelfth Night: a Folk Miracle-Play of Carolina," *Theatre Arts Monthly,* December, 1932.

CONKLE, E. P. "The Playwright and His Play," *The Players Magazine,* May-June, 1934.

"Dakota Playmakers, The," *The Quarterly Journal of the University of North Dakota,* Vol. IX, October, 1918.

DICKINSON, THOMAS H. "The Dawn of a New Dramatic Era," *Virginia Quarterly Review,* July, 1929.

DOBIE, CHARLES C. "The First California Authors," *The Bookman,* February, 1931.

DU BOIS, W. E. B. "The Drama Among Black Folk," *The Crisis,* August, 1916.

EATON, WALTER P. "Toward a New Theatre," *The Freeman,* July 12, 1922.

ERNST, ALICE H. "Dramatic Trails of the Northwest," *Theatre Arts Monthly,* September, 1927.

FARQUHAR, E. F. "University of Kentucky Experiment in Community Drama," *Theatre,* October, 1920.

FLANAGAN, HALLIE. "Federal Theatre Project," *Virginia Quarterly Review,* Spring, 1939.

———. "Florida Wheel," *Federal Theatre* (National Policy Board), 1939.

———. "Men at Work: Midwest," *Federal Theatre,* 1:13-17, 1935.

FLOWER, B. O. "Mask or Mirror: The Vital Difference Between Artificiality and Veritism on the Stage," *Arena,* August, 1893.

"Folk Playmaking," *Theatre Arts Magazine,* April, 1920.

FORD, PAUL L. "The Beginnings of American Dramatic Literature," *New England Magazine,* February, 1894.

GRANT, G. C. "Contributions of the Negro to Dramatic Art," *Journal of Negro History,* January, 1932.

GREEN, PAUL. "Drama and the Weather," *Theatre Arts Monthly,* August, 1934.

———. "Needed! A Native American Theatre," *Drama Magazine,* October, 1930.

———. "On the Theatre of the Imagination," *New York Times,* August 5, 1928.

HALPERT, HERBERT. "Federal Theatre and Folksong," *Southern Folklore Quarterly,* June, 1938.

HAMILTON, CLAYTON. "Paucity of Themes in the American Theatre," *Forum,* June, 1909.

HURSTON, ZORA N. "Hoodoo in America," *The Journal of American Folklore,* October-December, 1931.

HUTTON, LAURENCE. "The American Play," *Lippincott's,* March, 1886.

ISAACS, EDITH J. R. "The Carolina Playmakers: Their Contributions to American Art," *American Magazine of Art,* September, 1930.

JAMES, FARREN E. "One-Act Play Contests in the United States," *The Players Magazine,* May-June, 1936.

JOHNSTON, WINIFRED. "The Case of Folk Drama," *Folk-Say,* 1930.

———. "Cow Country Theatre," *Southwest Review,* October, 1932.

KOCH, FREDERICK H. "A California Folk-Play," *The Carolina Play-Book,* March, 1930.

———. "A Folk Theatre in the Making," *Theatre Arts Monthly,* September, 1924.

———. "A Playmaker from Mississippi," *The Carolina Play-Book,* December, 1930.

———. "Folk Playmaking," *The Scholastic,* April 13, 1929.

———. "Folk Playmaking in Dakota and in Carolina," *Playground,* January, 1925.

———. "Making a Native Folk Drama," *Southern Folklore Quarterly,* September, 1937.

———. "Making a Pageant of the Northwest," reprint from the *Quarterly Journal of the University of North Dakota,* July, 1914.

———. "Making a Regional Drama," *A.L.A. Bulletin,* August, 1932.

———. "The Dakota Playmakers," *The American Magazine of Art,* September, 1918.

———. "The Yankee Playmaker," *The Carolina Play-Book,* September, 1930.

———. "Towards an American Folk Drama," *Theatre and School,* October, 1933.

———. "Towards a New Folk Theatre," *The Quarterly Journal of the University of North Dakota,* Spring, 1930.

LADSON, B. P. "Negro Drama for Negroes by Negroes," *Drama,* December, 1921.

LANCASTER, A. E. "Historical American Plays," *Chautauqua,* April-September, 1900.

LINDSTROM, D. E. "Drama Tournaments Spotlight Rural Productions," *The Players Magazine,* May-June, 1933.

———. "Rural Drama in Wisconsin," *Quarterly Journal of Speech,* April, 1930.

LITTELL, R. "Main Street in the Theatre," *New Republic,* December 24, 1924.

MACKAYE, PERCY. "For the Theatre and the Drama," *The Carolina Play-Book,* June, 1933.

———. "Poetic Drama in Kentucky Mountains," *Literary Digest,* January 26, 1924.

MACLEOD, NORMAN. "Notes on Regionalism," *Sewanee Review,* October-December, 1931.

MALONE, ANDREW E. "An American Folk Dramatist: Paul Green," *The Dublin Magazine,* April-June, 1929.

MAXWELL, GERALD. "Revival of Folk-Drama," *Nineteenth Century and After,* London, December, 1907.

MEADE, J. R. "Paul Green," *The Bookman,* January-February, 1932.

MOSES, MONTROSE J. "The American Note in Drama," *Current History,* October, 1933.

———. "Cobwebs of Antiquity," *The North American Review,* January, 1931.

"Negro Theatre," *New Theatre,* July, 1935.

ODUM, HOWARD W. "Notes on the Study of Regional and Folk Society," *Social Forces,* December, 1931.

"A Pageant of the Prairies," *The Survey,* July 4, 1914.

PERRIGO, L. "The First Two Decades of Theatricals in Central City, Colorado," *Colorado Magazine,* July, 1934.

QUINN, ARTHUR HOBSON. "The American Spirit in the American Drama," *The Nation,* April 12, 1919.

"Regionalism: Pro and Con," *Saturday Review of Literature,* November 28, 1936.

"Renaissance of the Folk-Play in the American College," *Current Literature,* October, 1911.

RIGGS, LYNN. "When People Say 'Folk Drama,'" *The Carolina Play-Book,* June, 1931.

SCHONBERGER, E. D. "Community Drama," *North Dakota Quarterly Journal,* May, 1925.

STECHHAN, H. O. "Community Drama in Pasadena," *Drama*, March-April, 1920.

SUCKOW, RUTH. "The Folk Idea in American Life," *Scribner's*, September, 1930.

———. "Middle Western Literature," *English Journal*, March, 1932.

THATCHER, MOLLY DAY. "Drama in Exile," *New Theatre*, October, 1934.

"The Negro in the American Theatre," *Theatre Arts*, August, 1942.

TOTHEROH, DAN. "The Open Air Theatre," *Theatre Arts Monthly*, September, 1928.

TUPPER, V. G. "Negro Folk Music Drama Given in Charleston, S.C.," *Etude*, March, 1937.

VESTAL, STANLEY. "Lynn Riggs: Poet and Dramatist," *Southwest Review*, Autumn, 1929.

WEISHAAR, W. M. "Des Moines, Iowa, Community Drama Association," *Drama*, April, 1928.

"Within the Type: For a Dramatist's Note Book," *Theatre Arts Monthly*, August, 1934. (Illustrated with photographs.)

"Work of Pasadena Community Players," *Theatre*, October, 1920.

IV. SELECTED PERIODICALS
CONTAINING REGIONAL ARTICLES AND PLAYS

The Carolina Magazine, a quarterly. The University of North Carolina, Chapel Hill, N.C., May, 1927 to April, 1929.

The Carolina Play-Book, a quarterly. The Carolina Playmakers and the Carolina Dramatic Association, University of North Carolina, Chapel Hill, N.C., March, 1928, to June, 1945.

The Drama Magazine, eight times a year. The Drama League of America, Chicago, Ill., Vols. I to XXIV, 1911 to 1931.

Folk-Say, a Regional Miscellany, edited by B. A. Botkin. The Oklahoma Folklore Society, Norman, Okla., Vols. I to IV, 1929 to 1932. Bibliographies.

The Frontier, three or four times a year. Montana State University, Missoula, Mont., May, 1920, to Summer, 1939.

Holland's Magazine, a monthly. Title varies. Texas Farm and Ranch Publishing Company, Dallas, Tex., April, 1919, to date.

Journal of American Folklore, a quarterly. Founded, 1888. The American Folklore Society, Menasha, Wisconsin.

The Midland: A Magazine of the Middle West, edited by John T. Frederick. Iowa City, Iowa, 1915 to 1933. Absorbed by *The Frontier,* November, 1933, which changed title to *The Frontier and Midland.*

New Theatre, a monthly. New Theatre League, New York, 1934 to 1936.

One Act Play Magazine, a monthly. New York and Boston, May, 1937, to May-June, 1942.

Play Book, a monthly. Wisconsin Dramatic Society, Madison, Wis., Vols. I and II, 1913 to May, 1915.

The Players Magazine, a monthly. Official publication of the National Collegiate Players, Cheyenne, Wyo., 1924 to date.

Poet Lore, a quarterly. Founded, 1889, at Philadelphia; moved to Boston, 1892. Files, 1889 to Winter, 1932, consulted.

Theatre Arts Magazine, a quarterly. Founded, November, 1916. Changed title, 1924, to *Theatre Arts Monthly.* Title changed, 1939, to *Theatre Arts,* a monthly. Theatre Arts, Inc., New York, to date.

V. REGIONAL AUTHORS AND PLAYS

A selective list of plays, short and long, including those already recorded at the end of each chapter, together with other pertinent items.

After each entry the region is indicated by one of the following symbols:

N.E.—New England	Gt. L.—Great Lakes
N.Y.—New York State	Mid.—Midwest or Mid-
Pa.—Pennsylvania	America
Negro—Negro	S.W.—Southwest
So.—South	Rk.—Rockies
App.—Southern Appalachians	Ore.—Oregon or Northwest
Oz.—Ozarks	Cal.—California
La.—Louisiana and environs	Ru.—Rural
	Ind.—Indian

ABBOTT, GEORGE, and ANN PRESTON BRIDGERS. *Coquette*. New York: Longmans, Green & Co, 1928.—So.

ACHESON, SAM. "We Are Besieged," *Southwest Review*, Autumn, 1941.—S.W.

ALEXANDER, HARTLEY. "Kills-with-Her-Man." In *Plays of American Life and Fantasy*, edited by Edith J. R. Isaacs. New York: Coward-McCann, 1929.—Ore.

———. *Manitou Masks*. New York: E. P. Dutton & Co., 1925.—Ind.

———. *Taiwa*. Los Angeles, Calif.: Primavera Press, 1934.—Ind.

———. "Wakuwapi," *The Play Book* (Madison, Wis.), April, 1915.—Gt. L.

ALEXANDER, JOHN F. "John Brown of Pottawatomie," *Carolina Play-Book*, March, 1934.—Mid.

ALLEN, GERTRUDE. "Homespun." In *Country Life Plays*. Boston, Mass.: Walter H. Baker Co., 1936.—So.

———. *The Grass Is Always Greener*. Boston, Mass.: Walter H. Baker Co., 1935.—Ru.

ALLEN, JAMES M. "The Wind Blows," *One Act Play Magazine*, March, 1939.—So.

ALLENSWORTH, CAROL. "Ring Once for Central," *One Act Play Magazine*, November-December, 1940.—N.E.

ANDERSON, LEE. "Mutiny." In *The Players' Book of One Act Plays*, first series. New York: W. V. McKee, 1928.—Gt. L.

ANDERSON, MAXWELL. *High Tor*. Washington, D.C.: Anderson House, 1937.—N.Y.

———. *Night Over Taos*. New York: Samuel French, 1932.—S.W.

ARCHIBALD, H. A. "Feet On the Ground." Federal Theatre script, 1936—Pa.

ARDREY, ROBERT. "God and Texas," *Theatre Arts*, September, 1943.—S.W.

ARMSTRONG, NOEL. "Marthe." In *Fifty More Contemporary One-Act Plays*, edited by Frank Shay. New York: D. Appleton & Co., 1928.—N.Y.

AUSTIN, MARY. "Fire," *The Play Book* (Madison, Wis.), October, 1914.—Cal.

———. "Sekala Ka'ajma," *Theatre Arts Monthly*, April, 1929.—S.W.

————. *The Arrow Maker.* New York: Duffield & Co., 1911.— Cal.

BAILEY, LORETTO C. "Black Water," *Carolina Play-Book,* March, 1929.—So.

————. "Cloey," *Carolina Play-Book,* March, 1931.—So.

————. "Job's Kinfolks." In *Carolina Folk-Plays,* third series, edited by Frederick H. Koch. New York: Henry Holt & Co., 1928.—So.

BAILEY, LORETTO C. and J. O. BAILEY. "Strike Song." (Based on Gastonia mill strike of April, 1929.) Script, December, 1932.—So.

BAILEY, RIETTA WINN. "Mourners to Glory." In *American Folk Plays,* edited by Frederick H. Koch. New York: D. Appleton-Century Co., 1939.—Negro.

————. "Washed in de Blood," *Carolina Play-Book,* March, 1938.—Negro.

BAIRD, GEORGE M. P. *Mirage.* Cincinnati, Ohio: Stewart Kidd Co., 1922.—S.W.

BAKER, CECIL. "A Bee in a Drone's Hive." In *The Little Country Theatre,* edited by Alfred G. Arvold. New York: The Macmillan Co., 1922.—Mid.

BAKER E. IRENE, and A. M. DRUMMOND. "A Day in the Vineyard." In *The Lake Guns of Seneca and Cayuga,* edited by A. M. Drummond and Robert E. Gard. Ithaca, N.Y.: Cornell University Press, 1942.—N.Y.

BAKER, GEORGE PIERCE. *The Pilgrim Spirit: A Pageant.* Boston, Mass.: Marshall Jones Co., 1921. N.E.

BAKER, VIRGIL L. "Ol' Captain." In *Twenty Short Plays on a Royalty Holiday,* edited by Margaret G. Mayorga. New York: Samuel French, 1941.—Gt. L.

————. "Spanish Diggin's." In *Contemporary One-Act Plays,* edited by William Kozlenko. New York: Charles Scribner's Sons, 1938.—Oz.

————. "When the Sap's A'Runnin'," *One Act Play Magazine,* February, 1940.—Oz.

————. "Witchin' Racket." In *Yearbook of Short Plays,* fifth series. Evanston, Ill.: Row, Peterson & Co., 1939.—Oz.

BANKS, WILLIAM S. "Mennonite." In *Yale One-Act Plays,* Vol. II, edited by Walter P. Eaton. New York: Samuel French, 1937.—Pa.

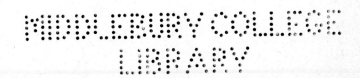

BARKER, JAMES NELSON. *Superstition.* Philadelphia, Pa.: A. R. Poole, 1826.—N.E.

BARNARD, CHARLES, and NEIL BURGESS. *The Country Fair.* New York: Samuel French, 1922.—Ru.

BARNES, ELEANOR. "Close to the Wind," *Poet Lore,* Winter, 1929.—N.E.

BARRY, MAY HOWLEY. "The Combing Jacket." In *New York Rural Plays,* Chicago, Ill.: The Dramatic Publishing Co., 1935.—N.Y.

BASSHE, EM JO. *Earth.* New York: The Macaulay Co., 1927.—So.

BATES, ESTHER WILLARD. "Garafelia's Husband." In *Plays of the Harvard Club,* Vol. III, second series. New York: Brentano's, 1919.—N.E.

BATES, WILLIAM O. "Merry Mount," *The Drama,* July-September, 1920.—N.E.

BEACH, LEWIS. "Brothers." In *Four One-Act Plays.* New York: Brentano's, 1921.—Gt. L.

BEAN, ORESTES UTAH. "Corianton." (Based on the Book of Mormon.) Script, 1933.—Rk.

BEARD, MILDRED MARIE. "R.F.D." In *Midwest Prize Plays.* Chicago, Ill.: The Dramatic Publishing Co., 1938.—Mid.

BECK, WARREN. "No One Can Say." In *Midwest Prize Plays.* Chicago, Ill.: The Dramatic Publishing Co., 1938.—Gt. L.

BECKER, EDNA. "Cheese It." In *New York Rural Plays.* Chicago, Ill.: The Dramatic Publishing Co., 1935.—N.Y.

BEIN, ALBERT. *Let Freedom Ring.* (Based on the novel *To Make My Bread,* by Grace Lumpkin). New York: Samuel French, 1936.—So.

BELASCO, DAVID. *The Girl of the Golden West.* New York: Samuel French, 1933.—Cal.

BENÉT, STEPHEN VINCENT. *The Devil and Daniel Webster.* New York: Dramatists Play Service, 1938.—N.E.

BENTON, RITA. "Margaret of Salem." In *Franklin and Other Plays.* New York: The Writers Publishing Co., 1924.—N.E.

BLAKE, EUGENE H. *Tangled Trails.* Columbia, S.C.: The State Company, 1936.—So.

BLAND, MARGARET. *Dead Expense.* Franklin, Ohio: Eldridge Entertainment House, 1929.—App.

———. "Lighted Candles." In *Carolina Folk-Plays,* third series,

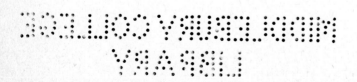

edited by Frederick H. Koch. New York; Henry Holt & Co., 1928.—So.

——. *Pink and Patches*. New York: Samuel French, 1928.— App.

BOMSTEAD, BEULAH. "The Diabolical Circle." In *Dakota Playmaker Plays*, first series. Boston, Mass.: Walter H. Baker Co., 1923.—N.E.

BOUCICAULT, DION. "The Octoroon, or Life in Louisiana." In *Representative American Plays*, edited by Arthur Hobson Quinn. Fifth edition; New York: D. Appleton & Co., 1930.—La.

BOWEN, SYBIL SPANDE. *Through the Gate*. Salt Lake City, Utah: General Boards, M.I.A., 1928.—Rk.

BOYCE, NEITH. "Winter's Night." In *Fifty More Contemporary One-Act Plays*, edited by Frank Shay. New York: D. Appleton & Co., 1928.—Ru.

BRADFORD, CLINTON. "Arkansas Folk Plays." Script.—Oz.

BRADFORD, ROARK. "How Come Christmas?" *Harper's Magazine*, December, 1930.—Negro.

——. *John Henry* (with music). New York: Harper & Bros., December, 1930.—Negro.

BRANDLEY, ELSIE TALMADGE. "Conversion." In *M.I.A. Book of Plays, Vol. XIV*. Salt Lake City, Utah: General Boards, M.I.A., 1942.—Rk.

BRAY, LOUISE W. "Mis' Mercy." In *Harvard University: Plays of the 47 Workshop*, third series, edited by George Pierce Baker. New York: Brentano's, 1922.—N.E.

BRITT, JANIE MALLOY. "Nancy Hanks, Bondwoman." In *American Folk Plays*, edited by Frederick H. Koch. New York: D. Appleton-Century Co., 1939.—App.

BROWN, ALICE. *Children of Earth*. New York: The Macmillan Co., 1915.—N.E.

——. *One Act Plays*. New York: The Macmillan Co., 1921.— N.E.

BROWN, G. "Wait Till We Grow Up." *Pasadena Playhouse Theater*, March, 1930.—Ru.

BROWN, H. CLARK. *See* Thistle, Donald.

BROWNE, THEODORE. "The Natural Man." (Based on the legend of John Henry.) Promptbook, Federal Theatre, Seattle, 1937.—Negro.

BRUCE, RICHARD. "Sahdji, an African Ballet." In *Plays of*

Negro Life, edited by Alain Le Roy Locke and Montgomery Gregory. New York: Harper & Bros., 1927.—Negro.

BUERMANN, HOWARD. "Country Slicker." In Stage Magazine, comp., *Forty-Minute Prize Plays,* edited by Grant Wood and Jewell B. Tull. New York: Dodd, Mead & Co., 1936.—Ru.

BURKE, CHARLES. "Lita's Man." In *All University One-Act Plays.* Franklin, Ohio: Eldridge Entertainment House, 1931.—Mid.

BURNET, DANA. "Rain," *The Drama,* October, 1923.—N.E.

BURRILL, MARY. "Aftermath," *Liberator,* April, 1919.—Negro.

BUSH, C. W. *Miss Marsh.* Privately Printed. Abbotsford, Wis.—Ru.

BUSSE, BARBARA. "The Front Door." In *Twenty Short Plays on a Royalty Holiday,* edited by Margaret G. Mayorga. New York: Samuel French, 1941.—Gt. L.

BUTCHER, JAMES W. JR., "The Seer," *Negro Caravan,* edited by Sterling A. Brown and others. New York: The Dryden Press, 1941.—Negro.

BUTTITTA, ANTHONY. "Singing Piedmont," *One Act Play Magazine,* August, 1937.—Negro.

CAIN, JAMES M. "Hemp," *American Mercury,* April, 1927.—Negro.

CAMPBELL, BARTLEY. "My Partner." In *Favorite American Plays of the Nineteenth Century,* edited by Barrett H. Clark. Princeton, N.J.: Princeton University Press, 1943.—Cal.

CANNON, JOSEPH J. "Defense." In *The Battle Front.* Salt Lake City, Utah: General Boards, M.I.A. No date.—Rk.

——. "Flight." Script.—Rk.

——. "Love One Another." Script.—Rk.

——. *The Battle Front.* Salt Lake City, Utah: General Boards, M.I.A. No date.—Rk.

——. "The Emigrants." In *M.I.A. Book of Plays, XVII.* Salt Lake City, Utah: General Boards, M.I.A., 1940.—Rk.

——. "The Great Fig Tree." Script.—Rk.

CARROLL, ELSIE C. *Success.* Salt Lake City, Utah: General Boards, M.I.A., 1929.—Rk.

CARROLL, WALTER. "De Lost John," *Carolina Play-Book,* September, 1942.—Negro.

CARVER, ADA JACK. "The Cajun." In *The American Scene,*

edited by Barrett H. Clark and Kenyon Nicholson. New York: D. Appleton & Co., 1930.—La.

CHAMBERLAIN, ERNEST. "Banners of the Soil." Federal Theatre script.—S.W.

CHAPMAN, PHYLLIS. *Betsy Anne.* New York: Samuel French, 1928.—N.Y.

CHARMLEY, BEULAH. "The Chest." In *International Plays.* Chicago, Ill.: The Dramatic Publishing Co., 1936.—Gt. L.

CHILDS, ALICE. "Mr. Greatheart," *The Players Magazine,* May-June, 1935.—App.

CLARK, CALISTA BARKER. "Barred." In *Wisconsin Community Plays.* Chicago, Ill.: The Dramatic Publishing Co., 1935.—Gt. L.

———. "Dreams." In *Wisconsin Rural Plays.* Chicago, Ill.: The Dramatic Publishing Co., 1931.—Gt. L.

———. "The Bohemian Shawl." In *International Plays.* Chicago, Ill.: The Dramatic Publishing Co., 1936.—Gt. L.

CLARK, J. AUDREY. "The Quarry." In *The American Scene,* edited by Barrett H. Clark and Kenyon Nicholson. New York: D. Appleton & Co., 1930.—N.E.

CLARKE, DWIGHT L. "Desert Smoke." In *Boston Theatre Guild Plays.* Boston, Mass.: Walter H. Baker Co., 1924.—Cal.

CLEMENTS, COLIN. "Across the Border." In *The American Scene,* edited by Barrett H. Clark and Kenyon Nicholson. New York: D. Appleton & Co., 1930.—S.W.

CLOUSER, GORDON. "Stick 'Em Up." In *American Folk Plays,* edited by Frederick H. Koch. New York: D. Appleton-Century Co., 1939.—S.W.

(Club. *Deseret Deserted; or, The Last Days of Brigham Young.* New York: Samuel French, 1858.—Rk.

COBB, LUCY M. "Gaius and Gaius, Jr." In *Carolina Folk-Plays,* second series, edited by Frederick H. Koch. New York: Henry Holt and Co., 1924.—So.

COFFIN, GERTRUDE WILSON. "A Shotgun Splicin'." In *Carolina Folk-Plays,* third series, edited by Frederick H. Koch. New York: Henry Holt & Co., 1928.—App.

———. "Magnolia's Man." In *Carolina Folk-Plays,* fourth series, edited by Frederick H. Koch. New York: Henry Holt & Co., 1931. App.

COLEY, MARION K. "Fixin's." In "Blackfriar Series of

Original Plays, No. 2." University, Ala.: University of Alabama, 1940. Script.—La.

COMPTON, WILLIAM A. "The Provider." In *University of Michigan Plays,* Book three, edited by Kenneth T. Rowe. Ann Arbor, Mich.: George Wahr, 1932.—Gt. L .

CONKLE, E. P. "Bill and the Widow-Maker." Script.—S.W.

———. *Crick Bottom Plays.* New York: Samuel French, 1928.—Mid.

———. "Forty-Nine Dogs in a Meat House." Script.—Mid.

———. "Gold Is Where You Don't Find It." In *The Best One-Act Plays of 1939,* edited by Margaret G. Mayorga. New York: Dodd, Mead & Co., 1940.—S.W.

———. "Hawk A'Flyin'." In *Contemporary One-Act Plays,* edited by William Kozlenko. New York: Charles Scribner's Sons, 1938.—Mid.

———. *In the Shadow of a Rock.* New York: Samuel French, 1936.—Mid.

———. "Johnny Appleseed." Script.—Pa.

———. *Loolie and Other Short Plays.* New York: Samuel French, 1935.—Mid.

———. "Oxygenerator." Script.—Mid.

———. "Paul and the Blue Ox." Script.—Ore.

———. "Prologue to Glory." In *Federal Theatre Plays.* New York: Random House, 1938.—Gt. L.

———. "Th' Feller from Omaha." In *One-Act Plays for Stage and Study,* eighth series. New York: Samuel French, 1934.—Mid.

CONNELLY, MARC. *The Green Pastures.* New York: Farrar & Rinehart, 1930.—Negro.

CONWAY, WILLIAM OAKLEY. "Indiana: a Pageant in Five Acts, 1669-1892." 1916. Script.—Mid.

COOKSEY, CURTIS. "Mountain Laurel." In *Fifty More Contemporary One-Act Plays,* edited by Frank Shay. New York: D. Appleton & Co., 1928.—App.

COONTZ, KATHLEEN READ. "Patriots and Pirates," *Holland's,* January, 1933.—La.

CORMACK, LIEUT. BEALE. *See* Hare, Walter Ben.

CORNELIUS, ORRELLE F. *Mother's Old Home.* Chicago, Ill.: T. S. Denison & Co., 1927.—App.

———. "The Tie That Binds." In *The American Scene,*

edited by Barrett H. Clark and Kenyon Nicholson. New York: D. Appleton & Co., 1930.—App.

————. "The Whippoorwill," *The Cue,* St. Louis, Mo., 1937. —App.

COURLANDER, HAROLD. *Home to Langford County.* Troy, Mich.: The Blue Ox Press, 1938.—Negro.

————. *Swamp Mud.* Detroit, Mich.: Printed by M. S. Kaplan, 1936.—Negro.

COVINGTON, W. P., III. "Shirt-Tail Boy." In *20 Prize-Winning Non-Royalty One-Act Plays,* edited by Betty Smith. New York: Greenberg, 1943.—Gt. L.

COX, MARCIA B. "Short Cut." In *Wisconsin Rural Plays.* Chicago, Ill.: The Dramatic Publishing Co., 1931. Gt. L.

COX, WILLIAM NORMENT. "The Scuffletown Outlaws." In *Carolina Folk-Plays,* third series, edited by Frederick H. Koch. New York: Henry Holt & Co., 1928.—So.

CROCKETT, HAROLD K. "Storm Clouds and Wheat." Federal Theatre script.—S.W.

CROFFUT, W. A. *Deseret; or, A Saint's Afflictions.* (Libretto by W. A. Croffut, music by Dudley Buck.) New York, 1880.—Rk.

CRONYN, GEORGE W. "A Lady and the Law." In *Fifty More Contemporary One-Act Plays,* edited by Frank Shay. New York: D. Appleton & Co., 1928.—Rk.

CROWELL, J. F. *Three Cape Cod Plays.* Yarmouthport, Mass.: The Register Press, 1934.—N.E.

CRUM, CAROLINE HART. "Got No Sorrow," *Southern Literary Messenger,* April, 1940.—Negro.

CUDDY, LUCY. *Thanksgiving in Plymouth.* Chicago, Ill.: Rand McNally & Co., 1925.—N.E.

CULBERTSON, ERNEST H. *Goat Alley.* Cincinnati, Ohio: Stewart Kidd Co., 1922.—Negro.

————. "Rackey." In *Plays of Negro Life,* edited by Alain Le Roy Locke and Montgomery Gregory. New York: Harper & Bros., 1927.—So.

————. "The End of the Trail." In *The Appleton Book of Short Plays,* edited by Kenyon Nicholson. New York: D. Appleton & Co., 1926.—Ore.

CULLEN, COUNTEE. "One Way to Heaven." Script.—Negro.

CULLEN, COUNTEE, and ARNA BONTEMPS. "St. Louis Woman." Prompt copy.—Negro.

CULLEN, COUNTEE, and OWEN DODSON. "The Third Fourth of July." Script.—Negro.

DALY, AUGUSTIN. "Horizon." In *American Plays,* edited by Allan G. Halline. New York: American Book Co., 1935.—Cal.

DANIEL, ELLA MAE. *Hunger.* Minneapolis, Minn.: Northwest Press, 1938.—So.

DAVENPORT, SAMUEL R. "Sky River Drive." In *Midwest Prize Plays.* Chicago, Ill.: The Dramatic Publishing Co., 1938.—Gt. L.

DAVIS, ALLAN, and CORNELIA C. VENCILL. *On Vengeance Height.* New York: Samuel French, 1914.—App.

DAVIS, OWEN. *Icebound.* Boston, Mass.: Little, Brown & Co., 1923.—N.E.

———. *The Detour.* Boston, Mass.: Little, Brown & Co., 1922.—N.Y.

DAVIS, OWEN, and DONALD DAVIS. *Ethan Frome* (A dramatization of Edith Wharton's novel). New York: Charles Scribner's Sons, 1936.—N.E.

DAY, ANNE MARJORIE. *The Guiding Light: Pilgrim Tercentenary Pageant Play.* Boston, Mass.: R. G. Badger, 1921.—N.E.

DAZEY, CHARLES T. *In Old Kentucky.* New York, 1893.—App.

DEAN, ALEXANDER. "Just Neighborly," *The Drama,* October-November, 1921.—N.E.

DEAN, ELOISE EARLE. *Stockin' Money.* New York: Longmans, Green & Co., 1929.—App.

DE CAMP, ROSEMARY SHIRLEY. "Conchita." In *American Folk Plays,* edited by Frederick H. Koch. New York: D. Appleton-Century Co., 1939.—S.W.

DE KAY, MABELLE. "Veedauwoo" ("Earth-born"), a pageant. Federal Theatre script, 1935.—Rk.

DENISON, MERRILL. "The Weather Breeder." In *Fifty More Contemporary One-Act Plays,* edited by Frank Shay. New York: D. Appleton & Co., 1928.—Gt. L.

DICKEY, JESTON, and BESSIE L. D. ROSELLE. *Pageants and Plays of Pioneers.* San Antonio, Tex.: Carleton Printing Co., 1935.—S.W.

DILLAYE, INA. *Ramona: A Play in Five Acts.* (Adapted from Helen Hunt Jackson's novel.) Syracuse, N.Y.: F. Le C. Dillaye, 1887.—Cal.

DOBIE, CHARLES C. "The Cracked Teapot." In *The Banner Anthology of One-Act Plays,* edited by Leslie H. Carter. San Francisco, Calif.: Banner Play Bureau, 1929.—Cal.

DODSON, OWEN. "The Divine Comedy." Excerpts in *Negro Caravan,* edited by Sterling A. Brown and others. New York: The Dryden Press, 1941.—Negro.

DORTCH, HELEN. "Companion-Mate Maggie." In *Carolina Folk Comedies,* fourth series, edited by Frederick H. Koch. New York: Samuel French, 1931.—Negro.

DOWDY, JAMES B. "Light and Shadow." In *Folk Plays for Contests.* Chicago, Ill.: T. S. Denison & Co., 1940.—So.

DRANSFIELD, JANE. *Blood o' Kings.* New York: Samuel French, 1923.—N.Y.

———. *Joe.* New York: Samuel French, 1928.—N.Y.

DRUMMOND, A. M., and ROBERT E. GARD. "The Cardiff Giant." Script. Cornell University Theatre, Spring, 1939.—N.Y.

DU BOIS, W. E. B. "The Star of Ethiopia." Script, 1913.—Negro.

DUNBAR, OLIVIA HOWARD. "Blockade." In *Plays of American Life and Fantasy,* edited by Edith J. R. Isaacs. New York: Coward-McCann, 1929.—N.E.

DUNCAN, THELMA MYRTLE. "Black Magic." In *Yearbook of Short Plays,* first series. Evanston, Ill.: Row, Peterson & Co., 1931.—Negro.

———. "Sacrifice." In *Plays and Pageants from the Life of the Negro,* edited by Willis Richardson. Washington, D.C.: The Associated Publishers, 1930.—Negro.

———. "The Death Dance." In *Plays of Negro Life,* edited by Alain Le Roy Locke and Montgomery Gregory. New York: Harper & Bros., 1927.—Negro.

DUNCAN, THOMAS W. "Flotsam." In *Prayers for Passel and Other Prize Plays,* edited by A. C. Cloetingh. New York: Samuel French, 1931.—La.

DUNN, JOHN W. "Chisbaohoyo: the Sweetheart of the Corn." Federal Theatre script, 1939. A marionette play.—S.W.

DURHAM, FRANK. "Fire of the Lord." In *Twenty Short Plays on a Royalty Holiday,* edited by Margaret G. Mayorga. New York: Samuel French, 1941.—So.

EASTMAN, FRED. "Bread." In *Plays of American Life.* New York: Samuel French, 1934.—Mid.

———. "Our Lean Years." *Ibid.* Mid.

———. "The Doctor Decides." *Ibid.*—App.

EATON, WALTER PRICHARD. *Grandfather's Chair.* New York: Samuel French, 1930.—N.E.

EDMONDS, RANDOLPH. *Shades and Shadows.* Boston, Mass.: Meador Publishing Co., 1930.—Negro.

———. *Six Plays for a Negro Theatre.* Boston, Mass.: Walter H. Baker Co., 1934.—Negro.

———. *The Land of Cotton and Other Plays.* Washington, D.C.: The Associated Publishers, 1942.—Negro.

EDWARDS, LAURA. "Heaven-Bound." Negro Unit: Federal Theatre script, 1940.—Negro.

ELLIOT, HARRISON. "The Call of the Cumberlands." (A folk opera.) Script, June, 1935.—App.

ELSER, FRANK B., and MARC CONNELLY. "Low Bridge: a Play of the Old Erie Canal," or "The Farmer Takes a Wife." Promptbook, 1934.—N.Y.

ELSEY, MYRTLE GIARD. *Fingerprints.* Syracuse, N.Y.: The Willis N. Bubgee Co., 1931.—Ru.

ENGLISH, THOMAS DUNN. *The Mormons; or, Life at Salt Lake City.* New York: Samuel French, 1858.—Rk.

ERNST, ALICE HENSON. *High Country; Four Plays from the Pacific Northwest.* Portland, Ore.: The Metropolitan Press, 1938.—Ore.

EVANS, JAMES W. "Spirit of Idaho." (A pageant.) Script, 1925.—Ore.

FELTON, MRS. CARL. "Goose Money." In *Wisconsin Rural Plays.* Chicago, Ill.: The Dramatic Publishing Co., 1931.—Gt. L.

———. "This Way Out." In *Wisconsin Community Plays.* Chicago, Ill.: The Dramatic Publishing Co., 1935.—Gt. L.

FERRING, ANNE. "Compensation." In *New York Rural Plays.* Chicago, Ill.: The Dramatic Publishing Co., 1935.—Mid.

FIELD, CHARLES K. "The Man in the Forest"; music by Joseph D. Redding. (First Bohemian Club Grove Play, 1902.) Unpublished.—Cal.

FIELD, ELLIOT. *Tenant Farmers.* Boston, Mass.: Walter H. Baker Co., 1941.—S.W.

FIELD, RACHEL. "Greasy Luck." In *The American Scene,* edited by Barrett H. Clark and Kenyon Nicholson. New York: D. Appleton & Co., 1930.—N.E.

FINCH, ROBERT. "From Paradise to Butte." In *25 Non-*

Royalty One-Act American Comedies, edited by William Kozlenko. New York: Greenberg, 1943.—Ore.

———. "Good-Bye to the Lazy K." In *One Hundred Non-Royalty One-Act Plays,* edited by William Kozlenko. New York: Greenberg, 1940.—Ore.

FINCH, ROBERT, and BETTY SMITH. "Summer Comes to the Diamond O." In *The Best One-Act Plays of 1940,* edited by Margaret G. Mayorga. New York: Dodd, Mead & Co., 1941.—Ore.

FISHEL, H. L. "Jericho." Negro Unit: Federal Theatre script, 1937.—Negro.

FLAGG, ISAAC. *Three Plays.* Berkeley, Calif.: The Studio Bookshop, 1936.—Cal.

FORTUNE, JAN ISABELLE. "Texas History Play (The Cavalier from France)." In *Prize-Winning One-Act Plays,* edited by Billie Oneal. Dallas, Tex.: Southwest Press, 1930.—S.W.

FOWLER, RICHARD B. "A Half-Hour Reformation." In *All University One-Act Plays.* Franklin, Ohio: Eldridge Entertainment House, 1931.—Oz.

FOX, JOSEPH PHILIP. "Hollyhocks," *Carolina Play-Book,* September, 1930.—N.E.

FRANK, YASHA. "Timberline Tintypes." Federal Theatre script, 1938.—Ore.

FRANKLIN, PEARL. *A Mountain Wedding.* New York: Samuel French, 1926.—App.

FREEMAN, MARY E. WILKINS. *Giles Corey, Yeoman.* New York: Harper & Bros., 1893.—N.E.

FROST, ROBERT. "A Way Out," *Seven Arts,* February, 1917.—N.E.

FUSSLER, IRENE. "Ever' Snitch." In *Carolina Folk Comedies,* fourth series, edited by Frederick H. Koch. New York: Samuel French, 1931.—So.

GALE, ZONA. "Neighbors." In *Wisconsin Plays,* edited by Thomas H. Dickinson. New York: B. W. Huebsch, 1914.—Gt. L.

———. "Uncle Jimmy." In *Types of Modern Dramatic Composition,* edited by Leroy Phillips and Theodore Johnson. Boston, Mass.: Ginn & Co., 1927.—Gt. L.

GAMBLE, HAZEL V. "Little Fish," *The Drama,* February, 1924.—Ru.

GARD, ROBERT E. "Let's Get on with the Marryin'." In *The*

Lake Guns of Seneca and Cayuga, edited by A. M. Drummond and Robert E. Gard. Ithaca, N.Y.: Cornell University Press, 1942.—N.Y.

——. "Mixing Up the Rent." *Ibid.*—N.Y.

——. "Raisin' the Devil." *Ibid.*—N.Y.

——. "Wild Hills." Script, 1941.—N.Y.

GARDNER, EMELYN E. "Raising the Devil," *Poet Lore,* Spring, 1928.—N.Y.

GARLAND, HAMLIN. *Under the Wheel.* Boston, Mass.: The Barta Press, 1890.—Mid.

GAULT, LYNN. "His Boon Companions." In *American Folk Plays,* edited by Frederick H. Koch. D. Appleton-Century Co., 1939.—Gt. L.

GEDDES, VIRGIL. "As the Crow Flies." In *Native Ground.* New York: Samuel French, 1932.—Mid.

——. "Mud on the Hoof," *Folk-Say,* IV (1932).—Mid.

——. *Native Ground.* New York: Samuel French, 1932.—Mid.

——. *Pocahontas and the Elders,* Chapel Hill, N.C.: M. A. Abernathy, 1933.—Mid.

——. *The Earth Between.* New York: Samuel French, 1930.—Mid.

——. "The Ploughman's Gleam." In *Native Ground.* New York: Samuel French, 1932.—Mid.

GEPHART, BESSE P. *Blindness.* New York: Dramatists Play Service, 1937.—App.

GIBBS, HARRY C. "Chico." In *Twenty Short Plays on a Royalty Holiday, II,* edited by Margaret G. Mayorga, New York: Samuel French, 1944.—S.W.

GILL, WILLIAM, and RICHARD GOLDEN. "Jed Prouty; the Man from Maine" (or "Old Jed Prouty"). Unpublished, 1889.—N.E.

GINTY, ELIZABETH B. *Missouri Legend.* New York: Random House, 1938.—S.W.

GLADYS, CHARLES, and GEORGE SAVAGE. "Keep Me a Woman Grown." In *25 Non-Royalty One-Act American Comedies,* edited by William Kozlenko. New York: Greenberg, 1943.—App.

GLASPELL, SUSAN. "Trifles." In *Types of Modern Dramatic Composition,* edited by Leroy Phillips and Theodore Johnson. Boston, Mass.: Ginn & Co., 1927.—N.E.

GOLD, MICHAEL. "Hoboken Blues." In *The American Caravan*. New York: The Macaulay Co., 1927.—Negro.

GOODRICH, FRANCES, and ALBERT HACKETT. *The Great Big Doorstep*. Chicago, Ill.: The Dramatic Publishing Co., 1943.—La.

GRAY, FRANCES. "The Beaded Buckle." In *Carolina Folk-Plays*, second series, edited by Frederick H. Koch. New York: Henry Holt & Co., 1924.—So.

GREEN, CLARA MAE. "Jumpin' the Broom." In *One-Act Plays for Stage and Study, fifth series*. New York: Samuel French, 1929.—So.

GREEN, ELIZABETH LAY. *Balanced Diet*. New York: Samuel French, 1928. *See also* Lay, Elizabeth.—N.Y.

GREEN, ERMA, and PAUL GREEN. "Fixin's." In *Carolina Folk-Plays*, second series, edited by Frederick H. Koch. New York: Henry Holt & Co., 1924.—So.

GREEN, PAUL. "Blue Thunder." In *One-Act Plays for Stage and Study*, fourth series. New York: Samuel French, 1928.—Negro.

———. "Granny Boling" (rewritten as "The Prayer Meeting"), *The Drama*, 1921.—Negro.

———. *Hymn to the Rising Sun*. New York: Samuel French, 1936.—So.

———. "In Abraham's Bosom." In *Lonesome Road: Six Plays for the Negro Theatre*. New York: Robert M. McBride Co., 1926.—Negro.

———. "In Aunt Mahaly's Cabin," *The Reviewer*, Richmond, Va., 1924.—Negro.

——— *In the Valley and Other Carolina Plays*. New York: Samuel French, 1928.—Negro and So.

———. *Lonesome Road: Six Plays for the Negro Theatre*. New York: Robert M. McBride Co., 1926.—Negro.

———. "Old Wash Lucas," *Poet Lore*, Summer, 1924.—So.

———. "Quare Medicine." In *In the Valley and Other Carolina Plays*. New York: Samuel French, 1928.—So.

———. *Roll, Sweet Chariot* (revision of *Potter's Field*). New York: Samuel French, 1935.—So.

———. "Sam Tucker" (rewritten as "Your Fiery Furnace"), *Poet Lore*, Summer, 1923.—Negro.

———. *Shroud My Body Down*. Iowa City, Iowa: Clio Press, 1935.—So.

————. "Supper for the Dead." In *In the Valley and Other Carolina Plays.* New York: Samuel French, 1928.—Negro.

————. "The Common Glory." Unpublished.—So.

————. "The End of the Row," *Poet Lore,* Spring, 1924.—Negro.

————. "The Field God." In *American Plays,* edited by Allan G. Halline. New York: American Book Co., 1935.—So.

————. *The Highland Call.* Chapel Hill, N.C.: The University of North Carolina Press, 1941.—So.

————. "The Hot Iron," *Poet Lore,* Spring, 1924.—Negro.

————. *The House of Connelly.* New York: Samuel French, 1931.—So.

————. "The Last of the Lowries." In *Carolina Folk-Plays,* first series, edited by Frederick H. Koch. New York: Henry Holt & Co., 1922.—So.

————. "The Lord's Will," *Poet Lore,* Autumn, 1922.—Negro.

————. *The Lost Colony.* Chapel Hill, N.C.: The University of North Carolina Press, 1937.—So.

————. "The Man Who Died at Twelve O'Clock." In *In the Valley and Other Carolina Plays.* New York: Samuel French, 1928.—Negro.

————. "The No 'Count Boy," *Theatre Arts Monthly,* November, 1924.—Negro.

————. "The Prayer Meeting," *Poet Lore,* Summer, 1924.—Negro.

————. *The Southern Cross.* New York: Samuel French, 1938.—So.

————. "Tread the Green Grass." In *The New American Caravan.* New York: The Macaulay Co., 1929.—So.

————. "Unto Such Glory." In *In the Valley and Other Carolina Plays.* New York: Samuel Fernch, 1928.—So.

————. "White Dresses." In *Contemporary One-Act Plays,* edited by B. R. Lewis. New York: Charles Scribner's Sons, 1922.—Negro.

GREENE, PATTERSON. *Papa Is All.* New York: Samuel French, 1942.—Pa.

GREENSFELDER, ELMER. *Broomsticks, Amen!* New York: Longmans, Green & Co., 1931.—Pa.

————. *Swing Low.* New York: Longmans, Green & Co., 1929.—Negro.

GREGORY, WAYNE. *No Hidin' Place.* San Francisco, Calif: Banner Play Bureau, 1938.—Negro.

GRIFFITH, ALICE MARY MATLOCK. *Westward the Course of Empire.* Austin, Tex.: The E. L. Steck Co., 1924.—S.W.

GRIMKÉ, ANGELINA W. *Rachel.* Boston, Mass.: The Cornhill Co., 1920.—Negro.

GRINDER, MARION M. "The Maker of Fine Laces." In *International Plays.* Chicago, Ill.: The Dramatic Publishing Co., 1936.—Gt. L.

GROOMES, BERTHA. "Pretty Dress." In *Folk Plays for Contests.* Chicago, Ill.: T. S. Denison & Co., 1940.—Ru.

GROVER, HARRY GREENWOOD. *Thompson's Luck.* Cincinnati, Ohio: Stewart Kidd Co., 1923.—N.E.

HALE, NATHAN, and RUTH HALE. "It Shall Keep Thee." In *M.I.A. Book of Plays, XIII.* Salt Lake City, Utah: General Boards, M.I.A., 1941.—Rk.

———. *Light for Tomorrow.* Salt Lake City, Utah: General Boards, M.I.A., n.d.—Rk.

HALE, RUTH HUDSON. *Handcart Trails.* Salt Lake City, Utah: General Boards, M.I.A. 1940.—Rk.

HALEY, GLEN. "Sit Down to Supper." In *Tested One-Act Plays,* edited by Oscar E. Sams, Jr. New York: Noble and Noble, 1939.—Rk.

HAMER, BEVERLEY DU BOSE. "Funeral Flowers for the Bride." *Carolina Play-Book,* September, 1937.—App.

HARE, WALTER BEN. *Aaron Slick from Punkin Crick.* Boston, Mass.: Walter H. Baker Co., 1919. (Signed "Lieut. Beale Cormack.")—Ru.

———, *Deacon Dubbs.* Chicago, Ill.: T. S. Denison & Co., 1916.—Ru.

HARK, MILDRED and NOEL McQUEEN. "Through You I Live," *One Act Play Magazine,* March-April, 1941.—Ru.

HARRIS, BERNICE KELLY. *Folk Plays of Eastern Carolina.* Chapel Hill, N.C.: The University of North Carolina Press, 1939.—So.

HARTE, BRET. *Two Men of Sandy Bar.* (From his story, "Mr. Thompson's Prodigal.") Boston, Mass.: Houghton Mifflin Co., 1882.—Cal.

HATCH, MARY COTTAM. "Spring Storm." In *American Folk Plays,* edited by Frederick H. Koch. New York: D. Appleton-Century Co., 1939.—Rk.

HEFFNER, HUBERT. "Dod Gast Ye Both!" In *Carolina Folk-Plays,* first series, edited by Frederick H. Koch. New York: Henry Holt & Co., 1922.—App.

HERNE, JAMES A. *Shore Acres and Other Plays.* New York: Samuel French, 1928.—N.E.

HERRICK, MARVIN, and HOYT H. HUDSON. *That Upper Forty.* New York: Samuel French, 1928.—N.Y.

HEYWARD, DOROTHY and DUBOSE. *Mamba's Daughter.* New York: Farrar & Rinehart, 1939.—Negro.

——. *Porgy.* Theatre Guild Edition. New York: Doubleday, Page & Co., 1927.—Negro.

HEYWARD, DUBOSE. *The Brass Ankle.* New York: Farrar & Rinehart, 1931.—Negro.

HILTON, CHARLES. "Broken Pines," *Poet Lore,* Autumn, 1929.—Ore.

HOLME, GARNET. "Ramona Pageant." (Based upon the novel by Helen Hunt Jackson.) Script, 1923.—Cal.

HOPKINS, ARTHUR. "Moonshine," *Theatre Arts Magazine,* January, 1919.—App.

HOUSTON, NOEL. "Last Refuge." In *American Folk Plays,* edited by Frederick H. Koch. New York: D. Appleton-Century Co., 1939.—S.W.

HOWARD, FRED. "New Nigger" (or "Big John"), *Carolina Play-Book,* September, 1936.—Negro.

——. "Sharecropper." Script, February, 1938.—Negro.

HOWELL, CORRIE C. "The Forfeit," *Poet Lore,* Spring, 1925.—Negro.

HUDSON, ARTHUR P. "Get Up an' Bar the Door," *Carolina Play-Book,* December, 1930.—La.

HUGHES, GLENN. "Miguel," *The Players Magazine,* February, 1925.—Cal.

HUGHES, HATCHER. *Hell-Bent for Heaven.* New York: Harper & Bros., 1924.—App.

——. *Ruint.* New York: Harper & Bros., 1925.—App.

HUGHES, LANGSTON. "Don't You Want to Be Free?" *One Act Play Magazine,* October, 1938.—Negro.

——. "De Organizer: a Blues Opera in One Act." Script, 1940.—Negro.

——. "Soul Gone Home," *One Act Play Magazine,* July, 1937.—Negro.

HUGHES, LANGSTON, and ARNA BONTEMPS. "When the Jack Hollers." Script, 1936.—Negro.

HUGHES, LANGSTON, and MARTIN JONES. "Mulatto." Script, 1935.—So.

IOBST, CLARENCE. "En Quart Millich un en Halb Beint Raahm," *Pennsylvania German Folklore Society,* No. 4, 1939.—Pa.

———. "Salz." *Ibid.*—Pa.

JACKSON, PHYLLIS WYNN. "John Brown." In *Fourth Yearbook of Short Plays.* Evanston, Ill.: Row, Peterson & Co., 1938.—App.

JEFFERSON, JOSEPH, and DION BOUCICAULT. *Rip Van Winkle.* New York: Dodd, Mead & Co., 1899.—N.Y.

JENNINGS, S. E. *The Old Settlers' Picnic.* Chicago, Ill.: The Dramatic Publishing Co., 1935.—N.Y.

JENNINGS, TALBOT. "Footprints West; a Pageant." Script, 1926.—Ore.

———. *No More Frontier.* New York: Samuel French, 1931.—Ore.

———. "The Light on the Mountains." Script, 1923.—Ore.

JODER, ANNA BEST. "Dola's Learnin'." Script (no date).—Mid.

———. "The Dance." Script, 1938.—Mid.

JOHNSON, GEORGIA DOUGLAS. "Blue Blood." In *Fifty More Contemporary One-Act Plays,* edited by Frank Shay. New York: D. Appleton & Co.,1938.—Negro.

———. *Plumes.* New York: Samuel French, 1927.—Negro.

JOHNSON, HALL. "Run, Little Children." Negro Unit: Federal Theatre script, 1938.—Negro.

JOHNSON, SAMUEL D. *The Shaker Lovers.* New York: Samuel French, 1857?—Rk.

JONES, LEALON N. "And Cling to Thee." In *Folk Plays for Contests.* Chicago, Ill.: T. S. Denison & Co., 1940.—Oz.

———. "Heirloom." In *Midwest Prize Plays,* Chicago, Ill.: The Dramatic Publishing Co., 1938.—Oz.

———. "Swamp Spirit." In *Yearbook of Short Plays,* second series. Evanston, Ill.: Row, Peterson & Co., 1934.—Oz.

———. "Swappin' Fever." In *American Folk Plays,* edited by Frederick H. Koch. D. Appleton-Century Co., 1939.—Oz.

———. "Triflin'." In *25 Non-Royalty One-Act American*

Comedies, edited by William Kozlenko. New York: Greenberg, 1943.—Oz.

KAMARCK, EDWARD. "Chenango Crone." In *The Lake Guns of Seneca and Cayuga,* edited by A. M. Drummond and Robert E. Gard. Ithaca, N.Y.: Cornell University Press, 1942.—N.Y.

KANE, HELEN P. *The White Doe of Oneida,* New York: Samuel French, 1907.—N.Y.

——. *Yagowanea.* New York: Samuel French, 1900.—N.Y.

——. *Yot-Che-Ka.* New York: Samuel French, 1914.—N.Y.

KAPINGEN, ROSE. "Russian in Reverse." In *International Plays.* Chicago, Ill.: The Dramatic Publishing Co., 1936.—Gt. L.

KEELEY, MARY PAXTON. "The River Rat." In *Christian College Prize Plays.* Columbia, Mo.: Christian College, 1934.—Mid.

KELLEY, ESTELLA. "The Machine Age." In *Goin' Home and Other Plays of the 1927 Contest.* New York: Longmans, Green & Co., 1928. Rk.

KENNEDY, HARRIET L. *The Lion's Mouth.* New York: D. Appleton & Co., 1924.—Negro.

KERR, WALTER. *Rip Van Winkle.* New York: Samuel French, 1937.—N.Y.

KINER, GRACE. *Wedding Clothes.* New York: Samuel French, 1928.—N.Y.

KIRKLAND, JACK, and ERSKINE CALDWELL. *Tobacco Road.* New York: The Viking Press, 1934.—So.

KNAPP, JACK STUART. *Chloe.* Rock Island, Ill.: Frederick B. Ingram Publications, 1936.—Negro.

——. *Mother Minnetonka.* Boston, Mass.: Walter H. Baker Co., 1931.—Gt. L.

——. *The Blue Gate.* Boston, Mass.: Walter H. Baker Co., 1938.—Pa.

——. *The Heritage.* New York: Samuel French, 1930.—Ru.

——. "The Son's Wife." In *Country Life Plays.* Boston, Mass.: Walter H. Baker Co., 1936.—Ru.

KOCH, FREDERICK H., director. *A Century of Culture, a Pageant.* North Carolina Education Association, 1937.—So.

——. *Raleigh, the Shepherd of the Ocean.* Raleigh, N.C.: Edwards and Broughton Co., 1920.—So.

KOCH, FRED, JR. "Smoky Mountain Road." Unpublished thesis, University of North Carolina, 1939.—App.

————. "These Doggone Elections," *Carolina Play-Book,* September, 1939.—App.

————. "Wash Carver's Mouse Trap," *Carolina Play-Book,* December, 1938.—App.

LA FARGE, CHRISTOPHER. *Mesa Verde.* Norfolk, Conn.: New Directions, 1945.—S.W.

LARKIN, MARGARET. *El Cristo.* New York: Samuel French, 1926.—S.W.

LATHAM, LOIS. *Hit's Man's Business.* Evanston, Ill.: Row, Peterson & Co., 1940.—So.

LAWRENCE, ETHEL G. *Waitin' Fer Sun-up.* Franklin, Ohio: Eldridge Entertainment House, 1930.—App.

LAWRENCE, NATALIA GRIMES. *Hurricane.* Boston, Mass.: Walter H. Baker Co., 1931.—So.

LAY, ELIZABETH A. "Trista." In *Carolina Folk-Plays,* second series, edited by Frederick H. Koch. New York: Henry Holt & Co., 1924.—So.

————. "When Witches Ride." In *Carolina Folk-Plays,* first series, edited by Frederick H. Koch. New York: Henry Holt & Co., 1922. *See also* Green, Elizabeth Lay.—So.

LEMMON, ALLEAN. "Alsace in Missouri." In *Christian College Prize Plays,* edited by Mary Paxton Keeley. Columbia, Mo.: Christian College, 1934.—Oz.

————. *Last Flight Over.* Evanston, Ill.: Row, Peterson & Co., 1935.—Mid.

————. "The Hero." In *Christian College Prize Plays,* edited by Mary Paxton Keeley. Columbia, Mo.: Christian College, 1934.—Oz.

LEONARD, WILLIAM ELLERY. *Glory of the Morning.* Madison, Wis.: Wisconsin Dramatic Society, 1912.—Gt. L.

————. *Red Bird.* New York: B. W. Huebsch, 1923.—Gt. L.

LE PELLEY, GUERNSEY. "Two Hundred Riders." In *The Fifth Yearbook of Short Plays.* Evanston, Ill.: Row, Peterson & Co., 1939.—Rk.

LEVY, ADOLPH. "Go Down Moses." In *University of Michigan Plays,* series three, edited by Kenneth T. Rowe. Ann Arbor, Mich.: George Wahr, 1932.—Negro.

LEWIS, JACK W. "Shooting Star." In *Twenty Short Plays on a Royalty Holiday,* edited by Margaret G. Mayorga. New York: Samuel French, 1941.—Rk.

LEWIS, KATE PORTER. *Alabama Folk Plays.* Chapel Hill, N.C.: The University of North Carolina Press, 1943.—So.-Negro.

LINCOLN, JOSEPH C. *The Managers.* New York: D. Appleton & Co., 1925.—N.E.

LINDSTROM, DAVID E. "Sons of Soil." In *Wisconsin Rural Plays.* Chicago, Ill.: The Dramatic Publishing Co., 1931.—Gt. L.

LIPSCOMB, G. D. "Frances," *Opportunity,* May, 1925.—Negro.

LOBNER, JOYCE E. "The Golden Eagle Child." In *Banner Anthology of One-Act Plays,* edited by Leslie H. Carter. San Francisco, Calif.: Banner Play Bureau, 1929.—Cal.

LONDON, JACK. *The Acorn-Planter: a California Forest Play.* New York: The Macmillan Co., 1916.—Cal.

LORENZEN, RONALD. *Which Is the Way to Boston?* Chicago, Ill.: The Dramatic Publishing Co., 1936.—N.E.

LOY, TOM. "Glendale Plantation." *Carolina Play-Book,* December, 1931.—So.

LUTHER, VIVIAN. "One Head of Wheat." U.S. Department of Agriculture and the state of North Dakota, January, 1936. Mimeographed copy.—Mid.

McCAULEY, CLARICE V. *The Conflict.* Baltimore, Md.: The Norman Remington Co., 1921. Vagabond Plays, No. 6.—N.E.

McCLELLAN, WALTER. *The Delta Wife.* New York: D. Appleton & Co., 1924.—La.

McGROARTY, JOHN STEVENS. "The Mission Play." (Presented at San Gabriel, Cal., 1912-32). Unpublished.—Cal.

MACK, ORIN. "Last Day for Grouse." In *The American Scene,* edited by Barrett H. Clark and Kenyon Nicholson. New York: D. Appleton & Co., 1930.—Rk.

MACKAY, CONSTANCE D'ARCY. *Plays of the Pioneers.* Harper & Bros., 1915.—N.E.

McKAY, KATHRYN C. "Soul Mates." In *Six One-Act Plays, M.I.A. Book of Plays.* Salt Lake City, Utah: General Boards, M.I.A., 1929.—Rk.

MACKAYE, KEITH. *Honey Holler.* New York: Brentano's, 1930.—N.E.

MACKAYE, PERCY. *Kentucky Mountain Fantasies.* Revised edition; New York: Samuel French, 1933.—App.

———. *Masque of St. Louis.* St. Louis, Mo.: St. Louis Pageant Drama Association, 1914.—Mid.

————. *Rip Van Winkle; a Folk Opera.* (Music by Reginald de Koven). New York: Alfred A. Knopf, 1919.—N.Y.

————. *The Scarecrow; or the Glass of Truth.* New York: The Macmillan Co., 1908.—N.E.

————. *This Fine-Pretty World.* New York: The Macmillan Co., 1924.—App.

————. *Wakefield: a Folk-Masque of America.* H. V. Steele, 1932.—Ru.

————. *Yankee Fantasies.* New York: Duffield & Co., 1912.—N.E.

McKinney, Isabel. "Mud," *Poet Lore,* Autumn, 1919.—Ru.

McKnight, L. A. *Indiana: a Drama of Progress.* Fowler, Ind.: The Author, 1908.—Gt. L.

MacManus, Polly. *Detour Ahead.* Chicago, Ill.: The Dramatic Publishing Co., 1930.—Ru.

MacMillan, Dougald. "Off Nags Head or The Bell Buoy." In *Carolina Folk-Plays,* first series, edited by Frederick H. Koch, New York: Henry Holt & Co., 1922.—So.

MacMillan, Mary Louise. "Honey." In *More Short Plays.* Cincinnati, Ohio: Stewart Kidd Co., 1917.—App.

McMullan, Patricia. "Cottie Mourns." *Carolina Play-Book,* March, 1935.—So.

Malam, Charles. "The Second Time." In *Still Another Book of Miniature Plays.* Boston, Mass.: Walter H. Baker Co., 1938.—Ru.

Mansfield, Hiram E. "King Row." In *Wisconsin Rural Plays.* Chicago, Ill.: The Dramatic Publishing Co., 1931.—Gt. L.

Marley, Clare Johnson. "Crusoe Islanders," *Carolina Play-Book,* March, 1944.—So.

————. "Swamp Outlaw," *Carolina Play-Book,* March, 1940.—So.

————. "The Old Dram Tree," *The Southern Literary Messenger,* August, 1942.—So.

Martens, Anne Coulter. "Blue Beads." In *Fourth Yearbook of Short Plays,* Evanston, Ill.: Row, Peterson & Co., 1938.—Ru.

Martin, Helen R., and Frank Howe, Jr. *A Mennonite Maid.* New York: Longmans, Green & Co., 1924.—Pa.

Martin, Milward W. "Flood Control." In *Twenty Short*

Plays on a Royalty Holiday, edited by Margaret G. Mayorga. New York: Samuel French, 1941.—S.W.

MASTERS, EDGAR LEE. "Moroni." Prompt copy.—Rk.

MATHEUS, JOHN F. "Black Damp," *The Carolina Magazine,* April, 1929.—Negro.

———. "'Cruiter." In *Plays of Negro Life,* edited by Alain Le Roy Locke and Montgomery Gregory. New York: Harper & Bros., 1927.—Negro.

———. "Ti Yette." In *Plays and Pageants from the Life of the Negro,* edited by Willis Richardson. Washington, D.C.: The Associated Publishers, 1930.—La.

MATHEWS, CORNELIUS. *Witchcraft; or the Martyrs of Salem.* New York: Samuel French, 1852.—N.E.

MEADOW, HERB. "Barge Incident," *The Players Magazine,* November-December, 1938.—N.Y.

MEBLIN, ROSE C. "Dowry and Romance." In *Dakota Playmaker Plays,* first series. Boston, Mass.: Walter H. Baker Co., 1923.—N.E.

MECHEM, KIRKE. "John Brown," *Kansas Magazine.* Manhattan, Kansas: Kansas State College, c1939.—So.

MEEK, PETER G. *The Fourth Generation.* New York: Samuel French, 1935.—La.

MELLON, EVELYN EMIG. "Trains," *Poet Lore,* Autumn, 1930.—Rk.

MILHOUS, JOHN PHILIP. "Davy Crockett," *Carolina Play-Book,* March, 1933.—App.

MILLER, JOAQUIN. "An Oregon Idyl." In *Poems,* Vol. VI. San Francisco, Cal.: The California Publishing Co., 1910.—Ore.

———. *Forty-Nine: an Idyl Drama of the Sierras.* San Francisco, Calif.: The California Publishing Co., 1882.—Cal.

———. "Tally Ho!" In *Poems,* Vol. VI. San Francisco, Calif.: The California Publishing Co.,—1910.—Cal.

———. *The Danites in the Sierras.* San Francisco, Calif.: The The California Publishing Co., 1910.—Cal.

MILLER, LAURA. "It Took a Woman." In *Second Yearbook of Short Plays,* Evanston, Ill.: Row, Peterson & Co., 1934.—Ore.

MILLER, MARGARET. "Hannah's Pitcher." In *Country Life Plays.* Boston, Mass.: Walter H. Baker Co., 1936.—N.E.

MILLER, MAY. "Scratches," *The Carolina Magazine,* April, 1929.—So.

MITCHELL, RONALD ELWY. "Resurrection Ezra," *One Act Play Magazine,* August-September, 1938.—Pa.

MIX, MORTON. *The Woodpile.* New York: Samuel French, 1928.—N.Y.

MOODY, WILLIAM VAUGHN. *The Great Divide.* New York: The Macmillan Co., 1909.—S.W.

MOON, ILANON. *Texas; the Land of the Strong.* Austin, Texas: The E. L. Steck Co., 1936.—S.W.

MOORE, ALMA LOUISE. "Summer Ducks." In *Midwest Prize Plays.* Chicago, Ill.: The Dramatic Publishing Co., 1938.—So.

MOORE, BESSIE C. "On Bayou La Batre," *Poet Lore,* Winter, 1926.—La.

MORRELL, DELLA. "Things Not Seen." In *Six One-Act Plays, M.I.A. Book of Plays.* Salt Lake City, Utah: General Boards, M.I.A., 1929.—Rk.

MORROW, T. M. "The Catalogue." In *New York Rural Plays.* Chicago, Ill.: The Dramatic Publishing Co., 1935.—N.Y.

MOSS, GRANT. "Death Comes Creepin' in the Room." Script.—Negro.

MOWATT, ANNA CORA. *Fashion; or, Life in New York.* New York: Samuel French & Son, 1854?.—N.Y.

MULDROW, EDNA. "Dust." In *The Best One-Act Plays of 1938,* edited by Margaret G. Mayorga. New York: Dodd, Mead & Co., 1939.—S.W.

MUNSON, JOHN H. *The Old Timers' Bureau.* New York: Samuel French, 1928.—N.Y.

MURDOCK, FRANK H. "Davy Crockett" (as revised by Frank Mayo). In *Favorite American Plays of the Nineteenth Century.* Princeton, N.J.: Princeton University Press, 1943.—App.

MURRY, ANNE. "Wax Before the Fire." In *Folk Plays for Contests.* Chicago, Ill.: T. S. Denison & Co., 1940.—N.Y.

MYERS, SUSANNA. "The Giant Who Swallowed the Clouds," *School Arts,* March, 1935.—S.W.

MYGATT, TRACY D. "The Noose," *The Drama,* November, 1929.—Negro.

NEFF, ELIZABETH. *The Howl of the Wolf.* Chicago, Ill.: The Dramatic Publishing Co., c1935.—Ru.

NEUSBAUM, FRANK, and KATHRYN M. POPP. *Ephrata.* New

York: Dramatists Play Service (distributed by the Pennsylvania Book Service, Harrisburg, Pa.), 1943.—Pa.

NEWETT, JAMES H: "'Limination." In *Prize-Winning One-Act Plays,* edited by Billie Oneal. Dallas, Texas: Southwest Press, 1930.—S.W.

NICHOLSON, KENYON, and CHARLES ROBINSON. "The Apple of His Eye." Script, 1945.—Mid.

NIENDORFF, ARTHUR STARR. *A Mountain Tragedy.* New York: Samuel French, 1932.—App.

NIXON, NORA F. *Cunjer Joe.* New York: Samuel French, 1935.—Negro.

O'CONNELL, LOUISE. "Donalds O'Rourk." In *The Lake Guns of Seneca and Cayuga.* Ithaca, N.Y.: Cornell University Press, 1942.—N.Y.

O'CONNELL, WILKESON. "The Lie." In *Carolina Folk Comedies,* fourth series, edited by Frederick H. Koch. New York: Samuel French, 1931.—So.

——. "The Loyal Venture," *Carolina Play-Book,* March, 1932.—So.

O'DEA, MARK. *Red Bud Women.* Cincinnati, Ohio: Stewart Kidd Co., 1922.—Gt. L.

OLIVER, MARGARET SCOTT. "The Lost Child." In *Tea and Little Rice Cakes.* Boston, Mass.: R. G. Badger, 1926.—Ind.

O'NEILL, EUGENE. "All God's Chillun Got Wings." In *The Plays of Eugene O'Neill.* New York: Random House, 1941.—Negro.

——. "Desire Under the Elms." *Ibid.*—N.E.

ORDWAY, FRANK H. "Spring Storm." In *Country Life Plays.* Boston, Mass.: Walter H. Baker Co., 1936.—N.Y.

ORDWAY, PRISCILLA. "Onions." In *Country Life Plays.* Boston, Mass.: Walter H. Baker Co., 1936.—N.E.

OWEN, ROBERT DALE. *Pocahontas.* New York: G. Dearborn, 1837.—Ind.

PALMER, ANNIE D. *The Rescue.* Salt Lake City, Utah: General Board, Y.M.M.I.A., 1927.—Rk.

PARK, JAMES STANTON. "The Pageant of Old Detroit." In *Pageants of Our Nation,* edited by Anne P. Sanford. New York: Dodd, Mead & Co., 1929.—Gt. L.

PARKER, JOHN W. "Sleep On, Lemuel," *Carolina Play-Book,* December, 1932.—So.

PARKER, PHILIP GODDARD. "Ancient Heritage." In *American*

Folk Plays, edited by Frederick H. Koch. New York: D. Appleton-Century Co., 1939.—N.E.

PATTERSON, THOMAS, McEVOY. "American Primitive." Script, 1947.—Negro.

PAXTON, MARY. *The Kettle Singing.* Boston, Mass.: Walter H. Baker Co., c1930.—Ru.

PEET, TELFAIR. "The New Moon." In *Carolina Folk Comedies,* fourth series, edited by Frederick H. Koch. New York: Samuel French, 1931.—So.

PELÉE, LILLIAN SUTTON. "Ties of Blood," *Poet Lore,* December, 1921.—Cal.

PEMBERTON, ANEMONE. "Nelagony" ("Good Water"). Federal Theatre script, No. 41.—Ind.

PENDRAY, G. EDWARD, and KENYON NICHOLSON. "The Organ." In *The American Scene,* edited by Barrett H. Clark and Kenyon Nicholson. New York: D. Appleton & Co., 1930.—Mid.

PERRY, LOUISE S. "One Fine Day." In *Second Yearbook of Short Plays.* Evanston, Ill.: Row, Peterson & Co., 1934.—So.

——. "Saturday Market." In *First Yearbook of Short Plays.* Evanston, Ill.: Row, Peterson & Co., 1931.—So.

PETERS, PAUL, and GEORGE SKLAR. *Stevedore.* New York: Covici-Friede.—Negro.

PETERSON, AGNES EMILIE. "Roads." In *Goin' Home and Other Plays of the 1927 Contest.* New York: Longmans, Green & Co., 1928.—Mid.

——. "Star on the Trail." In *Fifth Yearbook of Short Plays.* Evanston, Ill.: Row, Peterson & Co., 1939.—Rk.

——. "The Winds," *The Drama,* May, 1925.—Cal.

PHARIS, GWEN. "Pasque Flowers," *Carolina Play-Book,* March, 1939.—So.

PIERRATT, ALICE. "Day's End." In *American Folk Plays,* edited by Frederick H. Koch. New York: D. Appleton-Century Co., 1939.—Cal.

PORTNER, MAYER. *Soil.* New York: Samuel French, 1928.—N.Y.

POST, EDWARD. "Tower," *One Act Play Magazine,* July-August, 1940.—So.

PRATT, THEODORE. "The Big Blow." Federal Theatre script, 1938.—So.

PRICE, DORIS D. "The Bright Medallion." In *University of*

Michigan Plays, book three, edited by Kenneth T. Rowe. Ann Arbor, Mich.: George Wahr, 1932.—Negro-S.W.

———. "The Eyes of the Old." *Ibid.*—Negro.

———. "Two Gods," *Opportunity,* December, 1932.—Negro.

PRIDE, LEO B. "Fortune's Hired Man." In *The Shadow of the Mine.* New York: Samuel French, 1929.—So.

PYLE, MARY THURMAN. "All the Rivers." In *Third Yearbook of Short Plays.* Evanston, Ill.: Row, Peterson & Co., 1936.—App.

RADCLIFFE, MARGARET. "Sigrid," *Carolina Play-Book,* September, 1934.—Mid.

RANCK, CARTY. *The Mountain.* Rock Island, Ill.: Frederick B. Ingram Publications, 1938.—App.

RANDALL, WILLIAM M. "Tobacco Alley." In *The Best One-Act Plays of 1937,* edited by Margaret G. Mayorga. New York: Dodd, Mead & Co., 1938.—App.

REDFORD, GRANT H. "Highway 91." In *M.I.A. Book of Plays, XIV,* Salt Lake City, Utah: General Boards, M.I.A., 1942.—Rk.

REED, MARK. "A Transfer of Property." In *One-Act Plays for Stage and Study,* eighth series. New York: Samuel French, 1934.—N.E.

REELY, MARY KATHARINE. "A Window to the South." In *Daily Bread.* New York: H. W. Wilson Co., 1919.—Mid.

———. "The Lean Years." *Ibid.*—Mid.

REESE, MARY HOYT. "Abram's Wife." Script, 1941.—App.

REIFSNYDER, M. S. *The Up Sign.* New York: Fritzgerald Publishing Corporation, 1937.—Pa.

RICE, CALE YOUNG. *The Swamp Bird.* New York: The Century Co., 1931.—So.

RICE, WALLACE, and KENNETH S. GOODMAN. "The Glorious Gateway of the West." In *Pageants of Our Nation,* edited by Anne P. Sanford and Robert Haven Schauffler. New York: Dodd, Mead & Co., 1929.—Gt. L.

RICHARDSON, HOWARD, and WILLIAM BERNEY. "Dark of the Moon." Promptbook, September, 1944.—So.

RICHARDSON, WILLIS. "Compromise." In *The New Negro,* edited by Alain Locke. New York: A. & C. Boni, 1925.—Negro.

———. "The Broken Banjo." In *Plays of Negro Life,* edited

by Alain Le Roy Locke and Montgomery Gregory. New York: Harper & Bros., 1927.—Negro.

——. "The Chip Woman's Fortune." In *Fifty More Contemporary One-Act Plays,* edited by Frank Shay. New York: D. Appleton & Co., 1928.—Negro.

——. "The Flight of the Natives." In *Plays of Negro Life,* edited by Alain Le Roy Locke and Montgomery Gregory. New York: Harper & Bros., 1927.—Negro.

——. "The Idle Head," *The Carolina Magazine,* April, 1929.—Negro.

RIGGS, LYNN. "A Lantern to See By." In *Two Oklahoma Plays.* New York: Samuel French, 1928.—S.W .

——. *Big Lake.* New York: Samuel French, 1927.—S.W.

——. *Green Grow the Lilacs.* New York: Samuel French, 1931.—S.W.

——. *Knives from Syria.* New York: Samuel French, 1928.—S.W.

——. "Rancor." Script with Samuel French, New York.—S.W.

——. "Reckless." In *One-Act Plays for Stage and Study,* fourth series. New York: Samuel French, 1928.—S.W.

——. *Roadside* (or *Borned in Texas).* New York: Samuel French, 1930.—S.W.

——. *Russet Mantle.* New York: Samuel French, 1936.—S.W.

——. "Sump'n Like Wings." In *Two Oklahoma Plays.* New York: Samuel French, 1928.—S.W.

——. *Cherokee Night.* New York: Samuel French, 1936.—S.W.

——. "The Cream in the Well." Promptbook, 1941.—S.W.

RITCHEY, JOHN. "Beating Wings." In *Country Life Plays.* Boston, Mass.: Walter H. Baker Co., 1936.—Pa.

ROBINSON, HORACE W. "The Promised Land." In *Amateur Acting and Play Production,* edited by W. Campbell. New York: The Macmillan Co., 1931.—S.W.

ROBINSON, THOMAS P. *Darick Clausen.* New York: Longmans, Green & Co., 1931.—N.Y.

ROCKWELL, ETHEL THEODORA. *Children of Old Wisconsin, a Pageant Based on the History of Wisconsin and Representing the Children of Different Periods.* Madison, Wis.: University of Wisconsin, 1935.—Gt. L.

——. *The Centennial Cavalcade of Wisconsin, a Pageant.* Madison, Wis.: University of Wisconsin, 1936.—Gt. L.

ROGERS, JOHN W. JR. *Bumblepuppy.* New York: Samuel French, 1927.—S.W.

———. *Judge Lynch.* New York: Samuel French, 1924.—Negro.

———. "The Rescue of Cynthia Ann." In *One-Act Plays for Stage and Study,* fifth series. New York: Samuel French, 1929.—S.W.

———. "Westward People," Southwest Review, Autumn, 1934. —S.W.

ROSE, TURNER. "Marked for Rest." In *University of Virginia Plays.* New York: Samuel French, 1932.—Negro.

ROSELLE, BESSIE LEE DICKEY. *Dramas of Daring Deeds.* San Antonio, Texas: The Naylord Co., 1936.—S.W.

ROSENTHAL, CARLA F. *The Little Shakeresses.* Chicago, Ill.: Old Tower Press, 1923.—N.Y.

ROSS, JOHN M. "Wanga Doll." Script, 1947.—La.

RUSSELL, MARY MARGARET. "The Devil Doll," *Poet Lore,* Spring, 1935.—N.E.

RUTHERFORD, ALETRICE, and OTHERS. "Dust Unto Dust." In *Folk Plays for Contests.* Chicago, Ill.: T. S. Denison & Co., 1940.—Ru.

RYERSON, FLORENCE, and COLIN CLEMENTS. *Men Folk.* New York: Samuel French, 1928.—N.E.

ST. CLAIR, ROBERT. "Fire Trap," *One Act Play Magazine,* July-August, 1941.—Cal.

SAMPLEY, ARTHUR McC. "Share-Croppers," *The Players Magazine,* March-April, 1939.—S.W.

SCOTT, NATALIE V. "Zombi." In *Plays of American Life and Fantasy,* edited by Edith J. R. Isaacs. New York: Coward-McCann, 1929.—La.

SEARS, WILLIAM B. *Black Harvest.* Chicago, Ill.: The Dramatic Publishing Co., 1938.—Mid.

SELNICK, EUGENE. "The Gold Machine," *The Drama,* March, 1930.—Negro.

SHAFROTH, JANET DURRIE. "Bonanza." Script. Chevy Chase, Md.—Rk.

SHAVER, JOHN D. *The Resignation of Bill Snyder.* New York: Samuel French, 1928.—Rk.

SHELDON, EDWARD. *The Nigger.* New York: The Macmillan Co., 1910.—So.

SHERWOOD, ROBERT E. *Abe Lincoln in Illinois.* New York: Charles Scribner's Sons, 1940.—Mid.

SHUMWAY, MERLINE H. *Back to the Farm (University of Minnesota Bulletin,* General Series, No. 12). Minneapolis, Minn.: University of Minnesota, 1914.—Gt. L.

SINCLAIR, SUSIE SMITH. "For Better or Worse." In *25 Non-Royalty One-Act American Comedies,* compiled by William Kozlenko. New York: Greenberg, 1943.—App.

———. "Graveyard Day." In *25 Non-Royalty One-Act Plays for All-Girl Casts.* New York: Greenberg, 1942.—App.

SKIDMORE, HOBERT. "Books for the Dead," *The One-Act Theater,* Vol. II. New York: Samuel French, 1936.—Gt. L.

SMITH, BETTY. "The Boy Abe," *One Act Play Magazine,* March-April, 1941.—Mid.

———. "Young Lincoln." In *Plays of Democracy.* New York: Dodd, Mead & Co., 1944.—Mid.

SMITH, BETTY, and ROBERT FINCH. "Montana Night." In *American Folk Plays,* edited by Frederick H. Koch. New York: D. Appleton-Century Co., 1939.—Ore.

———. *Murder in the Snow.* New York: Samuel French, 1938. —Ore.

———. *Western Night.* New York: Dramatists Play Service, 1938.—Ore.

SMITH, BETTY, and CHASE WEBB. "Manana Bandits." In *The Best One-Act Plays of 1938,* edited by Margaret G. Mayorga. New York: Dodd, Mead & Co., 1939.—S.W.

SMITH, BOYD. "The Patriarch." In *Yale Plays.* New York: Samuel French, 1926.—App.

SMITH DORIS. "Rosario, the Pageant of the Rose." Script, 1925.—Ore.

SMITH, EARL HOBSON. *Eleanor of Cumberland Mountain.* Lexington, Ky.: Kentucky Playmakers, 1926.—App.

———. *Stephen Foster, Or Weep No More, My Lady.* Knoxville, Tenn.: The Foster Players, 1935.—App.

SMITH, EDGAR VALENTINE. "'Lijah." In *Types of Modern Dramatic Composition,* edited by Leroy Phillips and Theodore Johnson. Boston, Mass.: Ginn and Co., 1927.—So.

SMITH, GRACE E., and GERTRUDE KNEVELS. *The Arrow-Maker's Daughter.* New York: Samuel French, 1913.—Ind.

SMITH, HOWARD FORMAN. *Blackberryin'.* Boston, Mass.: Rockwell and Churchill Press, 1922.—Ru.

SMITH, JANET KATHERINE. "Concise Account." In *Fifth Year-*

book of Short Plays. Evanston, Ill.: Row, Peterson & Co., 1939.—N.E.

SMITH, JOHN. *Out of the Night.* New York: Samuel French, 1928.—N.Y.

SNEED, VIRGINIA LEE. "Drifters," *The Players Magazine,* January-February, 1938.—La.

SOLLENBERGER, JUDITH K. "The Marriage Gown." In *Indiana Prize Plays.* Indianapolis, Ind.: Bobbs-Merrill Co., 1924. —N.E.

SPEARMAN, WALTER. *Country Sunday.* Atlanta, Ga.: Association of Southern Women for the Prevention of Lynching, 1936.—Negro.

SPENCE, EULALIE. *The Fool's Errand.* New York: Samuel French, 1927.—Negro.

———. "The Hunch," *The Carolina Magazine,* May, 1927.—Negro.

———. "The Starter." In *Plays of Negro Life,* edited by Alain Le Roy Locke and Montgomery Gregory. New York: Harper & Bros., 1927.—Negro.

———. "The Undertow," *The Carolina Magazine,* April, 1929. —Negro.

STAADT, EDWARD. *Cabbages.* New York: Samuel French, 1927.—Gt. L.

STACY, AUGUSTA. "Home Ties." In *Country Life Plays.* Boston, Mass: Walter H. Baker Co., 1936.—Mid.

STALLINGS, LAURENCE. "Deep River: an Operetta;" music by Frank Harling. Script, 1926.—La.

STEELE, WILBUR DANIEL. *The Giant's Stair.* New York: D. Appleton & Co., 1924.—App.

STEPHENS, NAN BAGBY. "Charivari," *Theatre Arts Monthly,* November, 1928.—La.

STEVENS, DANA J. *Old Acre Folks.* Boston, Mass.: Walter H. Baker Co., 1900—Ru.

STEVENS, HENRY BAILEY. "Early Frost." In *Country Life Plays.* Boston, Mass.: Walter H. Baker Co., 1936.—Ru.

———. *Johnny Appleseed and Paul Bunyan: a Pageant* (presented at Wilton, N.H., May 19, 1935). Boston, Mass.: Walter H. Baker Co., 1930.—Gt. L.

STEVENS, THOMAS WOOD. "The Coronado Pageant." Unpublished, 1940.—S.W.

————. *Pageant of St. Louis.* St. Louis, Mo.: St. Louis Pageant Drama Association, 1914.—Mid.

————. "Pageant of the Old Northwest." Unpublished, 1911.—Gt. L.

STOKER, E. "The Boomer." In *University of Utah Plays,* edited by Roland B. Lewis. Boston, Mass.: Walter H. Baker Co., 1928.—Rk.

STOKES, R. L. *Paul Bunyan.* New York: G. P. Putnam's Sons, 1932.—Ore.

STONE, WELDON. *A Darksome Furriner.* New York: Samuel French, 1937.—Oz.

————. "Cloud over Breakshin." In *The Best One-Act Plays of 1938,* edited by Margaret G. Mayorga. New York: Dodd, Mead & Co., 1939.—Oz.

————. "Courtin' Maisie." In *Widwest Prize Plays.* Chicago, Ill.: The Dramatic Publishing Co., 1938.—Oz.

————. *Devil Take a Whittler.* New York: Samuel French, 1938.—Oz.

————. *Mammon and the Whittler.* New York: Samuel French, 1938.—Oz.

————. "Quarrytown," *The Players Magazine,* September-October, 1936.—Oz.

————. "Rainbows in Heaven." In *The Best One-Act Plays of 1940,* edited by Margaret G. Mayorga. New York: Dodd, Mead & Co., 1941.—Oz.

————. *The Flute and the Vine.* New York: Samuel French, 1941.—Oz.

————. "We Write a Play," *One Act Play Magazine,* June-July, 1938.—Oz.

STORM, JUDE. *Woman's Might.* New York: Samuel French, 1934.—Mid.

STOUT, OAKLEY. *Harvest.* New York: Longmans, Green & Co., 1929.—Gt. L.

STOUT, WILBUR. "In Dixon's Kitchen." In *Carolina Folk-Plays,* third series, edited by Frederick H. Koch. New York: Henry Holt & Co., 1928.—So.

————. "Dogwood Bushes." In *Carolina Folk Comedies,* fourth series, edited by Frederick H. Koch. New York: Samuel French, 1931.—So.

STRICKLAND, TERESA. *White Hawk: a Legend of the Shawnee*

Indians; music by Lily Strickland. Philadelphia, Pa.: Theodore Presser Co., 1933.—S.W.

STURGIS, ROBERT. "The Red Land." Script.—S.W.

SULLIVAN, ELIZABETH H. "The Strongest Man." In *Harvard University: Plays of the 47 Workshop,* edited by George Pierce Baker. New York: Brentano's, 1925.—La.

SUNDGAARD, ARNOLD. "Everywhere I Roam." Script, 1938.—Ru.

SUTHERLAND, EVELYN GREENLEAF. *Po' White Trash.* New York: Duffield & Co., 1909.—So.

SWAYZE, KATE LUCY. *Ossawattomie Brown; or the Insurrection at Harper's Ferry.* New York: Samuel French, 1859? —App.

SZEKELY, SARI. "Transplanted." In *International Plays.* Chicago, Ill.: The Dramatic Publishing Co., 1936.—Gt. L.

TABER, GLADYS BAGG. "Miss Manda," *Poet Lore,* Autumn, 1927.—Gt. L.

TANNER, VIRGINIA. *A Pageant of Portsmouth.* Concord, N.H.: Rumford Press, 1923.—N.E.

THISTLE, DONALD. *Johnny Appleseed.* Charles City, Iowa: The Torrence Printing Co., 1927.—Mid.

THOMPSON, DENMAN, and G. W. RYER. *The Old Homestead* (sequel to *Joshua Whitcomb).* Boston, Mass.: Walter H. Baker Co., 1927.—N.E.

THOMPSON, DORIS K., and JANE ASSUR. "Salvage," *The Drama,* May, 1931.—App.

THURSTON, ELLA L. "Family Co-operative." In *The Lake Guns of Seneca and Cayuga,* edited by A. M. Drummond and Robert E. Gard. Ithaca, N.Y.: Cornell University Press, 1942.—N.Y.

TOOMER, JEAN. "Balo." In *Plays of Negro Life,* edited by Alain Le Roy Locke and Montgomery Gregory. New York: Harper & Bros., 1927.—Negro.

TORRENCE, RIDGELY. "The Danse Calinda," *Theatre Arts Magazine,* July, 1919.—La.

———. *Plays for a Negro Theatre.* New York: Macmillan Co., 1917.—Negro.

TOTHEROH, DAN. "Distant Drums." Promptbook, 1932.—Ore.

———. "Good Vintage." In *One Act Plays for Everyone.* New York: Samuel French, 1931.—Cal.

———. "In the Darkness." *Ibid.*—Ore.

———. *Wild Birds.* New York: Samuel French, 1930.—Mid.

TOWNSEND, CHARLES. *A White Mountain Boy.* Philadelphia, Pa.: The Penn Publishing Co., 1914.—N.E.

——. *The Golden Gulch.* New York: Wehman Brothers, 1893.—Cal.

——. *Uncle Josh.* Chicago, Ill.: T. S. Denison & Co., 1891,— Ru.

——. *Uncle Rube. Ibid.*, 1899—Ru.

TOY, JANE. "Agatha." In *Carolina Folk Comedies,* fourth series, edited by Frederick H. Koch. New York: Samuel French, 1931.—So.

TROYER, HOWARD. "Oak," *The Players Magazine,* May-June, 1930.—N.E.

TRUMBAUER, WALTER H. "When the Dead Live On." Script. —Pa.

TULL, JEWELL BOTHWELL. "Carnival," *The Players Magazine,* November-December, 1935.—Mid.

——. "Dead Men Can't Hurt You," *The Players Magazine,* January-February, 1933.—Mid.

——. "Heat," *The Players Magazine,* March-April, 1934.— Mid.

——. "Michael Has Come Back," *The Players Magazine,* September-October, 1938.—Mid.

VAN NORMAN, C. ELTA. "A Light on the Crossroads." In *New York Rural Plays.* Chicago, Ill.: The Dramatic Publishing Co., 1935.—N.Y.

VINJE, ANNETTE. "Hay Harvest." In *International Plays.* Chicago, Ill.: The Dramatic Publishing Co., 1936.—Gt. L.

VOLLMER, LULA. *Moonshine and Honeysuckle.* New York: Samuel French, 1934.—App.

——. *Sun-Up.* New York: Brentano's, 1924.—App.

——. "The Dunce Boy." Script, 1925.—App.

——. *The Hill Between.* New York: Longmans, Green & Co., 1937.—App.

VON HESSE, MAXEDA. "Traficante." In *American Folk Plays,* edited by Frederick H. Koch. New York: D. Appleton-Century Co., 1939.—So.

VORSE, MARY H., and COLIN C. CLEMENTS *Wreckage.* New York: D. Appleton & Co., 1924.—N.E.

WALLACE, BERTHA E. *Too Busy.* New York: Samuel French, 1928.—N.Y.

WALSH, CHAD. "The Hanging." In "The Mountaineer and Other Plays." Script, 1940.—Negro.

WALSH, JOHN E. "Public Citizen Number First." In *Folk Plays for Contests.* Chicago, Ill.: T. S. Denison & Co., 1940.—S.W.

WARD, H. GLYNN. "The Aftermath," *Poet Lore,* Winter, 1926.—Gt. L.

WARD, THEODORE. "Big White Fog." New York: New Theatre League, 1937.—Negro.

————. "Our Lan'." Promptbook, 1947.—Negro.

————. "Shout Hallelujah." Script, 1940.—Negro.

————. "Sick and Tiahd." Script, 1936.—Negro.

WARE, ALICE H. *Mighty Wind A-Blowin'.* New York: New Theatre League, 1936.—Negro.

WAYNE, ROLLO. "Carry Me Long" (with songs of Stephen Foster). Script.—App.

WEAVER, J. CLARK. "Cloudburst." In *One-Act Plays,* edited by Marie A. Webb. New York: The Macmillan Co., 1940.—Ore.

WEAVER, VIRGINIA B. "The Reign of Minnie Belle." In *25 Non-Royalty One-Act American Comedies,* edited by William Kozlenko. New York: Greenberg, 1943.—S.W.

WEBB, ALLA. "Larnin'." In *The One-Act Theater,* Vol. I. New York: Samuel French, 1936.—App.

WEBB, CHASE. *Frontier Night.* Evanston, Ill.: Row, Peterson & Co., 1936.—S.W.

————. "Muley." In *Fourth Yearbook of Short Plays.* Evanston, Ill.: Row, Peterson & Co., 1938.—App.

————. "The Woman from Merry River," *Carolina Play-Book,* March, 1941.—App.

WELLS, FRANK B. "John Henry." Federal Theatre script No. 6, 1936.—Negro.

WHIPKEY, STELLA D. "Door Mats," *Poet Lore,* Spring, 1929.—Oz.

————. "Very Crude Oil," *The Drama,* May, 1930.—S.W.

WHITE, ARTHUR CORNING. "Maze," *Poet Lore,* Spring, 1925.—N.E.

WHITE, CLEMON, and BETTY SMITH. "West from the Panhandle." In *American Folk Plays,* edited by Frederick H. Koch. New York: D. Appleton-Century Co., 1939.—S.W.

WHITE, HELEN. *The Crippled Heart* (or *The Swap*). Des Moines, Iowa: Ivan Bloom Hardin Co., 1938.—Oz.

———. "Feet First." In *Sixth Yearbook of Short Plays*. Evanston, Ill.: Row, Peterson & Co., 1940.—Oz.

WHITEHAND, ROBERT. "Derricks on the Hill." Script.—S.W.

———. "Precious Land." Script, 1937.—S.W.

WHITING, ELEANOR. "Common Ground," *Poet Lore,* January, 1921.—N.E.

WILDER, THORNTON. "Queens of France." *Yale Review,* September, 1931.—La.

———. *Our Town.* New York: Coward-McCann, 1938.—N.E.

WILLIAMS, GRACE. "Bride Out of Beaver." In *Plays from the Drama Workshop,* Number Two. Mills College, Calif.: Eucalyptus Press, 1937.—Cal.

WILLIAMS, LAUREN. "Over Fourteen: and Single." In *The Lake Guns of Seneca and Cayuga,* edited by A. M. Drummond and Robert E. Gard. Ithaca, N.Y.: Cornell University Press, 1942.—N.Y.

WILLIAMS, SARAH M. "The Turkey Girl." In *University of Utah Plays,* edited by Roland B. Lewis. Boston, Mass.: Walter H. Baker Co., 1928.—S.W.

WILLIAMS, TENNESSEE. "Landscape with Figures." In *American Scenes,* edited by William Kozlenko. New York: The John Day Co., 1941.—La.

———. *27 Wagons Full of Cotton and Other One-Act Plays.* Norfolk, Conn.: New Directions, 1947.—La.

WILLIAMSON, HAROLD. "Peggy." In *Carolina Folk-Plays,* first series, edited by Frederick H. Koch. New York: Henry Holt & Co., 1922.—So.

WILSON, ELIZABETH. "The Wishful Taw." (Avery Hopwood Prize Winner). University of Michigan, 1943. Script.—Oz.

WILSON, FRANK H. "Meek Mose." Script, 1928.—S.W.

———. "Sugar Cane." In *Plays of Negro Life,* edited by Alain Le Roy Locke and Montgomery Gregory. New York: Harper & Bros., 1927.—Negro.

———. "Walk Together, Chillun." Negro Unit: Federal Theatre script, 1936.—Negro.

WITHERSPOON, KATHLEEN. "Jute," *Southwest Review,* Spring, 1931.—Negro.

WOLFE, THOMAS CLAYTON. "The Return of Buck Gavin." In

Carolina Folk-Plays, second series, edited by Frederick H. Koch. New York: Henry Holt & Co., 1924.—So.

———. "The Third Night," *Carolina Play-Book,* September, 1938.—So.

WOLL, JAN. "Lumbering Love." In *Midwest Prize Plays.* Chicago, Ill.: The Dramatic Publishing Co., 1938.—Gt. L.

WOOD, GRANT, and JEWELL BOTHWELL TULL. "They That Mourn." In Stage Magazine, comp. *Forty-Minute Prize Plays,* edited by Grant Wood and Jewell B. Tull. New York: Dodd, Mead & Co., 1936.—Mid.

WOOD, H. CLEVELAND. "Amor, . . . or a Pretty Shakeress," a musical comedy. (Music by L. C. Walter.) Harrodsburg, Ky. Script.—So.

WOOD, J. KARL. "Pageant Dramas: Another Witness; Elijah, the Prophet; Faith Points the Way; The Messenger." Scripts. No dates.—Rk.

WOOD, JAMES MILTON. "Death Valley Scotty," *Carolina Play-Book,* March, 1930.—Cal.

WOODBURY, DAVID O. *Forever Credulous.* Boston, Mass.: Walter H. Baker Co., 1936.—N.E.

WOODFORD, BESSIE (VAN DYKE). *Somebody.* New York: Fortuny's, 1937.—So.

WOODS, WALTER. "Billy the Kid." In *The Great Diamond Robbery and other Recent Melodramas,* edited by Garret Hasty Leverton. Princeton, N.J.: Princeton University Press, 1940.—S.W.

Works Progress Administration. Federal Theatre Project. "Out of the Wilderness: The Salem Years of Abraham Lincoln," presented at New Salem State Park, September 26, 27, 28, 1940. Federal Theatre script.—Mid.

WRIGHT, RICHARD. "Fire and Cloud." In *American Scenes,* edited by William Kozlenko. New York: The John Day Co., 1941.—So.

YATES, ELIZABETH. "The Slave." In *Small Plays for Small Casts.* Philadelphia, Pa.: The Penn Publishing Co., 1926. —Negro.

YOUNG, PAULINE RODGERS. "Off the Road." *Poet Lore,* Summer, 1925.—S.W.

YOUNG, STARK. *Three One-Act Plays.* Cincinnati, Ohio: Stewart Kidd Co., 1921.—La.

Index

NOTE: No attempt has been made here to duplicate the names of authors and the titles contained in the Bibliography. Only the main body of the text is covered by this index.

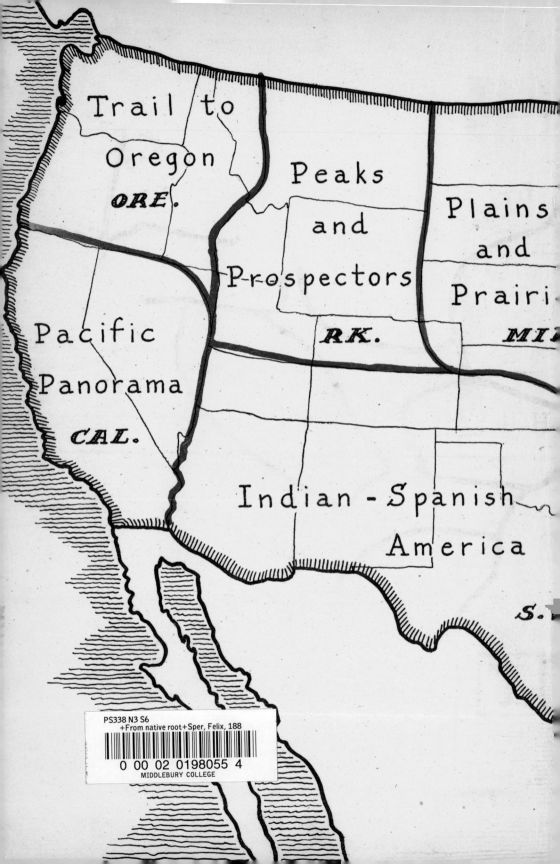

Trail to Oregon *ORE.*

Peaks and Prospectors

Plains and Prairi-

RK.

MI

Pacific Panorama *CAL.*

Indian - Spanish America

S.